Interpreting STANDARDIZED TEST SCORES

For Kate and Addy . . .
Thanks for putting up with me while I wrote another one!
The two of you are my entire world!

Interpreting STANDARDIZED TEST SCORES

STRATEGIES FOR DATA-DRIVEN INSTRUCTIONAL DECISION MAKING

CRAIG A. MERTLER
Bowling Green State University

SAGE Publications
Los Angeles • London • New Delhi • Singapore

For information:

Sage Publications, Inc.
2455 Teller Road
Thousand Oaks, California 91320
E-mail: order@sagepub.com

Sage Publications India Pvt. Ltd.
B 1/I 1 Mohan Cooperative
Industrial Area
Mathura Road, New Delhi 110 044
India

Sage Publications Ltd.
1 Oliver's Yard
55 City Road
London EC1Y 1SP

Sage Publications Asia-Pacific Pte. Ltd.
33 Pekin Street #02-01
Far East Square
Singapore 048763

Printed in the United States of America

Library of Congress Cataloging-in-Publication Data

Mertler, Craig A.
Interpreting standardized test scores: Strategies for data-driven instructional decision making/Craig A. Mertler.
     p. cm.
Includes bibliographical references and index.
ISBN 978-1-4129-3718-4 (cloth)
ISBN 978-1-4129-3719-1 (pbk.)
  1. Educational tests and measurements—United States—Interpretation.
2. Examinations—United States—Interpretation. 3. Teaching—Decision making. I. Title.

LB3060.8.M47 2007
371.26′2—dc22

                                        2006101370

Printed on acid-free paper.

07   08   09   10   11   10   9   8   7   6   5   4   3   2   1

Acquiring Editor:	Diane McDaniel
Editorial Assistant:	Ashley Plummer
Production Editor:	Sarah K. Quesenberry
Copy Editor:	Renee Willers
Proofreader:	Joyce Li
Indexer:	Will Ragsdale
Typesetter:	C&M Digitals (P) Ltd.
Cover Designer:	Bryan Fishman
Marketing Manager:	Nichole M. Angress

7454708

TABLE OF CONTENTS

PREFACE

PURPOSE OF THE TEXT

I have been involved in public PreK–12 education for nearly 20 years. I have been a high school teacher, a supervisor for elementary-level student teachers, a researcher at various levels, a consultant to individual schools as well as school districts, and, currently, a professor of educational research and measurement. I have worked extensively with teachers and district-level administrators, particularly on topics related to both classroom assessment and large-scale assessment. In my work with teachers and administrators, it has become apparent to me that these professionals—the educators for whom scores resulting from standardized tests are so potentially vital and informative—have literally never received formal training regarding how to interpret these scores and, more importantly, how to use them to aid their instructional decision making. They admittedly do not like standardized tests (although who among us really does?). They tend to administer them because their respective states, or the federal government in the case of the No Child Left Behind (NCLB) Act and its associated Adequate Yearly Progress (AYP) require-ments, force them to do so. Many teachers are so overwhelmed with the test reports they receive back on their students—I have actually heard teachers com-ment that "there is so much information here that I don't even know where to begin!"—that they make the conscious decision to do nothing with them, simply filing them away in students' cumulative folders.

The basic purpose of this book is to provide teachers and administrators with a manual, of sorts, designed to help them understand the nature of standardized tests and, in particular, the scores that result from them. The ultimate purpose of the book is to help them develop the skills necessary to incorporate these test scores into various types of instructional decision making—a process known as data-driven decision making—necessitated by the needs of their students.

AUDIENCE FOR WHOM THE TEXT IS INTENDED

This book was written with teachers and administrators as the primary audience. Specifically, this audience includes preservice teachers (seeking initial certification or licensure), K–12 classroom teachers (seeking either master's or doctoral degrees) and K–12 administrators (typically seeking doctoral degrees). I believe that this book is appropriate for educators in all areas of education (e.g., elementary and secondary; mathematics, science, social studies, languages, music, art, physical education, special education). Considering the stress that is being placed on educational accountability in this country, the importance of understanding student performance on standardized tests and knowing how to use that information only continues to grow. This book could serve as a supplement to any course that incorporates standardized testing as a topic, including but not limited to courses in classroom assessment, educational psychology, content methods, reading, special education, curriculum, literacy, administration, the principalship, and the superintendency. In addition to undergraduate and graduate education courses, individual practitioners (e.g., classroom teachers and building or district administrators) seeking professional development opportunities can also gain benefit from this book.

ORGANIZATION AND PEDAGOGICAL FEATURES OF THE TEXT

The treatment of the content is fairly expansive, due to the narrow focus of the book. It does, by necessity, incorporate some measurement-related conceptual information; however, I have tried to make these concepts and subsequent discussions as applied as is possible (e.g., I have tried to avoid the excessive use of statistical formulas!). The coverage of the material is a new presentation of existing knowledge, focusing on the applicability of this knowledge to and by the K–12 professional educator. This is something that has not typically been done when presenting material related to understanding and using standardized test scores. The basic content outline is as follows:

Section I: Overview of Standardized Testing: Concepts and Terminology
      Module 1: What Is "Standardized" Testing?
      Module 2: The Importance of Standardized Testing
      Module 3: Standardized Test Administration and Preparation

Section II: Standardized Test Scores and Their Interpretations
      Module 4: Test Reports
      Module 5: Criterion-Referenced Test Scores and Their Interpretations
      Module 6: Norm-Referenced Test Scores and Their Interpretations

Section III: Using Standardized Test Scores in Instructional Decision Making
        Module 7: Group-Level Decision Making
        Module 8: Student-Level Decision Making
        Module 9: Value-Added Analysis and Interpretation

Section IV: Case Studies: Interviews With Teachers and Administrators

Interview Transcripts
        Teachers
        Administrators

There are very few textbooks that focus their coverage solely on standardized testing. Most books that do discuss the topic give it a brief chapter, somewhere near the end of the book. Along those lines, most instructors give it brief mention, if any at all. There are four main pedagogical means by which this occurs in the book.

First, numerous samples of printouts resulting from well-known standardized tests are presented and discussed in detail. This list—which includes achievement, aptitude, and diagnostic tests—is comprised of the following standardized tests:

- Dynamic Indicators of Basic Early Literacy Skills (DIBELS),
- Iowa Tests of Basic Skills (ITBS),
- Gates-MacGinitie Reading Tests (GMRT),
- Ohio Achievement Tests (third and eighth grades),
- Otis-Lennon School Ability Test (OLSAT),
- Stanford Achievement Test 10 (SAT10),
- TerraNova (2nd ed.), and
- Wechsler Intelligence Scale for Children IV (WISC-IV).

Second, following the presentation of the process to be used for incorporating test results into instructional decision making (in Module 3), several specific examples are provided and thoroughly discussed. Highlighted in these discussions are explanations of the purposes of a given test, a description of either (1) a student and her/his scores (including an actual test report) or (2) an entire class and their scores (including a class test report), and an account of how a teacher, or group of teachers, would proceed through the process of using the test scores to aid in making decisions about future instruction.

Third, each module contains several "Activities for Application and Reflection." The nature of these activities are quite varied; some are appropriate for seasoned teachers and administrators (by capitalizing on their classroom and other school-based experiences) while others have been designed to address the needs of preservice teachers in helping them understand the process of data-driven instructional decision making.

Finally, in Section IV, I have presented case studies, consisting of interviews conducted by me with district-level administrators, building administrators, and classroom teachers. These individuals, all from one school district, have been engaged in a process of incorporating test scores into decision making for several years. Several end-of-module activities and discussion starters are tied directly to these interview transcripts.

A FINAL NOTE . . .

I honestly do not know anyone who loves standardized testing! But the standardized testing movement is not going away anytime soon. An examination of its impact on this country's educational system over the past 40 years will confirm that. Therefore, I approach it from this perspective . . . and I strongly suggest that all professional educators adopt a similar attitude. Anytime we are given the responsibility of making decisions about children, we need as much information as possible in order for those decisions to be as accurate as possible. We ask students questions; we ask them to read to us; we require them to write for us; we test them over units of instruction; we observe them; we encourage them to be creative; we engage them in performance-based tasks; etc. The results from standardized tests are just another source of information—about student learning, about our teaching, and about our curriculum. Please use them as such—add them to your long list of various sources of information about student learning. They can only help improve the accuracy of the decisions that we make about our students, as well as our own instruction. Best of luck as you embark on this new, or perhaps not so new, endeavor!

ACKNOWLEDGMENTS

I would like to acknowledge the contributions of several individuals to this project.

First, I would like to recognize and sincerely thank my editorial team at Sage Publications, namely Dr. Diane McDaniel (Acquisitions Editor), along with Erica Carroll, Ashley Plummer (Editorial Assistants), and Sarah Quesenberry (Production Editor). After two projects with her, I can definitively attest to the fact that Dr. McDaniel is the most professional editor with whom I have had the pleasure to work, especially in terms of collaboratively developing a project from its initial conception to its ultimate completion.

I would like to recognize and thank the teachers and administrative staff at Bowling Green City Schools in Bowling Green, Ohio, for allowing me to work with them since 2001 on this concept of utilizing standardized test scores as a contributing source of information for instructional decision making. The completion of this book is just one more step in our continuing journey!

I would also like to thank those individuals who served as reviewers of both the original prospectus and the initial draft of this book—their comments and feedback were greatly appreciated and extremely helpful:

Prospectus Reviewers:

Rosemarie L. Ataya, University of South Florida

Gordon Brooks, Ohio University

Nancy Cerezo, Saint Leo University

Marietta Daulton, Walsh University

Leland K. Doebler, The University of Montevallo

Ramona A. Hall, Cameron University

Linda Karges-Bone, Charleston Southern University

Manuscript Draft Reviewers:

Nancy A. Cerezo, Saint Leo University

Ollie Daniels, Barry University

Marietta Daulton, Walsh University

Jack Dilendik, Moravian College

Linda Karges-Bone, Charleston Southern University

Terry Hunkapiller Stepka, Arkansas State University

And one reviewer who wished to remain anonymous

Finally, I would like to thank my wife, Kate, and our son, Addy, for their continued support of my extensive writing projects, and for Kate's feedback on various aspects of the book—always keeping me grounded with a classroom teacher's perspective.

—Craig A. Mertler

SECTION I

Overview of Standardized Testing

Concepts and Terminology

Module 1: What Is "Standardized" Testing?

Module 2: The Importance of Standardized Testing

Module 3: Standardized Test Administration and Preparation

Module 1

WHAT IS "STANDARDIZED" TESTING?

This book focuses on the examination and interpretation of standardized test scores for the purposes of helping to inform instructional decisions. However, before we delve into improving our understanding of test scores and their interpretations, it is imperative that we have a clear understanding of the nature of standardized testing. In this module, we will examine various aspects of standardized testing, including the characteristics of a standardized test, a recent history of testing, how standardized tests are developed and revised, and the various types of standardized tests.

WHAT MAKES A TEST "STANDARDIZED"?

In essence, a *standardized test* is any test that is administered, scored, and interpreted in a standard, consistent manner. It does not matter if the test is administered to students in Ohio or Oregon, Maine or Michigan, Connecticut or California; there is a standard set of procedures for administering the test to those students. Nearly all nationally standardized tests are distributed by commercial testing companies, most of which operate on a "for-profit" basis (Popham, 2002). Examples of these test publishing companies—as well as some of their respective tests—include CTB/McGraw-Hill (TerraNova), Harcourt Assessment (Stanford Achievement Test, Metropolitan Achievement Test, WISC–Wechsler Intelligence Scale for Children, OLSAT–Otis-Lennon School Ability Test), and Riverside Publishing Company (ITBS–Iowa Tests of Basic Skills, Gates-MacGinitie Reading Test, Stanford-Binet Intelligence Scales, Woodcock-Johnson Tests of Achievement). There are a few not-for-profit organizations, such as the Educational Testing Service, that also distribute standardized tests.

Undoubtedly, it is likely that you have administered a standardized test to students. If you have not had the opportunity to do so, think back to when you were a student and all of the standardized tests you took. Recall reading—or being read to—the directions for taking the test. They might have appeared something like the following:

SAY: I am going to give you your test booklet. Don't open your booklet until I tell you to do so.

Distribute the test booklets, making sure that each student receives the correct booklet. Next, distribute the answer sheets to each student.

SAY: Open your test booklet to Page 1. Find the section titled "Reading Comprehension." Next, on the answer sheet, find the section titled the same.

Make sure that all students have identified the appropriate locations both in the test booklet and answer sheet.

SAY: Read the directions to yourself as I read them aloud. . . .

Look—or sound—familiar? One of the primary characteristics of any standardized test is that it includes a set of directions—somewhat like a script to be read aloud and verbatim—that are designed to ensure that the particular test is administered in a consistent manner, regardless of the geographic location of the students. Additionally, standardized tests are timed, ensuring that all students are provided with the same amount of time to complete each given section or an entire test. I am sure that we all remember the ever-popular—or was it the ever-dreaded?—phrase spoken by teachers for decades: *Stop. Put your pencils down and close your test booklet.*

A second characteristic of standardized tests is that the answers provided by students are also scored in a consistent manner. Traditionally, standardized tests consisted almost exclusively of *selected-response items*. These types of test items have only one correct answer and that correct answer actually appears as part of the question; the student's task is to simply identify, or select, the correct option. For the most part, multiple-choice and true-false items make up the majority of selected-response items. Since there is only one correct answer to these types of items, student responses are quite easy to score—they are either right or they are wrong. They can be scored quite efficiently and in a consistent manner through the use of scannable answer sheets that are then scored by computer. Since there are no judgments being made by actual scorers, the scoring process remains very consistent. This practice of including only selected-response items on standardized tests has begun to change in recent years. With greater frequency, developers of standardized tests are including more performance-based, constructed-response items along with the selected-response items, although they are doing this more on state-mandated tests (Airasian, 2005). In answering a *constructed-response test item*, students must recall from their own memories, or otherwise create, their responses. Because there may be more than one correct answer—or perhaps only one correct answer, but different ways to arrive at that answer or to explain it—judgment on the part of the scorer does play a part in the scoring process. However, by specifying ahead of time the particular scoring criteria, this subjectivity is kept to a relative minimum and scoring remains, for all intents and purposes, consistent.

You might be asking yourself, "Why the need for all of this standardization?" The answer lies within one of the underlying purposes of standardized testing. Standardized tests, in general, are designed to determine how well students are performing (e.g., achieving, mastering, learning) a common set of broadly based goals (Gronlund, 2006). Furthermore, standardized tests are designed to allow comparisons of a student's individual performance (expressed as a variety of scores) to the performance (i.e., scores) of similar students who have taken the same test under the same conditions. Without this level of standardization, we would continually be trying to compare apples to oranges, as the saying goes.

A BRIEF HISTORY OF STANDARDIZED TESTING IN AMERICAN EDUCATION

Large-scale testing in American education began in the 1800s, although initially was not widespread (Hamilton & Koretz, 2002). By the latter part of that century, large-scale standardized tests were being used to monitor the effectiveness of instructional programs and to compare schools and, in some cases, even teachers. The first standardized achievement test battery, the Stanford Achievement Test, was first published in 1923, after which time the role of testing began to grow dramatically (Hamilton & Koretz, 2002). Testing programs between World War II and the 1960s were primarily geared toward assessing individual students and evaluating curricula. With few exceptions, tests were not used to monitor educational systems or to hold schools—or their teachers—accountable for student performance.

It was not until the late 1960s that large-scale testing programs became much more prevalent. The creation of the National Assessment of Educational Progress

(NAEP)—often called the "Nation's Report Card" (National Center for Educational Statistics [NCES], 2006)—as a recurring national assessment program was really the first step toward using these types of assessments in order to monitor aggregate student achievement. The enactment of the Elementary and Secondary Education Act (ESEA) was also a major step during this decade. This act established the Title I programs and required that they be evaluated. Standardized testing became the primary means of evaluating these national programs (Hamilton & Koretz, 2002).

Statewide testing soon followed these national testing movements. By the end of the 1970s, over half of the states in the country had statewide testing programs in place. At that time, many of these programs were minimum-competency testing programs. Students were required to pass basic-skills tests as a requirement for graduation and even as a requirement for promotion between grades, in some instances (Hamilton & Koretz, 2002). Minimum-competency testing programs did not stick around very long, but their impact was lasting. They created a new function for large-scale testing programs: making students—and, therefore, their teachers—accountable for student test performance. These programs essentially changed the link between test scores and educational improvement (Hamilton & Koretz, 2002). More and more tests were being designed and used so that their results could be used to generate changes in educational practice. This was most likely the beginning of data-driven instruction.

The 1980s could be called the decade of educational reform. Increased testing, along with greater attention being paid to the results of those tests, began to highlight aspects of an educational system that many saw as failing. Student performance on standardized tests demonstrated that many were failing to demonstrate mastery of very rudimentary skills. Concerns regarding these issues sparked a national educational reform movement that, of course, resulted in the increased use of standardized tests. New testing programs were developed, existing programs were broadened, and tests were made more difficult. This new era of testing was used primarily for accountability purposes, with serious consequences for students and educators tied to the test results. This era was also the beginning of states' experimentation with financial incentives and the threat of state intervention for schools that were performing poorly (Hamilton & Koretz, 2002). This movement, however, resulted in a variety of reactions from educators; most of them, negative (Hamilton & Koretz, 2002). Specifically, there were two negative effects: tainted instructional practices (with some teachers focusing on unethical forms of test preparation and inappropriately teaching to the test) and inflated test scores (that were not accompanied by increased levels of achievement). The 1990s saw what some called the "second wave of educational reform" (Hamilton & Koretz, 2002, p. 18). Numerous states began to establish formal systems of financial rewards (for improved scores) and sanctions (for poor performance) for educators that were directly tied to test scores. Furthermore, two major changes within testing programs were called for. First, new tests were developed so that, if most instruction focused on helping students do well on a given test, the students would still be receiving quality instruction. Second, policymakers wanted to see tests that began to concentrate more on higher-order thinking skills. These new formats relied less on multiple-choice items (as had been done in the past) and more on hands-on performance assessments, portfolios, essays, and short-answer questions.

In 2002, the stakes were raised to an even higher level when the No Child Left Behind Act (NCLB) of 2001 was implemented. Along with the passage of NCLB, Congress reauthorized the ESEA of 1965—the original federal law that affected K–12 education in our country. NCLB raises the expectations—and the associated educational accountability—for all states, school districts, and individual schools in terms of ensuring that all students meet or exceed state standards in reading and mathematics prior to completing their K–12 educational programs (Essex, 2006). Furthermore, NCLB requires all states to develop statewide academic standards, as well as a statewide system of testing. A key cornerstone of the NCLB legislation is the notion of Adequate Yearly Progress (AYP), which is defined as a year-to-year measure of student achievement on statewide assessments (Essex, 2006). States are instructed to work diligently toward the goal of closing the achievement gap among racial and disadvantaged groups in order to ensure that all students achieve academic proficiency; AYP is the mechanism for continuously monitoring school, district, and state progress toward this goal. It is important to note that NCLB is not limited to academic proficiency. It is a wide-reaching act with numerous federal education programs included within it. These include such programs as Education for the Disadvantaged, Reading First/Early Reading First, Safe and Drug-free Schools, Bilingual and Migrant Education, Education Technology, Teacher Quality, and Rural Education (Kubiszyn & Borich, 2007). You will undoubtedly notice that neither assessment nor testing appear anywhere in these program titles, but funding for these programs is very closely linked to state, district, and school compliance with NCLB (Kubiszyn & Borich, 2007).

Alongside these movements was the nationwide effort to create sound state-level content and performance standards (Hamilton & Koretz, 2002). The tests would then be designed to parallel these new standards. This notion of data-driven instruction continues to be embedded within testing programs today. Its basic characteristic is the idea that both instruction and standardized tests are developed from state-level content standards. Those resulting test scores (as a mechanism for identifying student strengths and weaknesses) can then be used to guide future instruction. This process, of course, is the focus of this book.

HOW STANDARDIZED TESTS ARE DEVELOPED

As we are well aware, commercial standardized tests are quite different from teacher-made or textbook tests that are designed to be administered in individual classrooms. Not only are the final products quite different, but also is the process used to develop them. A comparison of the steps used in constructing teacher-made tests and those used to create a standardized test are shown in Figure 1.1. Airasian (2005) has identified three characteristics of well-constructed commercially-available standardized tests:

- they are carefully constructed, with item tryouts, analyses, and revisions occurring before the final versions of tests are completed;
- there are written directions and procedures for administering and scoring the test; and
- score interpretation is based on the test having been administered to a carefully selected sample of students from across the country.

This final characteristic is an important feature of standardized tests. The national sample of students, known as a *norm group*, serves as the basis for the comparison for the scores attained by a given local group of students. This group is randomly selected from schools around the country such that representation is based on characteristics including gender, race, ethnicity, culture, and socioeconomic status (Mertler, 2003). In addition to being representative, norm groups must also be current. This information regarding a test's norm group(s) typically appears in the technical manual that accompanies the test (Mertler, 2003). For example, the norm groups for the current *TerraNova* test (2nd ed.) included 100,000 K–12 students for the item tryout phase (during spring and fall of 1998) and over 275,000 K–12 students for the standardization phase (fall 1999 and spring 2000) (CTB/McGraw-Hill, 2001).

Standardized tests go through an extensive development process, beginning with the identification of the educational objectives to be addressed by the test. On a teacher-made classroom test, the objectives that served as the focus of instruction are those that are also assessed. In contrast, the objectives assessed by a standardized test are those that are commonly taught across the country at a specific grade level. These are typically identified through an examination of widely used textbooks and state curriculum guides (Airasian, 2005). Those objectives, content, and skills that are common across different textbooks and various curriculum guides are included in the test. Obviously, therefore, standardized tests may not address some objectives that a particular classroom teacher emphasizes throughout the year.

Once objectives have been identified, the test publisher must begin to write potential test items. A test publisher must develop a collection of potential test

Figure 1.1   Comparison of the Steps in Constructing Teacher-Made and Standardized Tests
(adapted from Airasian, 2005)

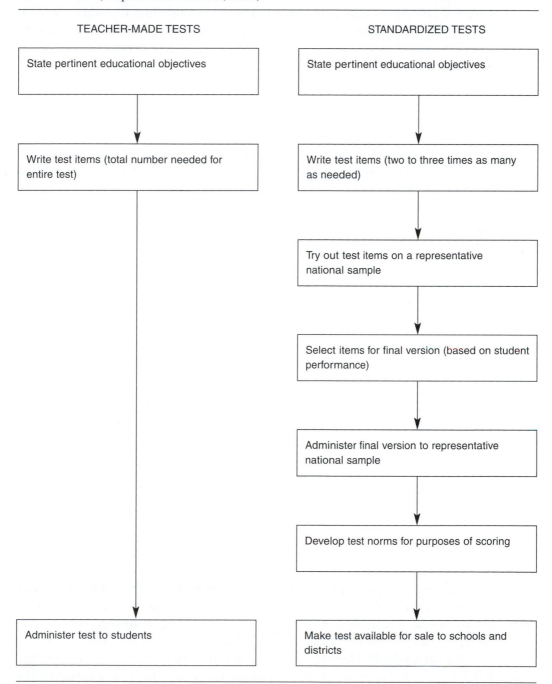

SOURCE: From Peter W. Airasian, *"Classroom Assessment,"* 5/e (2005), McGraw-Hill Publishing. Reproduced with permission of McGraw-Hill Companies.

questions, known as an item pool, consisting of two to three times as many as will actually be used on the test (Airasian, 2005). A staff of professional items writers develops these items, which then go through several iterations of review and revision before being accepted for use on an actual test. Reviews are conducted by several groups of individuals, each representing a different perspective (Airasian, 2005). Curriculum specialists examine the items for appropriate objective and content coverage. Individuals with expertise in test construction examine the items for quality, ensuring that the items are well written and avoid ambiguities or clues to correct answers. The items are also reviewed to ensure that they are not biased toward any specific group of students.

Once the initial pool of items has been developed, the items are tried out on students, and those that are more valid and reliable are retained for the final version of the test. *Validity* is defined as the extent to which a test—and, more specifically, the resulting information it provides about a given student—is sufficient and appropriate in order to make various educational decisions for which the information is intended. In other words, test publishers must address the issue of whether or not (or the extent to which) their test provides the right information for the decisions that schools need to make about their students' achievement. *Reliability* is a secondary, but still important, characteristic of standardized tests. Reliability is defined as the degree to which the scores on a given test are consistent. Here, test publishers are concerned with the issue of whether or not (or the extent to which) scores on their test would be similar if they were collected at some different point in time. Obviously, if a test score is to be a meaningful measure, it must be consistent (i.e., it should not vary from one day to the next). Validity and reliability information is typically provided by a test publisher in the technical manual.

It is impossible to know how well a particular item will work until it has been tried out with a group of students, who are selected for this task because they are characteristically similar to those students who will eventually be taking the final version of the test. There are two essential reasons for trying out items (Airasian, 2005). First, the test publisher wants to be sure that items are clearly written so that they can be easily understood by students. Ones that are not can be revised or discarded altogether. Second, items that are selected for inclusion on the final version of the test must ensure an adequate spread in scores among the students taking the test (remember, the basic purpose of standardized tests is to compare students, which could not occur if they all scored at roughly the same level).

This determination of spread in scores is accomplished through the examination of various statistical properties of each item. Specifically, two important indices are examined. The *difficulty index* of a test item is equal to the proportion of students who answer the item correctly. This value ranges between .00 (a very difficult item) and 1.00 (a very easy item). A difficulty index of .85 simply means that 85% of the examinees answered the item correctly. *Item discrimination* is a measure of how well students who scored high on the entire test perform on an individual item as compared to the performance on that item by students who scored low on the entire test. Generally speaking, if substantially more high-scoring students than low-scoring students answer an item correctly, then the item has functioned quite effectively to discriminate between those students who know the material (as evidenced by their high scores on the total test) and those who do not (again, as evidenced by their low scores).

Once a final version of the test has been established through the procedures described above, the test must be normed. *Test norms* describe how a representative national sample of students performed on the actual final test. This process is important because it provides the information necessary to be able to compare the scores for an individual student to the national sample of similar students. For example, if a test publisher wants to obtain information about how a representative group of fourth graders will perform on its fourth-grade achievement test, it must first select a large representative sample of students in the fourth grade. It must then administer its test to those students. Once the tests have been scored, the set of score information for that sample serves to represent the performance of fourth graders across the country. That information is then used as the comparison group, so to speak, for all other fourth graders who will eventually take the test. Once again, a test's technical manual typically describes the process used to norm its test.

TEST BIAS

Critics of standardized tests sometimes assume that these tests are unfair to certain minority groups—that is to say, the tests demonstrate bias toward those groups. Furthermore, they claim that the tests are occasionally used to deprive members of those groups of access to educational and employment opportunities (Borich & Tombari, 2004; Thorndike, 2005). There is, of course, some truth to this assertion. Historically, some factions of our society have performed less well on standardized tests, and, to the extent that these tests are used for admissions, employment, or other high-stakes decisions, members of these groups have been disproportionately rejected during those types of decision making processes (Thorndike, 2005). The real concern with respect to *test bias* is the extent to which the poor performances are unjust and unfair, resulting from various characteristics of the test itself.

Test bias can appear in several forms. For example, tests may be biased because they contain information or words that favor one racial, ethnic, or gender group over another. Or they may be biased because they contain pictures or references to other specialized topics of greater significance to one group than to others (Borich & Tombari, 2004). These types of biases are known as *group biases*. Specific examples of group test biases might include test items that utilize stereotypes such as female nurses and male doctors, routinely feature males in supervisory roles and females in subordinate roles, or use sexist titles such as fireman (as opposed to firefighter) or foreman (instead of supervisor). In addition, whenever illustrations or photographs are used, the habitual exclusion of people of color, for example, would constitute bias. Similarly, the use of illustrations presenting only females as teachers is biased.

Another type of bias occurs when certain cultural groups do not have adequate representation in the norm group, the group to which student test performance will ultimately be compared. This type of bias is known as *sample bias*. It is for this reason that test publishers take great care in selecting the schools whose students will constitute the norm group and serve as the basis for comparisons of students from around the country.

As with other important information regarding the characteristics of a given test, most publishers will include information regarding their attempts to reduce any inherent test bias within the test's technical manual. For example, the technical manual for the Metropolitan Achievement Test, version 8 (MAT8), includes a section titled "Statistical Procedures for Identifying Potential Bias." In addition, the manual includes a section titled "Standardization—Sampling Procedures," which includes the specification of the main stratification variables (i.e., socio-economic status, urbanicity, and ethnicity) that were used to select the representative norm group (Harcourt Assessment, 2002).

TYPES OF STANDARDIZED TESTS BASED ON PURPOSE

Any given standardized test is designed with a specific purpose in mind. These purposes are typically defined by the types of decisions for which the ultimate scores will be used. One of the most basic ways to categorize a standardized test is to classify it by its respective purpose. There are four basic groupings of standardized tests, based on this categorization scheme. These are achievement tests, aptitude tests, diagnostic tests, and state-mandated tests.

Achievement Tests

Achievements tests are arguably—at least from an educational standpoint—the most common type of standardized test. The main purpose of an achievement test is to measure how much students have learned in specific, clearly defined content areas including but not limited to reading, mathematics, science, and social studies (McMillan, 2001). They may also be used to determine eligibility for special education services, to identify the need for remedial services, and to evaluate the effectiveness of teachers and curricula (Spinelli, 2006). These tests can consist of a battery of tests, or may be used to measure only an individual subject or skill area. Because they are used throughout the country, they typically cover a broad range of content that is common to most school districts. This is an important characteristic of achievement tests because this broad coverage of content is what permits comparisons with the achievement levels of other similar students from across the country. The disadvantage of this coverage is that there may not be a good match between the test coverage and a particular district's local curriculum (McMillan, 2001).

Some examples of commonly used standardized achievement tests include the following:

- Comprehensive Tests of Basic Skills
- Iowa Tests of Basic Skills
- Metropolitan Achievement Tests
- Stanford Achievement Tests
- TerraNova (the newer versions of the California Achievement Tests)

Aptitude Tests

An *aptitude test* is used to determine an individual's cognitive ability such as one's potential or capacity to learn, which in the past was thought to be innate (i.e., intelligence). Historically, these types of tests were collectively referred to as intelligence tests (Kubiszyn & Borich, 2007; Linn & Miller, 2005). Since newer theories have emerged, standardized aptitude tests are sometimes also referred to as *ability tests*, implying that both innate and experiential influences are being measured (McMillan, 2001). In addition, since these tests are used for predicting achievement and for describing learning disabilities, other terms have also been used in place of aptitude test, including learning ability tests, school ability tests, cognitive ability tests, scholastic aptitude tests (Linn & Miller, 2005), as well as intelligence tests or IQ tests (Kubiszyn & Borich, 2007). The aptitude that is measured by these tests is influenced by both in-school and out-of-school experiences, what Thorndike (2005) refers to as "general life experiences" (p. 238). The fact that out-of-school experiences are included is what differentiates an aptitude test from an achievement test (McMillan, 2001). Therefore, aptitude tests typically measure a much broader set of skills. Scores resulting from the administration of an aptitude test are used to ascertain what an individual might be capable of doing at some time in the future. Essentially, then, the basic purpose of an aptitude test is to predict future performance in some activity (Linn & Miller, 2005).

Most aptitude tests administered in schools are group tests, similar to the way in which achievement tests are administered. Aptitude tests administered to groups are primarily used as screening devices to identify students whose abilities differ substantially from the norm (McMillan, 2001). Individual aptitude tests are administered by a trained examiner to one examinee at a time and are usually administered orally face-to-face. These types of tests are characteristically used to identify educational disabilities that may be used to qualify a particular student to receive special education services and/or to be placed in special education programs (McMillan, 2001).

Some examples of commonly used standardized aptitude tests include the following:

- Cognitive Abilities Test (group)
- Otis-Lennon School Ability Test (group)
- Stanford-Binet Intelligence Scale (individual)
- Test of Cognitive Skills (group)
- Wechsler Intelligence Scale for Children (individual)
- Woodcock-Johnson Psycho-Educational Battery (individual)

Diagnostic Tests

A *diagnostic test* is a specialized version of an achievement test. Once it has been determined—from an achievement battery or perhaps classroom observations— that a student is not making satisfactory progress in one or more subject areas (e.g., math or reading), a diagnostic test may be administered to the individual student (Thorndike, 2005). The main purpose of the diagnostic test is to identify the specific areas of weakness the student may be encountering. Analysis of subtest scores can provide insight into a student's respective academic strengths and weaknesses. Some examples of standardized diagnostic tests include the following:

- Metropolitan Reading Diagnostic Test
- Stanford Diagnostic Mathematics Test
- Stanford Diagnostic Reading Test

State-Mandated Tests

Most standardized tests are national in scope, meaning that they are intended to be administered to students across the country. However, some tests have been developed either by state departments of education or by testing companies with the intention of only being administered by school districts within that particular state. These *state-mandated tests* are named such because they are typically developed and implemented to meet some sort of legislative mandate within a particular state and have been implemented for accountability purposes. These state-mandated tests are achievement tests by design; state departments of education do not develop aptitude tests (Popham, 2002). Many of these state testing programs focus on the administration of *high-stakes tests*, so called because their results can have substantial consequences. Most states in the country now have mandated statewide systems of assessment. These states have typically adopted statewide curriculum frameworks or content standards. These standards are used to guide instruction as well as assessment. Instruction and assessment—both classroom assessments and state tests—are designed to parallel a particular state's content standards (Airasian, 2005). Furthermore, results from statewide assessments can inform decision making for future instruction. These reciprocal relationships are depicted in Figure 1.2.

As previously mentioned, high-stakes tests typically have important consequences, especially in light of the increased testing requirements specified in NCLB. In some cases, the consequences are felt by teachers, schools, and districts; in others, they are felt by the individual student. In several states, teachers, schools, and districts are rated based on the performance of their students on these statewide tests. Schools that have a history of poor performance may receive sanctions or reduced federal funding or may be put on probation or even closed altogether. Individual students may be placed in remedial programs, retained at a given grade level, or denied a high school diploma. At the other end of the spectrum, schools, administrators, and teachers with records of high student performance may receive merit pay or other incentives (Airasian, 2005).

Figure 1.2   The Relationships Between Standards, Instruction, and Assessments

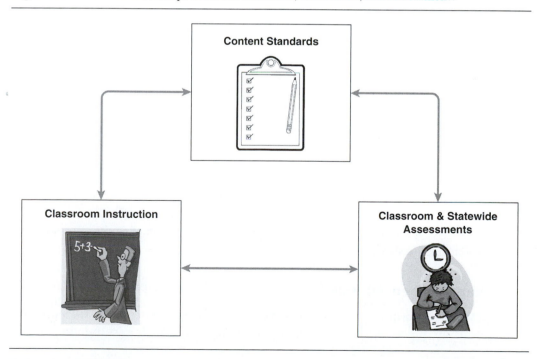

Some examples of state-mandated achievement tests include the following:

- California High School Exit Examination
- Florida Comprehensive Assessment Test
- Michigan Educational Assessment Program
- New York State Level Assessments
- North Carolina End-of-Grade Tests / End-of-Course Tests / Competency Tests
- Ohio Achievement Tests / Ohio Graduation Test
- Texas Assessment of Knowledge and Skills
- Virginia State Standards of Learning Tests

TYPES OF STANDARDIZED TESTS BASED ON SCORES

A second common way to categorize standardized tests is by the types of scores that are used to report student performance. As with the previous categorization scheme, this classification also affects the types of decisions that are made following examination of student results. Test scores are reported in either a *criterion-referenced* or *norm-referenced* format. These types of scores serve very different purposes and answer very different questions about student academic performance.

Criterion-Referenced Tests

The results from the administration of a criterion-referenced standardized test enable teachers to draw inferences about the level of student performance relative to a large domain of content. Individual student scores are not dependent on, and are therefore not compared with, the performance of other students (Mertler, 2003). The interpretation of criterion-referenced scores is not based on statistical analyses; rather, they are based on the establishment of *cut scores*. These types of test scores provide information that helps educators answer the following questions:

- What does this student know?
- What can this student do?
- What content and skills has the student mastered?

You will learn more about the types of criterion-referenced scores provided by standardized tests in Module 5.

Norm-Referenced Tests

When a norm-referenced standardized test is administered to students, the results are reported in a way that permits comparisons with a well-defined norm group. Therefore, a student's score on an individual subtest, for example, is dependent on the performance of the thousands of students making up the comparison group (Mertler, 2003). These types of scores are based on statistical analyses. Norm-referenced test scores provide information that enables educators to answer the following questions:

- What is the relative standing of this student across this broad domain of content?
- How does the student compare to other similar students?

You will learn more about the numerous types of norm-referenced scores provided by standardized tests in Module 6.

Incorporation of Criterion- and Norm-Referenced Results

With increasing frequency, tests publishers are incorporating both criterion- and norm-referenced scores on many of their test reports. However, McMillan (2004) is quick to point out that these tests are still norm-referenced; they are providing some criterion-referenced information on the reports by simply indicating the number of items answered correctly within a given subtest. Since the primary purpose of these tests is to compare student performance, the criterion-referenced information provided is typically not as detailed or meaningful. Therefore, it is important to note that there is a distinct difference between a criterion-referenced test and criterion-referenced interpretations (McMillan, 2004). This type of information is commonly used to supplement and to better understand the norm-referenced results.

Summary

Standardized tests are those that are administered, scored, and interpreted in a consistent manner, regardless of where the test is administered. These tests are characterized by a scripted set of directions and consistent scoring procedures and are designed to measure how well students are learning a common set of broadly-based educational goals. This standardization also allows for comparisons of students' performance with that of similar students who have taken the same test under the same conditions.

Although large-scale testing in American schools began in the 1800s, it did not become widespread until the 1950s and 1960s. The creation of the NAEP and the enactment of the ESEA prompted the need for continuous standardized testing. Statewide testing programs soon followed, with many states requiring students to pass tests as a requirement for graduation. For the first time, large-scale testing programs were being used to make students and their teachers accountable for performance. The decades that followed saw an increase in testing and in the attention paid to the results. Testing was now being used primarily for accountability purposes, with potentially serious consequences being tied to the results. After the turn of the century, NCLB functioned to raise the stakes even higher. The notion of data-driven instruction, where both instruction and tests are developed from state content standards, continues to be embedded in testing programs.

Standardized tests are developed through a thorough process of item construction, trial with representative samples, item analysis, and revision. The composition of the representative norm group is a critical step in this process, as is the determination of the validity and reliability of individual items. Items are carefully written to avoid the inclusion of bias. Standardized tests can be categorized based on their purpose (i.e., achievement, aptitude, diagnostic, and state-mandated tests) or by type of score provided (i.e., criterion-referenced and norm-referenced).

Activities for Application and Reflection

1. Most school districts possess the technical manuals from any standardized test they administer (these can usually be found in the assessment or curriculum offices). Ask for permission to review the technical manual for any standardized test. Locate, read, and summarize information pertaining to various aspects discussed in this module. Specifically, look for information addressing the following:

   - basic description of the test (e.g., type based on purpose and based on scores),
   - process used for item development,
   - selection criteria used for the norm group,
   - process used to limit test bias,
   - validity and reliability of test items, and
   - item analysis results.

2. In recent years, there has been a substantial reduction in the number of commercially available standardized aptitude tests in comparison to the number of available standardized achievement tests. Why do you suppose that this trend is occurring?

3. For your grade level or content area, examine your district's or state's curriculum guide. Select a standardized achievement test (preferably one that you actually administer). Which objectives appearing in the curriculum guide are adequately measured by the test? Which are not? In your opinion, how adequately is the content covered by the test?

4. Imagine that your state's legislature has passed a new law requiring all students to show proficiency in skills needed to be successful in everyday life before they can receive a diploma. What would be the relative advantages and disadvantages of using each of the following types of tests?

   • Tests constructed by each individual school district
   • A test developed by the state department of education
   • A nationally published test

Module 2

THE IMPORTANCE OF STANDARDIZED TESTING

In Module 1, you learned about standardized testing, from its history to the process used to develop tests, and about the various types of standardized tests. Now that we understand a bit more about the nature of standardized testing, we will take a look in this module at its relative advantages and disadvantages. Of course, there is no shortage of opinions among educators at all levels when it comes to standardized testing, so we will also examine why educators dislike testing and why they should like standardized testing.

APPROPRIATE USES OF STANDARDIZED TESTING IN EDUCATION

Standardized tests and their subsequent results have many uses and applications in educational settings. As you will see in this section, many of those uses are fundamentally good, positive, and beneficial to the overall educational process (see Figure 2.1). However, some uses—actually, misuses—are negative and detrimental, as you will see in the next section. Most of the appropriate uses for standardized tests focus on the instructional applications of the test results. These uses find applications at both the individual and group levels. First, standardized test results can be used quite effectively at the level of the individual student. Initially, test results can be used to efficiently describe individual students' learning abilities, as well as the educational levels that have been attained by given students (Linn & Miller, 2005; Nitko, 2004). This information can be used to help guide modifications or adaptations of instruction to meet individual students' needs. Norm-referenced tests can point out general areas of individual strengths and weaknesses, and criterion-referenced tests can indicate how well specific tasks are being mastered, especially since they are tied to specific instructional objectives (Linn & Miller, 2005). Standardized tests are also very useful at initially identifying the needs of exceptional students (Linn & Miller, 2005). Typically, their performance deviates so markedly from other students at their grade or age level that specialized instructional programs are warranted. Often, test results can be used to pinpoint—or, at least, narrow down—their problems of learning and development so further appropriate action may be taken. Standardized test results also permit comparisons between the performance of an individual student and that for a large group of similar students (i.e., who make up the norm group) at the same grade level from across the country. Finally, although teachers' reports of student academic progress and achievement are the most important source of information to parents, standardized test results can also provide a useful supplement (Linn & Miller, 2005). From the perspective of a parent, these results have the advantage of being independent of teacher opinions. As previously mentioned, they also have the advantage of providing to parents some normative comparisons with similar children across a wider context than that of an individual classroom or school.

> "You need an awful lot of information to be able to effectively educate each and every child that walks in a classroom."
>
> —Hugh Caumartin, District Superintendent

Second, and in my opinion, some of the most beneficial uses of test results have applications at the level of entire, intact groups of students. Prior to beginning instruction, test results may be used to a good indication of general ability levels of students in a class or grade level (McMillan, 2001). Prior to the beginning of a school year, the information resulting from the previous spring's test administration could be used for this purpose. Interpreting test results in this manner can help teachers establish reasonable student goals and can influence the nature of instruction and materials selected to support that instruction. These goals should be neither auspiciously low (for fear that the expectation becomes a self-fulfilling prophesy) nor unrealistically high. For example, if students in fifth grade generally score low on a test of reading comprehension (in the spring of fifth grade), the sixth-grade teachers may want to adjust their reading materials accordingly, at least at the beginning of the year.

Provided that the selected test is aligned with the district's curriculum and instructional objectives, the results can be used to identify areas of instructional strengths and weaknesses (Kubiszyn & Borich, 2007; Linn & Miller, 2005; McMillan, 2001). Curricular areas identified as weaknesses across a group of students (e.g., a class or a given grade level) may then be targeted for instructional revisions or, at a minimum, for a greater level of focused instruction. Trends or patterns in the test scores, as well as average scores across groups (i.e., a class, building, or school district), can be used in these types of decisions (Nitko, 2004). For example, if the majority of students in Grade 4 perform poorly on the geography subtest of a social studies

Figure 2.1   Appropriate Uses of Standardized Testing

Appropriate Uses of Standardized Testing in Education

For individual students, standardized test results can . . .
- Efficiently describe an individual's learning abilities and levels of achievement
- Guide modifications or adaptations of instruction to meet individual needs
- Identify general areas of strengths and weaknesses
- Initially identify various needs of exceptional students
- Pinpoint specific problems of learning and development
- Provide a useful supplement to the classroom teacher's measures of academic progress

For groups of students, standardized test results can . . .
- Provide a good indication of general ability levels prior to instruction
- Be used to establish reasonable classroom goals
- Help shape the nature of instruction and supplemental instructional materials
- Identify areas of instructional strengths and weaknesses across classes, grade levels, or school buildings
- Provide one source of data about the effectiveness of instruction

---

battery, teachers in that grade level may want to spend more time teaching geography or may want to alter the ways in which they teach the material, reinforce the concepts, or assess student learning within their classes. Similarly, curricular areas identified as strengths can be profited from by using those areas of stronger student performance to support areas of weaker performance. For example, if students performed well on a subtest of writing, perhaps writing activities could be used to support future instruction and reinforcement of concepts in geography.

Of course, another use for test results addresses the need for educational accountability (Kubiszyn & Borich, 2007). Although some experts disagree with its appropriateness for this purpose, standardized testing can provide a somewhat uniform means of measuring student academic performance. For example, No Child Left Behind (NCLB) requires each state to define Adequate Yearly Progress (AYP) for schools and districts. In defining AYP, states essentially set a minimum level of improvement—as measured by student performance on standardized tests—that individual schools and districts must achieve within time frames established by the law (Essex, 2006). Each state must set a starting point that is based on the performance of its lowest-performing demographic group or of the lowest-achieving schools in the state, whichever is higher. The state then establishes the level of student achievement that a school or district must make each year to meet AYP. The thresholds must increase at least once every three years until all students in the state are achieving at the proficient level by 2014. Although many believe this to be a lofty and unrealistic goal, it is nonetheless a goal to which schools and districts are being held accountable (Essex, 2006).

Other appropriate uses of standardized test results involve the provision of data that can help to provide information about the effectiveness of instruction. For example, test data can help educational evaluators describe the relative effectiveness of alternate methods of instruction and identify factors that influence the success of the particular instructional program (Nitko, 2004). Similarly, school superintendents can use standardized test scores, across a school or district, to describe to school boards, as well as other interested stakeholders, the relative effectiveness of the local educational system (Nitko, 2004).

MISUSES OF STANDARDIZED TESTING IN EDUCATION

Unfortunately, there are also abundant misuses of standardized test scores that cause harm to the overall educational process. One of the most important misuses of test scores is the use of the results of a single assessment to make important decisions about individual students, particularly involving decisions for which the results of the standardized test were not intended. For example, the results of standardized tests have sometimes been used by teachers as the basis for assigning course grades (Linn & Miller, 2005; Nitko, 2004). For several, and hopefully obvious, reasons, this is an undesirable practice. Nationally administered tests, and sometimes even state-mandated tests, are seldom closely related to the instructional objectives of a particular course (Linn & Miller, 2005). Also, they tend to measure only a portion of the desired learning outcomes emphasized in a particular course (Linn & Miller, 2005). Therefore, their content may not match the skills actually taught within the classroom; in other words, these tests were not designed specifically with your students or teaching style in mind.

A second misuse of standardized tests involves their use to assign a student to a remedial program or to retain the student altogether (Linn & Miller, 2005; Nitko, 2004). In either situation, much more information is required to make such an important decision. Information such as a student's background, prior learning experiences, and teacher observations of classroom behavior and academic performance needs to be factored into decisions such as these. Although standardized tests can provide additional information to help guide these types of decisions, they certainly should not be used in isolation for these purposes (Linn & Miller, 2005).

Third, it is critical for educators (teachers and administrators alike) to avoid a common misinterpretation of the norms for a given standardized test. Often, educators view the norms for a test as an absolute goal that is designed to be reached by all students (Payne, 2003). This tendency is often exacerbated by the fact that educators may criticize students who fail to meet the typically rigid standards. This, in turn, has a substantial detrimental effect on students' motivation and confidence in their academic abilities.

Another very serious misuse of standardized tests is to use them as a means of evaluating teachers and teaching effectiveness, as well as overall school effectiveness. First and foremost, standardized tests are not designed for this purpose and should therefore not be used for this purpose (McMillan, 2001). Furthermore, each school year brings a new group of students complete with different skills, knowledge, motivation, cultural background, and group dynamics than those of the previous year. The effects of all of these factors, along with many others, influence student academic learning and cannot be separated from the effect that an individual teacher has (Linn & Miller, 2005; McMillan, 2001; Nitko, 2004). Additionally, and as previously discussed, the content and skills appearing on the test will not match perfectly with a local curriculum or with how or what a given teacher may have emphasized during instruction. Therefore, blaming teachers for poor student performance on standardized tests is an extremely inappropriate application of test results. Unfortunately, evidence of this occurrence can be observed when teachers, feeling the pressure from this kind of blame, resort to unethical test preparation or administration practices (see Module 3).

It is important to note that many of these misuses may seem to you to be a bit obvious and perhaps even contrived. The reason that I have chosen to discuss them here is because educators—as well as the general public and the mass media—really have engaged in these types of inappropriate practices, and many continue to do so today. It is imperative that educators are aware of these inappropriate uses of standardized tests and their results.

Even though it was discussed earlier as an appropriate use, I would be remiss if I did not also discuss accountability in this section as a potential misuse of standardized tests. While many educators believe testing to be a positive accountability movement, countless others have criticized its use for this purpose. These critics argue that testing programs that consume weeks of teachers' and students' time each and every year are not the most productive or efficient way to collect performance measures of our students' learning. They claim that we cannot improve student learning by simply measuring students more often (perhaps you have heard the old saying, "You can't fatten a chicken by weighing it every day" or "You can't cure a child's cold by taking her temperature every day"). They believe that most states' accountability tests have nearly no value for improving teaching and learning (Airasian, 2005). At the risk of oversimplifying this debate, I would like to state that I disagree with this sentiment. What is being advocated in this book represents just the opposite attitude. Continual examination of students' standardized test results—and the subsequent revisions, adaptations, and modifications to curriculum and instruction that can result from them—is just one of many mechanisms for reflecting and refining our classroom practice.

WHY EDUCATORS DISLIKE STANDARDIZED TESTING

Many of the standardized testing critics are themselves educators. They tend not to like standardized testing because it does, admittedly, occupy a good deal of class time during the school year. Additionally, they do not like this notion of increased testing mandates because they typically originate from the federal government or from state legislatures—people whom educators believe do not really understand what it is like to be a teacher in today's schools. They question the accuracy of the measures themselves.

> " . . . standardized assessments have frustrated a lot of good teachers because they [are tempted to say], 'Okay I know what I need to teach, and I'll need to adjust this and do this, but now I have this big time bomb that's ticking;' that changes the way they typically do things."
>
> —Sue Garcia,
> *Primary Intervention Specialist*

Further, these educators tend to believe that the very notion of a commercially produced, external (i.e., not classroom-based), norm-referenced, summative, and quantitative instrument for measuring important educational outcomes is simply ridiculous (Nitko, 2004). They also argue that a single test cannot do an accurate job of measuring the whole person (Nitko, 2004). Human characteristics, motivation, behavior, attitudes, interests, values, and learning styles are just simply too complex to be measured by one test. They believe that these factors should be assessed regularly by schools (a point with which I would not disagree).

Finally, teachers do not like how the mass media has a tendency to portray them as the educational scapegoats for our children's "failing" education. Thanks to newspapers and local television news programs, the general public's perceptions of educational effectiveness are shaped by the media's reports of students' test performance (Popham, 2002). Although this is not earth shattering news, it is still seen as news by the general public—it sells newspapers and entices people to watch local television news broadcasts. Therefore, this practice of reporting district test scores and even ranking them accordingly will likely not end any time soon.

> "I didn't look at it as a measure of somebody looking down on me if things didn't quite go right. I looked at it as a measure of this is what I need to do to improve."
>
> —Martha Fether,
> *Elementary Principal*

WHY EDUCATORS (*SHOULD*) LIKE STANDARDIZED TESTING

Nitko (2004) argues that criticisms of a test or testing program are not the equivalent of a misuse of the test, and I would agree. There are certainly shortcomings of standardized tests, just as there are shortcomings (or limitations) of any method of educational assessment. Those weaknesses do not make the test or its results inherently bad. When administering a standardized test or interpreting its results, it is important to bear in mind one critical thing. As educators, I firmly believe that you will find standardized test results helpful to your instruction and classroom-based assessments, as well as to your students' learning and achievement, as long as you use that data with a full understanding of its limitations and as only a supplement to the data you gather from students on a daily basis. Often, the results of these tests will corroborate what you already know about your students (McMillan, 2001). Additional information from a new, or at least different, source may provide a positive influence on your teaching practices.

Also, since standardized testing is likely not going to go away, it is important for you to be able to help students and parents understand how to make sense out of the results of standardized test scores (Popham, 2002). These tests are important to them too, and they will likely seek your assistance in helping them sort out all of the different types of scores and what their interpretations mean.

I believe the bottom line is this: The results of standardized testing should be viewed as one source of information and not as the panacea of all educational assessment. No absolute decisions—especially those with substantial consequences to students—should be made solely on the basis of standardized test performance. Additionally, decisions about teachers and their relative instructional effectiveness in the classroom should not be grounded in students' standardized test scores. Teachers and administrators should use all sources of information at their disposal to make decisions about students, instruction, and curriculum. Since standardized testing is not likely to disappear in our immediate professional futures, we are stuck (not in a bad way, mind you!) administering tests and interpreting the results. The information in the form of test

"I think it's about attitude. It's about how you approach it. And you can accept it or not. And, we all need to accept it and deal with it. And if you really look at it as something that can be a really valuable tool and make you a better teacher, it's not a bad thing. That's a good thing."

—Megan Newlove,
High School English Teacher

" . . . if I make the choice to consciously and with a lot of effort try to change what I'm doing or gear it more towards the needs of the students, then I think it's very important."

—Ellen Sharp,
First- and Second-Grade Teacher

"Since we have to give the test and since your kids have to pass the test, why not use anything at your disposal that's going to help you help those kids?"

—Joe Hudok,
High School Social Studies Teacher

" . . . the tests are not going to go away. A lot of people in that 'I hate standardized tests' group think that they've been through a lot of transformations in the world of education and if they just lay low, it'll all pass. And I truly don't think that that's going to be the case."

—Cori Boos,
High School Mathematics Teacher

results will be returned to the schools and districts from the testing companies or state departments of education. We have the information; we might as well put it to good use.

Figure 2.2   Why Educators Dislike and (*Should*) Like Standardized Testing

Why Educators Dislike Standardized Testing	Why Educators (Should) Like Standardized Testing
• Takes up a good deal of instructional time • Testing mandates stem from governmental officials • Accuracy of standardized tests as measures of achievement and ability seems questionable • Single tests cannot measure the whole person • Mass media's unfair portrayal of teachers and programs, primarily in poorly performing schools	• All assessment methods have limitations; standardized tests are no different • Tests are not inherently bad • Standardized test results can be a helpful source of information about instruction and curriculum • Test scores can corroborate what is known about students • Need to help students and parents understand test results • Should be viewed as one additional source of information about student academic performance

Summary

Standardized testing has seen many uses of its results, both appropriate and in appropriate. At the individual student level, appropriate uses of standardized test results include the description of students' learning abilities, which can be used to guide modifications or adaptations of instruction. Test results are also useful for the initial identification of the needs of exceptional students. Results can be used to compare student performance to a large group of similar students. They also provide an alternative source of information independent from teachers' observations.

Standardized test results can also be used very effectively at the group level. Prior to instruction, the results can be used as an indication of general ability levels across a class or grade level. This information can ultimately be used to establish reasonable instructional goals. If the test is appropriately aligned with the curriculum and instructional objectives, results can be used to identify areas of instructional strengths and weaknesses. Test results can also be used as data for the evaluating the effectiveness of instruction, especially in the case of alternate methods of instruction. Finally, they can also be used as information about school system effectiveness when reporting to school boards or other interested stakeholders.

Standardized test results can also be, and are, misused. One of the most serious misuses of test data is to evaluate individual teachers and their relative effectiveness. Test scores are also misused when they are relied on as the sole source of information for decisions about remediation or retention and for assigning course grades. The norms for a given test should not be viewed as an absolute goal for all students to reach. Testing programs are also used for educational accountability. Depending on one's perspective, this can be either an appropriate or an inappropriate use of test results.

Educators typically dislike standardized testing because it takes time away from classroom instruction. Additionally, they disagree with the basic notion of a single measure of a whole person. Finally, local newspapers and television news programs have made it standard procedure to report standardized test results and even to rank local school districts. Educators often feel that this practice is quite unfair, often making educators the scapegoats for poor student performance.

However, educators should like standardized testing programs because they can provide some educational benefits. After factoring in the limitations of the tests, the resulting scores can be used very effectively to help guide decision making relative to instructional planning and delivery, as well as to classroom-based assessments. Since testing programs are not going away, educators should be better aware of how to use the information provided in a positive manner.

Activities for Application and Reflection

1. Describe some of the ways in which standardized tests might be used for instructional decision making in one of your teaching areas.

2. Based on your experiences as a current or future educator, can you identify additional appropriate uses for standardized test results, other than those you read about?

3. Based on your experiences as an educator, can you identify additional inappropriate uses for standardized test results, other than those you read about?

4. Carefully read the interview transcripts, which appear in Section IV of this book, for Sue Garcia, primary intervention specialist at Crim Elementary, and for Kathy Zachel, assistant superintendent of Bowling Green Schools. Compare and contrast their views toward and opinions of standardized testing. To what might you attribute their different perspectives?

5. Carefully read the interview transcript for Amy Kenyon, first- and second-grade teacher. Discuss her initial reaction when first required to interpret test scores and to use the resulting information. How and why did her initial reaction change?

6. Carefully read the interview transcript for Joe Hudok, high school social studies teacher. Discuss his explanations at the beginning of why he believes that some teachers do not like standardized testing. Do you agree or disagree with his opinions? Explain your answer.

7. Using the Internet, research more about your state's testing program. Find out how your state is complying with NCLB and AYP. Do you believe that this is "good" or "bad" accountability?

STANDARDIZED TEST ADMINISTRATION AND PREPARATION

In this module, we focus our attention on the administration of standardized tests. Although we touched on this process in Module 1, we will focus on aspects such as the types of preparation practices in which teachers engage with students—some of which they should do, and others that they should not do. We will examine various skills that students can gain to help facilitate their performances on these tests. Finally, we discuss the meaning behind the phrase *teaching to the test*.

STANDARDIZED ADMINISTRATION PROCEDURES

Since most standardized tests are given in classrooms—or, in the case of individually-administered tests, in some other school-based environment—teachers are typically responsible for administering them to students. The most crucial aspect of administering standardized tests to students is to follow the directions carefully and explicitly (Linn & Miller, 2005; McMillan, 2004). Strict adherence to the instructions provided by the test publisher is key to maintaining the comparability of the results, especially in the case of norm-referenced tests. The specific testing procedures are established to ensure standardization in the conditions under which students in different classrooms, buildings, districts, and states take the test. The directions that appear in a test's administration manual specify what you are to say, how you should respond to students' questions, and what you should do while students are working on the test. You owe it to yourself and to your students to familiarize yourself with the directions prior to reading them to your students

(Hogan, 2007; Kubiszyn & Borich, 2007). Even if you have administered a particular test consecutively over a number of years, avoid the temptation to paraphrase the directions or recite them from memory (McMillan, 2004). Published tests must be administered under the same conditions if the results are to be meaningfully interpreted (Linn & Miller, 2005); otherwise, the resulting interpretations will be nothing short of misleading (Airasian, 2005; Kubiszyn & Borich, 2007). For example, it would not be reasonable to compare the performance of a student who had 45 minutes to complete a subtest to that of the norm group of students who had 30 minutes (per the directions from the test publisher).

During the test, it is typically permissible to answer student questions about the directions or any procedures for answering test items. However, by no means should you provide assistance with an answer or with the interpretation of a test item (McMillan, 2004). Additionally, teachers are often tempted to give certain students hints to correct answers, to encourage them to move faster through the test, or even to slow down and think a little bit harder. It is necessary, but sometimes difficult, for educators to step out of the role of teacher and assume that of a test administrator for a few hours (Linn & Miller, 2005; McMillan, 2004). The bottom line is that educators must know what constitutes acceptable behavior and what does not. These are ultimately issues of conscientiousness and professional ethics.

Finally, the time limits must be rigorously followed. Once the time limit has expired for a given subtest, the completed answer sheets and tests must be promptly collected. To ensure test security, all copies of the test and answer sheets must be accounted for (McMillan, 2004).

To summarize the responsibilities of a teacher or other educator, five relatively simple tasks are listed and described below (Hogan, 2007; Kubiszyn & Borich, 2007; Linn & Miller, 2005). These tasks are expressed as follows.

- **Motivate the students**. As educators, we want our students to perform to the best of their abilities. To help students accomplish this goal, we should encourage them to do their best. The purpose of the test and how the results will be used should be clearly explained to students. Most importantly, however, may be the demonstration of a positive attitude toward the test results. This ultimately begins with a positive attitude coming from the teacher. If students are convinced that valid scores are beneficial to them, then their level of test anxiety tends to decrease and their level of motivation tends to increase.
- **Follow directions strictly**. The importance of strictly following testing directions has already been discussed, but cannot be overemphasized. If the test is not administered in complete accordance with the directions, the test scores will contain an unknown amount of error. This will result in misinterpretation and misuse of the results, typically meaning that numerous decisions—many of them containing substantial consequences—may simply be wrong decisions.

- **Keep time accurately**. One of the important aspects in the standardization process is ensuring that students, regardless of their geographic location, have the same amount of time to complete a test or subtest. It is crucial that time be kept—and, perhaps, even recorded—with the utmost precision.
- **Record significant events**. It is also important to carefully observe students during the administration of a test. You may want to record any unusual behavior or event that you witness that you believe could somehow influence test scores. For example, you might observe a student who seems very anxious or seems to be marking responses in a random manner without reading the test items. You should make note of your observation since it could certainly shed light on the interpretations of the student's test performance when the results are returned. Since test results are not returned sometimes for two or three months, it is not advisable to rely on your memory. Similarly, any interruptions to the testing period—including the nature and length of a given interruption—should be noted, for its occurrence could supply additional information for accurate test score interpretation.
- **Collect test materials promptly**. Once the testing time has ended, all materials should be collected promptly so that students are not able to work beyond the allotted time and so that all materials can be accounted for and secured.

> *"I think it's important for a teacher to show and have their students feel an aura of invincibility with tests and to feel confident. And if a teacher has a strong negative attitude about standardized tests I think that's very difficult to hide with students."*
>
> —Jeff Burkett,
> *Sixth-Grade Teacher*

TESTWISENESS SKILLS

There are numerous things that teachers can do to help students prepare for standardized tests. Many of these represent ethical and legitimate practices; however, other preparation practices do not. In this section, we will take a look at one category of student test preparation practices that is ethical and appropriate. In the next section of this module, we will examine a wide variety of additional practices, both appropriate and inappropriate.

There are numerous ways that teachers can help their students prepare to perform well on standardized tests. The single most important thing a teacher can do, first and foremost, is to provide sound instruction (Airasian, 2005; Hogan, 2007). Planning for and delivering instruction by incorporating periodic reviews; by clearly emphasizing important terms, concepts, and skills during instruction; by providing practice on key instructional objectives; and by providing an appropriate learning environment is simply good teaching. Furthermore, these practices also tend to result in good learning.

Beyond the provision of good, sound teaching, teachers can also help students develop a set of skills known as *testwiseness skills*. Students who possess testwiseness skills are those that have the ability to use test-taking strategies during a particular standardized test. Whenever students are required to take a standardized test, we want and expect them to put forth their best efforts and to demonstrate the extent to which they have mastered certain content learning and related skills. However, some students do not perform to the best of their abilities because they lack skills in test taking (Hogan, 2007; Linn & Miller, 2005). Students should be provided with training in test-taking strategies to prevent this type of inadequacy from lowering their test scores. Although this seems to be somewhat of a commonsense recommendation, instruction and practice in test-taking strategies are often not provided to students or may not be reinforced from year to year. These skills can be mastered fairly easily, but students need practice to develop them (Linn & Miller, 2005). Fortunately, many test publishers now provide practice tests that can be given prior to the actual tests. These give students and their teachers opportunities to become familiar with the testing format before it really counts. Among testwiseness skills that students should be taught and given the opportunity to practice are the following:

- listening to and/or reading test directions carefully (this includes following proper procedures for marking responses on the answer sheet);
- listening to and/or reading test items carefully;
- establishing a pace that will permit completion of the test or subtest;
- skipping difficult items (instead of wasting valuable testing time) and returning to them later;
- making informed guesses as opposed to just omitting items that appear too difficult;
- eliminating possible options (in the case of multiple-choice items), by identifying options that are clearly incorrect based on knowledge of content, prior to making informed guesses;
- checking to be sure that an answer number matches the item number when marking an answer; and
- checking answers, as well as the accuracy of marking those answers, if time permits (Linn & Miller, 2005).

It is important to note that there are some testwiseness skills that are considered to be unethical. In other words, application of these skills during a standardized test may result in the improvement of a student's score beyond that which would be attained from mastery of the content alone (Mertler, 2003). These techniques are seen as ways to eliminate incorrect answers—without knowing anything about the content—based purely on clues provided within the item. For example, the following clues could be used by students as a means of blindly guessing a correct answer (Airasian, 2005):

- If vague words (e.g., some, often, seldom, or sometimes) are used in one of the options, that option is likely to be the correct answer.
- The option that is the longest or the most precisely stated is more likely to be the correct answer.
- Any choice that has a grammatical or spelling error (which is not likely to occur on a published standardized test) is not likely to be the correct option.
- Choices that do not connect "smoothly" to the stem of a test question are not likely to be correct.
- Finally, there is an old adage among test-taking students: *When in doubt, pick C.* This belief stems from the fallacy that in any given standardized test, option *C* is correct more often than any other. Therefore, in situations when you simply do not know anything about a test item, *C* is most likely a good guess at the correct answer.

When students use these or similar strategies, they are, in essence, compensating for or overcoming their lack of content knowledge (Airasian, 2005). They end up with a score that is higher than their actual level of mastery.

DO'S AND DON'TS OF TEST PREPARATION

As educators, we always want our students to demonstrate what they have learned and what they are capable to doing to the best of their abilities. Helping them develop their testwiseness skills—those that are ethical and appropriate, of course—can go a long way in terms of providing more accurate test scores for valid instructional decisions. In this current age of increased accountability and pressure on both teachers and students to perform, it is easy to get carried away with test preparation practices. With increasing frequency, many teachers are focusing more of their attention on the contents of the standardized tests that they administer. Unfortunately, this can lead to poor instructional practices and inflated test scores (Linn & Miller, 2005).

For example, in a recent research study examining the impact of No Child Left Behind (NCLB) on teachers' instructional and assessment practices (Mertler, 2006), an overwhelming majority (93%) of teachers indicated that NCLB has changed the nature of instructional motivation for teachers and has placed more stress on teachers, and 73% of teachers believed that NCLB has changed the nature of academic motivation for and has placed more stress on students. Two-thirds of teachers

"There's pressure to have students perform because it's a reflection on ourselves as well as the student in the classroom and the school, the school district, the state, etc. So I think there's that issue. I have no problem being held accountable for what I teach."

—Jeff Burkett,
Sixth-Grade Teacher

agreed that NCLB has forced them to change the focus of their classroom instruction. The vast majority (84%) of teachers agreed that NCLB had influenced what or how instruction is provided to students. Additionally, 74% indicated that they have substantially decreased the amount of time spent on content that they knew was not tested on the state-mandated tests. Similarly, 82% responded that they had substantially increased the amount of time spent on content that they knew would appear on the state tests.

As you can see, this pressure to perform has become immense. I firmly believe that this pressure has the capability to produce the standardized testing version of good versus evil (see Figure 3.1). Within the most ethical of teachers, it can create an internalized tug-of-war. Teachers want their students to perform well—and, in doing so, provide evidence that they are highly effective educators—but at what cost? Care on the part of all educators must be exhibited to avoid the temptation to engage in student test preparation practices that would be considered unethical. Unethical test preparation practices will likely improve students' scores; however, in the end, they also result in scores whose validity is suspect, perhaps even highly questionable. It is important to remember that the ultimate purpose of any test is to improve teaching and learning (Kober, 2002).

We have already discussed some preparation practices—namely test-taking strategies—variations of which can be both ethical and unethical. There are numerous additional types of test preparation practices with which educators should be familiar. Although this scheme oversimplifies the situation, we typically discuss these practices as being ethical/appropriate or unethical/inappropriate. More appropriately, these types of practices exist on a continuum, ranging from most ethical and appropriate to least ethical and appropriate.

The majority of these practices can be categorized into one of five general areas of test preparation (Miyasaka, 2000) with each having their own respective range of appropriateness:

- curriculum and test content—practices that involve content objectives and curriculum standards;
- assessment approaches and item formats—practices that involve familiarizing students with a variety of assessment approaches (e.g., multiple-choice items, short answer items, extended response items, performance assessment) and item formats (e.g., different types of multiple-choice item formats);
- test-taking strategies—practices involving general test-taking or testwiseness strategies, unrelated to specific test content;
- timing of test preparation—practices conducted at various points in time before or during test administration; and
- student motivation—practices related to motivating students to perform to the best of their abilities.

Figure 3.1   The Standardized Testing Version of Good Versus Evil

Each of these five categories of test preparation practices will now be discussed in detail.

Test preparation practices related to curriculum and test content are arguably some of the most crucial, and sometimes the most easily confused and misunderstood. Much of this confusion is directly associated with specific phrases that are used to describe these practices. Educators, as well as measurement experts, tend to use the same phrase to refer to different types of practices. Miyasaka (2000) offers the following distinctions between these common phrases:

"Teaching to the curriculum objectives"	→	Teaching the objectives or the knowledge and skills in the curriculum content domain
"Teaching to the test"	→	Teaching/reviewing only the content objectives that are tested and including highly similar test item content
"Teaching the test"	→	Teaching the actual content/skills in the items appearing in the test

Most, if not all, standardized tests assess content that is part of national, state, and/or district curriculum standards and instructional objectives. In most states, teachers are required to teach to the standards that represent what students should know and be able to do. Regular classroom instruction and assessment that focuses on the adopted standards is test preparation. Therefore, teaching to the curriculum objectives (or standards) constitutes an ethical and appropriate test preparation practice—in addition to being good, sound teaching.

In contrast, teaching to the test can have a detrimental effect on the testing process. If instruction is designed to parallel only those standards and/or objectives that actually appear on the test, then the focus of instruction—and, therefore, test preparation—has simply been narrowed too much. This is especially problematic with tests where a small number of alternate forms of the test exist (Miyasaka, 2000). For example, if there is only one form of a test that is given each year, the actual objectives as well as actual items can become familiar to the teacher who administers (and therefore sees) the test each year. This is typically the situation when the good versus evil temptation begins to surface. Having the knowledge that certain material is tested and other material is not is sometimes too great a temptation to the teacher who really, *really* wants students to perform well. This would obviously result in an unethical and inappropriate type of test preparation. However, in situations when there are multiple forms of a given test, when the standards and objectives that are sampled on the various forms are different, and when the items differ from one form to another, teaching to the test results in the content and test prep focus to be much broader. This type of situation then would constitute an ethical and appropriate type of preparation practice. The difficulty, however, lies in the fact that teaching to the test is not necessarily a black and white issue; there exists a multitude of situations that would fall in the gray area in between the two scenarios presented here, which lie at the extreme opposite ends of the continuum.

In stark contrast to the two previous approaches to instruction and test preparation, teaching the test clearly represents an unethical and unacceptable form of test preparation. This practice takes the notion of a narrowed focus of instruction and test prep, as previously discussed, to the ultimate extreme. Here, teachers may become so familiar with the content tested, as well as with the format of actual test items, that this is all that they teach (Miyasaka, 2000). They actually abandon their content standards and teach only those topics (and perhaps even actual test items) that appear on the test.

With respect to this category, teachers should instruct, practice, and assess the entire domain of content knowledge including but not limited to those objectives covered on the test during regular classroom instruction. They may practice with actual content on previous forms or items of the test, provided they have been released by the publisher for use in this manner. Teachers should not teach or practice objectives that are based solely on the content objectives of the test.

Additionally, they should not teach or practice with highly similar test content on parallel forms of a test, nor should they teach or practice with actual test items from the current form of the test (Miyasaka, 2000).

The next category, assessment approach and item format test preparation practices, has previously been discussed. To reiterate, these practices focus on familiarizing students with various assessment approaches and various types of item formats that they are likely to encounter on standardized tests. Familiarizing students with different assessment approaches (e.g., selected-response items, such as multiple-choice and alternate-choice items, and constructed-response items, such as performance assessments and extended-response essay items) is a widely accepted type of test-taking strategy. This serves to expose students to the various types of test items that they can expect to see on diverse standardized tests. Furthermore, using a variety of assessment approaches as part of classroom instruction and assessment has the potential to enrich instruction as well as to better prepare students to take standardized tests. The main reason that this is an acceptable test preparation practice is that is occurs completely separate from the content of the test itself. With respect to this category, teachers should design and administer classroom assessments that include a wide range of assessment approaches and item formats. They may administer practice tests with samples of actual items only if the item format and not the content is the focus of the practice. They definitely should not administer classroom assessments that only contain item formats from the standardized test due to the limiting effect that this practice has on allowing students to demonstrate their learning in a variety of ways.

The third category, test-taking strategy test preparation practices, has also been previously discussed under the designations of test-taking strategies or testwiseness skills. Recall that the purpose of these skills is to familiarize students with the process of taking a standardized test. These preparation practices allow students to become familiar with the testing format prior to actually taking the test. Essentially, these skills prevent students from receiving a lower score due not to their lack of content knowledge but to their lack of basic knowledge of testing. For example, students should be exposed to and given opportunities to practice skills such as marking answer sheets, making educated guesses, and allocating and pacing their test-taking time. Teachers should incorporate these types of skills into their regular teaching.

> *"I think that [teaching kids the format of the test] is something that some really good teachers do.*
>
> —Sue Garcia,
> *Primary Intervention Specialist*

The fourth category of test preparation practices addresses the timing of test preparation practices. Test preparation practices can take place at various times during the instructional process: long before, just before, or during the administration of the standardized test. The earlier suggestion that test preparation involving content objectives, assessment approaches, and item formats be embedded within regular instruction implies that these various preparation practices can and should take place throughout the school year (Miyasaka, 2000). Cramming instruction or test preparation into the week or two immediately preceding the standardized test can typically do more harm than good, especially for lower-achieving students. Teachers should embed the various test preparation practices we have discussed into their regular instruction throughout the entire school year. In the weeks leading up to the test, they should teach and review a wide range of content objectives and assessment approaches and they may administer appropriate practice tests. Teachers should not review only those objectives that are tested. Additionally, once they may have seen the actual test, perhaps just before testing, teachers should most certainly not teach or review the actual test content nor should they administer practice items that actually appear on the test.

The final category of test preparation practices includes those related to student motivation. Test preparation practices should help students understand the importance of doing their best on the test without feeling inappropriately or excessively pressured (Miyasaka, 2000). One of the best ways teachers can help students prepare for standardized tests is to help them understand why schools are required to administer them, why students are required to take them, and how the scores are used to benefit both individual students as well as the school as a whole. It is important to note that positive student attitudes typically begin with a positive teacher attitude—if teachers are positive, or at least avoid being negative, students are more likely to react similarly to the notion of being required to take standardized tests.

Teachers should routinely discuss the importance of tests with their students (Hogan, 2007). They should encourage students to do their best and to persevere in completing the test. Encouraging students, by telling them and by sending notes home to parents, to get a good night's sleep and to eat a good breakfast on testing days are also beneficial and appropriate ways to prepare them. Teachers—as well as administrators—should take care in avoiding other types of external motivators, such as pep rallies or providing incentive awards if they do well. These types of practices are considered unethical because they take the focus off learning and create too much pressure, albeit it of a different kind, to do well on the tests.

Popham (2002) has provided two ethical standards that essentially encapsulate this discussion about the appropriateness of certain test preparation practices. Educators at all levels would be wise to keep these standards in mind and use them to judge whether or not individual teachers as well as entire schools are preparing students appropriately for standardized tests. The two ethical standards of test preparation are:

> "I see myself as a coach and they understand [that]. [I tell them] you are going to perform during 'the game' as well or not as well as you practiced. And so practicing the achievement tests is vital . . . you need to know your opponent.
> If you go into a game cold, then chances are you're not going to do as well. But we know our opponent. We know who we're 'playing.' We know the strategies they have. We know what plays they're going to run. So we work on meeting it."
>
> —Jeff Burkett,
> Sixth-Grade Teacher

Standard of Professional Ethics	No test preparation practice should violate the ethical standards of the education profession.
Standard of Educational Defensibility	No test preparation practice should increase students' test scores without simultaneously increasing student mastery of the content domain tested.

The do's and don'ts of test preparation practices are summarized in Figure 3.2.

Figure 3.2   Student Test Preparation Do's and Don'ts

Standardized Test Preparation Do's

- Instruct, practice, and assess entire domain of content knowledge
- Practice with actual content on previous forms or items of the test, provided they have been released by the publisher
- Design and administer classroom assessments that include a wide range of assessment approaches and item formats
- Administer practice tests with samples of actual items, only if the item format is the focus of the practice
- Practice test-taking skills such as marking answer sheets, making educated guesses, and allocating test-taking time
- Embed test preparation practices into regular instruction throughout the school year
- Teach and review a wide-range of content objectives and assessment approaches and administer appropriate practice tests prior to the test
- Routinely discuss the importance of tests with students
- Encourage students to do their best and to persevere in completing the test
- Encourage students to get a good night's sleep and eat a good breakfast

Standardized Test Preparation Don'ts

- Do not teach or practice objectives that are based solely on the content objectives of the test
- Do not teach or practice with highly similar test content or with actual test items from the current form of the test
- Do not administer classroom assessments that only contain item formats from the standardized test
- Do not review only those objectives that are tested
- Do not teach or review the actual test content or administer practice items that actually appear on the test
- Avoid using motivational techniques that provide external forms of motivation for students

"TEACHING TO THE TEST" VERSUS "TEACHING TO THE STANDARDS"—A FINAL WORD

Many people are confused or simply disagree about what the term "teaching to the test" exactly means (Kober, 2002). In its extreme unethical form, it means cheating —for example, giving students actual questions from a secure version of a standardized test. In its more common forms, it means direct preparation for a particular test, such as administering practice questions, teaching students how to fill in answer sheets, or focusing instruction on a limited number of skills (Kober, 2002). Although many of these practices may be permissible, they are not educationally sound. In its rarer—also extreme, but in this case ethical—form, instruction is focused on the most important knowledge and skills as outlined in national, state, or district content curriculum standards.

Initially, it is important to remember that three key components of the instructional process should always be aligned with one another: curriculum, instruction, and assessment (Mertler, 2003).

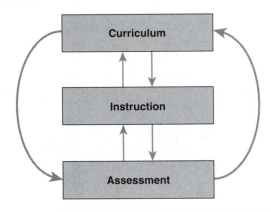

This visual representation of the process and the relationships among the three components implies that each of the three steps is dependent on and is informed by the other two. For example, when planning a unit on photosynthesis (based on curriculum or standards), science teachers might want to consider various approaches to teaching the content (delivery of instruction). In other words, the teachers would need to make decisions regarding the types of resources, materials, and visual aids to incorporate into the unit. In addition, they would need to consider how best to determine the level of student learning and the extent to which their students understood the photosynthetic process (assessment). Additionally, when developing particular assessments for the unit (assessment), they must consider not only the specific content that was taught (curriculum or standards), but also how it was presented to students (instruction). As suggested by this example, all three components must be aligned with one another for appropriate instruction and subsequent learning to occur. In other words, the instruction that is planned by a teacher (as reflected in curriculum standards) should directly relate to the actual instruction, and the assessments should closely reflect both the planned and delivered instruction (Mertler, 2003). In this sense, teaching to the test is not a bad thing. In contrast, it is an ethical and appropriate practice—it simply means that as a teacher you have taught your content standards, and your assessments of student learning reflect this fact.

"If you're not instructing what's going to be on the standardized tests, then you're not preparing your kids. And that's my job professionally, to prepare my kids not only for the test but for the future, and they're directly related. I can't do one without doing the other. If I don't use the data to drive my lessons to prepare my kids for the next step in their ventures, then I'm not doing my job."

—Cori Boos,
High School Mathematics Teacher

Of course, teaching to the test and actually teaching the test as described earlier can most emphatically be unethical practices. Narrowing or limiting the scope of instruction to only that content that is specifically covered on any assessment essentially deprives students from gaining additional skills and knowledge that still may be extremely important in their own right, even if not covered on a test. It is critical to remember that any standardized test is intended to serve as just one measure of an extremely large domain of content knowledge and skills. The scores resulting from that test are only a single indicator of a student's possible performance in the larger domain implied by the complete content standards (Nitko, 2004). One of the goals of any assessment is to be able to generalize from students' performances on the assessment to the larger domain of knowledge and skills. However, if actual instruction or test preparation practice focuses only on a limited number of tasks, the ability to generalize students' learning to broader learning targets—one of the real goals of education—is equally limited (Nitko, 2004). In essence, even though students may score higher, this type of practice actually invalidates their standardized test performance (Airasian, 2005).

"Some people are nervous about accountability. You know, their complaint is about 'teaching to the test.' Well, you're always teaching to a test, so I can't say that that's a good excuse. I think it's more because it's different; it's a change that it makes them more accountable."

—Martha Fether,
Elementary Principal

Unfortunately, the phrase teaching to the test has developed a substantially negative connotation. Most people, educators included, interpret the phrase to mean only those unethical test preparation practices we have discussed. I would like to strongly suggest that we, as professional educators, cease using the phrase "teaching to the test." Instead, I would like to suggest that we replace it with two alternatives: "teaching to the content represented by the test" or "teaching to the standards" (see Figure 3.3). In the case of either alternative, we are making it clear that we are teaching that knowledge and those skills that we are supposed to be teaching. And guess what? For the most part, the standardized test will be covering the same material. Therefore, our students should be able to demonstrate their best performance since they have been taught a very broad range of knowledge and skills, many of which will also appear on the test.

Figure 3.3   Alternatives to the Phrase "Teaching to the Test"

EDUCATORS SHOULD AVOID USING THE PHRASE:

"*Teaching to the test*"

TRY TO SAY INSTEAD:

"*Teaching to the content represented by the test*"

OR:

"*Teaching to the standards*"

Summary

The administration of standardized tests involves procedures that must be followed carefully and explicitly. Teachers and administrators must adhere to the publisher's directions. Violations of these standardization procedures invalidate any possible comparisons of resulting scores. It is permissible to answer student questions during the test, provided they are questions of a procedural nature. Assistance with actual test questions should be avoided at all cost. Any educator who is acting in the role of a test administrator has a responsibility to motivate students to do their best, follow directions strictly, keep the testing time accurately, record any significant events that could effect test scores, and collect test materials promptly.

There are numerous things that teachers can do to help students prepare for standardized tests. Some of these practices are ethical and appropriate, but others are neither. First and foremost, teachers should provide good, sound instruction. They can also help students develop testwiseness skills. These skills consist of various test-taking strategies. Practice in developing testwiseness skills permits students to become familiar with testing directions, proper procedures for completing an answer sheet, pacing their progress through a given test, and checking answers, among others. It is important to note that some testwiseness skills are considered unethical.

The application of any test-taking strategy that results in the improvement of students' scores beyond that which would be attained from content mastery alone is unethical. In other words, these techniques enable students to blindly guess correct answers when they do not know anything about the content.

The pressure for students to perform on standardized tests has become immense—for both students and teachers. It is crucial that teachers avoid the temptation to raise student scores at any cost. This attitude or approach often results in higher test scores; however, they are typically considered to be invalid due to the strategies used to achieve them. Five categories of test preparation practices exist, most of which fall on a continuum ranging from highly ethical and appropriate to unethical and inappropriate. These categories are curriculum and test content, assessment approaches and item formats, test-taking strategies, timing of test preparation, and student motivation. Educators should adhere to two important ethical standards of test preparation:

- No test preparation practice should violate the ethical standards of the education profession.
- No test preparation practice should increase students' test scores without simultaneously increasing student mastery of the content domain tested.

Since curriculum, instruction, and assessment should always be aligned with one another, the notion of teaching to the test is not necessarily a bad one, as many in and out of the education profession have come to believe. If instruction and test preparation practices are specifically limited to only those content areas and skills that appear on the test, then teaching to the test (or teaching the test) is an unethical practice. However, if instruction is designed to parallel the broader content standards, which are also assessed by the standardized test, then teaching to the test is an appropriate practice. Perhaps the best solution to this ethical dilemma is to avoid using the phrase teaching to the test and replace it with teaching to the standards.

Activities for Application and Reflection

1. Make a list of any test preparation practices that you use with your students. Classify each along the ethical continuum as highly ethical, somewhat unethical, or highly unethical. Assuming that you will stop doing anything that is highly unethical, what could you do to improve the appropriateness of those practices you may have classified as somewhat unethical?

2. Using the two ethical guidelines for standardized test preparation as presented in this module, evaluate the appropriateness of each of the following practices:

    a. The school uses the latest version of a particular standardized test. A teacher uses a version of the test that is no longer being administered in the school to give students special practice.

    b. A teacher copies test items from a version of the test that is currently being used in the school and provides these items to students for practice.

    c. A district's curriculum guide calls for learning various rules of addition of two-digit numbers that are covered by the standardized test used in its schools. Several teachers instruct students on how to use these rules to answer the same format of items that appears on the test, but do not provide practice numbers larger than two digits.

    d. A district's curriculum guide calls for learning various rules of addition of two-digit numbers that are covered by the standardized test used in its schools. Several teachers instruct students on how to use these rules to answer the same format of items that appears on the test and on how to apply these same rules to numbers larger than two digits.

3. Imagine that you receive a note from the parents of one of your more high-achieving students. The note says the following: "Why do you spend so much valuable class time teaching to the test? Shouldn't our children be learning more than just what's on the test?" How would you respond to this comment/question? Compose a brief note in response to the parents.

4. Carefully read the interview transcripts, which appear in Section IV, for Jeff Burkett, sixth-grade teacher, and Sue Garcia, intervention specialist, paying particular attention to techniques they use to help prepare students for standardized tests. Comment on the usefulness of these techniques for your current and/or future students.

5. Carefully read the interview transcript for Ellen Sharp, first- and second-grade teacher, paying particular attention to her comment that "assessment drives instruction." What do you think this means? How does this compare or contrast with teaching to the test and teaching to the standards?

6. Carefully read the interview transcript for Cori Boos, high school math teacher, paying particular attention to her comment that teaching test-taking skills "needs to be part of the daily classroom." Do you agree or disagree with this comment? Explain your answer.

7. Carefully read the interview transcripts for Sara Caserta and Megan Newlove, high school English teachers, paying particular attention to their discussion of the importance of providing positive motivation for students in advance of taking standardized tests. Do you believe that this is important? Why or why not?

SECTION II

Standardized Test Scores and Their Interpretations

Module 4

TEST REPORTS

In this module, we begin the process of inspecting various types of test performance reports that result from the administration of standardized tests. We will discuss the major types of reports namely reports of individual student performance, reports of the performance across a class of students, and reports of performance across even larger groups of students (e.g., for students across an entire school or district at a particular grade level). Several samples of test score reports are provided in this module. Examination of these test reports will undoubtedly leave you asking further questions such as "What does each of these scores actually mean?" Detailed discussions of the reports and the specific scores they contain will follow in Modules 5 and 6. In addition, these various reports, along with other examples we will consider later, will serve as the basis for our discussion of data-driven instructional decision making in Modules 7, 8, and 9 of Section III.

OVERVIEW OF TEST REPORTS

There are many types of reports that are produced from standardized tests. These include, but are not limited to, reports of performance for individual students, classes, schools, or districts (McMillan, 2001). There are also versions of individual student reports designed for parents. Reports of standardized test performance are designed to convey a great deal of information in a relatively limited space, often on only a single page. Because of this, test score reports frequently appear complicated and difficult to interpret (McMillan, 2001). There are typically several different scores provided, along with graphs in some cases. Some reports provide norm-referenced scores and interpretations while others provide criterion-referenced scores. Other standardized tests, depending on their purpose, provide both types of scores and interpretations.

Depending on the purpose of the test and the nature of the score report (including its intended audience), standardized test performance can be reported in a variety of ways. A single report may include various scores across all subtests for an individual student, may encapsulate the performance for each student in a class, or may provide summaries of the performance of the class as a whole or perhaps the school building or school district as a whole. There are also reports that show the level of mastery for a class or for individual students across a set of content standards or learning objectives. Although there are a common set of standard test score reports, many test publishers utilize their own unique reporting format and sometimes even their own unique types of scores (some of which will be discussed in Module 6).

One of the keys to standardized test score interpretation is understanding what is being provided on a particular report. We will begin the process of critically examining test score reports shortly, starting in this module with the general formats of several types of reports. First, however, I want to list and categorize the various tests along with their reports that will be utilized as examples in this module and throughout the remainder of the book. I have chosen to use eight different tests, categorized by the type (achievement versus aptitude) and by the format of administration (group versus individual), and a total of 31 different test reports. A listing of these tests and their respective reports are presented in Table 4.1.

INDIVIDUAL STUDENT REPORTS

There are four basic types of reports or formats for reporting individual student performance on a standardized test: (1) reports of student performance on content tests and subtests, (2) reports of student performance (i.e., mastery) of various standards or objectives, (3) narrative reports of student performance, and (4) reports of student performance designed for parents. Each of these is limited to reporting only the test performance of one student—not to be confused with reports to be discussed later that may list the performance of all students across an entire class, for example.

Sample Student Reports

The first type of individual student report is one that provides a variety of scores across subtests of a battery of tests, either achievement or aptitude. This type of report is often referred to as a student profile report. These reports may include norm-referenced scores, criterion-referenced scores, or in some cases both types of scores. An example of this type of report is the Student Report from the Stanford Achievement Test (SAT10). This report is shown in Figure 4.1.

You will undoubtedly notice from this report that numerous types of scores are provided on a typical student performance report. This report provides scores on

Table 4.1 Standardized Tests and Respective Reports Used as Examples

Test	Publisher	Type of Test	Method of Administration	Type(s) of Scores Reported	Test Reports Utilized
Dynamic Indicators of Basic Early Literacy Skills (DIBELS)	University of Oregon Center on Teaching and Learning	Achievement (Reading)	Individual	Criterion-Referenced	• Individual Student Report[a] • School Report[c]
Iowa Tests of Basic Skills (ITBS)	Riverside	Achievement (Battery)	Group	Criterion-Referenced and Norm-Referenced	• Individual Performance Profile[a] • Class Narrative Summary[b] • List of Student Scores[b] • System Narrative Summary[c]
Gates-MacGinitie Reading Tests (GMRT)	Riverside	Achievement (Reading)	Group	Criterion-Referenced and Norm-Referenced	• Individual Student Report[a] • List Report of Student Scores[b] • Building Averages Report[c]
Ohio Achievement Tests (Third and Eighth Grades)	Ohio Department of Education	Achievement (Reading & Mathematics)	Group	Criterion-Referenced	• Grades 3 & 8 Class Reading & Math[b] • Grades 3 & 8 Reading/Math District Report[c] • Grades 3 & 8 Reading/Math School Report[c]
Otis-Lennon School Ability Test (OLSAT)	Harcourt	Aptitude	Group	Criterion-Referenced and Norm-Referenced	• Individual Student Report[a] • Student Roster Report[b] • District Summary Graph[c] • District Summary Report[c]
Stanford Achievement Test 10 (SAT10)	Harcourt	Achievement (Battery)	Group	Criterion-Referenced and Norm-Referenced	• Individual Student Report[a] • Student Performance Standards Report[a] • Home Report[a] • Group Report[b]
TerraNova (2nd ed.)	CTB/ McGraw-Hill	Achievement (Battery)	Group	Criterion-Referenced and Norm-Referenced	• Individual Profile Report—Objectives[a] • Group Performance Level Report[b] • Group List Report[b] • Class Objectives Report[b]
Wechsler Intelligence Scale for Children IV (WISC-IV)	Harcourt	Aptitude	Individual	Criterion-Referenced and Norm-Referenced	• Interpretive Report[a] • Scoring Assistant Report[a]

a. Denotes a report of individual student performance.
b. Denotes a report of group (e.g., class) performance.
c. Denotes a report of school building or district performance.

Figure 4.1 Sample Individual Student Test Score Report

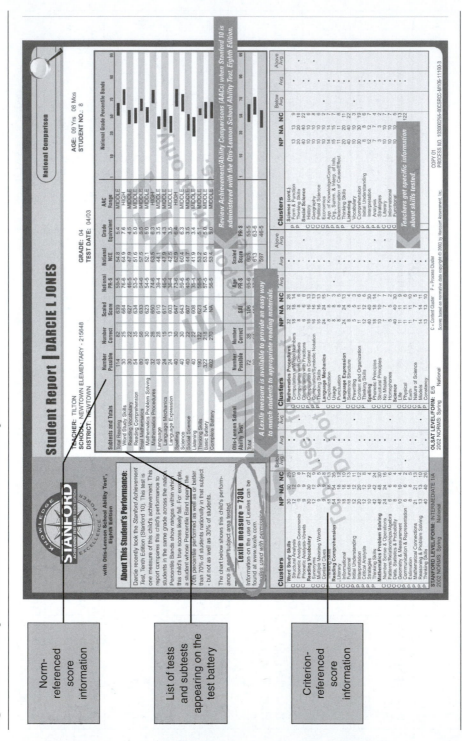

subtests of the battery that compare the student's performance to that of the national norm group. This norm-referenced information appears in the upper half of the report. The lower half of the report provides criterion-referenced information about test performance across the same content subtests but further broken down into specific skills tested.

Another example of an individual student test report is provided in Figure 4.2. The Individual Student Report from the Gates-MacGinitie Reading Tests (GMRT) contains much less information than the SAT10 student report shown in Figure 4.1. This is largely because the GMRT is a reading-only achievement test and not a more comprehensive test battery covering several content areas. Similarly, however, this test report provides several norm-referenced scores for the student. Additionally, a narrative interpretation is provided in the shaded box in the lower-half of the report.

The second type of report of individual student performance focuses on the student's mastery of specific content standards or instructional objectives. An example of this type of report is the TerraNova Individual Profile Report on Objectives (see Figure 4.3). This type of report presents information on specific student strengths and weaknesses based on criterion-referenced test performance. Notice that this particular test and report organizes student mastery of instructional objectives under the content sections of reading, language, mathematics, science, and social studies. On this particular report, actual scores are reported for the student on the subskills of each content area, but then coded in terms of a mastery level. These levels are high mastery, medium mastery, and low mastery. Again, this information can be used to help identify an individual student's general strengths and weaknesses.

A third type of report differs a bit from the previous two formats. Narrative reports are often utilized when standardized tests are administered to individual students instead of to large groups of students simultaneously. Although these reports may also offer some numerical scores (primarily norm-referenced in nature), they primarily focus on the presentation of student performance in narrative form. Excerpted pages from a sample Interpretive Report for the Wechsler Intelligence Scale for Children IV (WISC-IV) are shown in Figure 4.4. From the pages included in Figure 4.4, it should be clear that, although norm-referenced scores are included (e.g., "Haley's ability to sustain attention, concentrate, and exert mental control is in the Average range. She performed better than approximately 55% of her age-mates in this area . . ."), the report focuses more on the interpretation of what the scores mean for Haley. This type of report is typically more feasible, and appropriate, when a particular test is administered individually to a child.

The final type of individual student test report is intended for an altogether different audience—the parents of the child. Typically, these reports are not much different from the first type of report we examined (i.e., the profile report, as in Figure 4.1) with the exception that they contain much less information, usually in the form of fewer scores. An example is the Home Report of the SAT10 shown

(Text continues on page 60)

Figure 4.2 Sample Individual Student Test Score Report

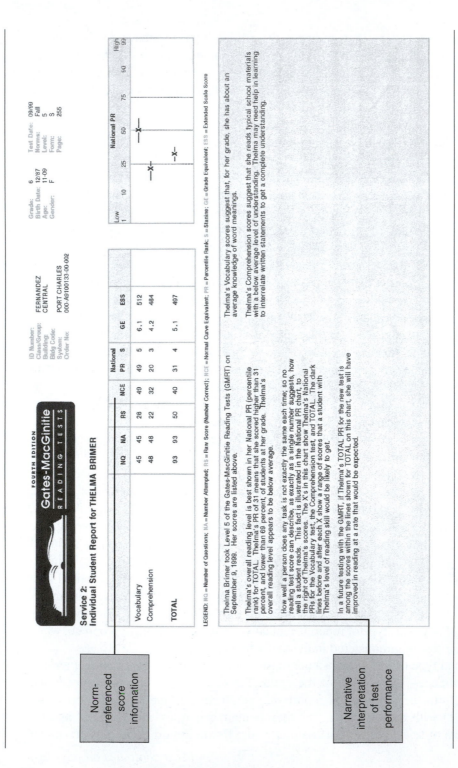

54

Figure 4.3   Sample Individual Student Test Score Report for Objectives

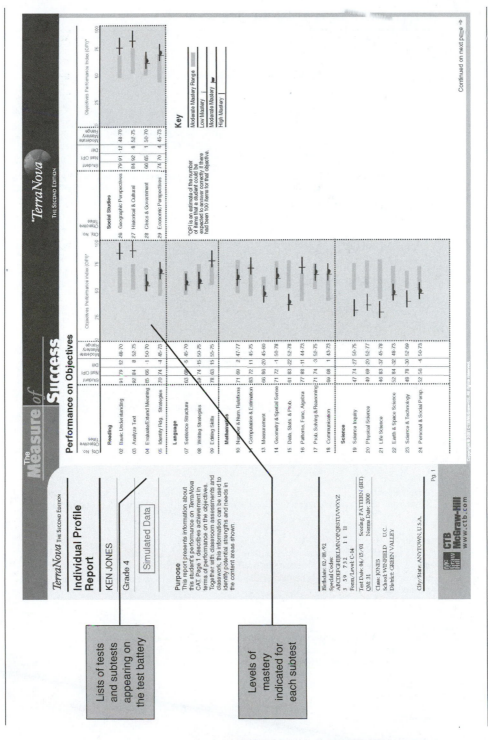

Figure 4.4   Sample Pages from a Narrative Student Test Report

WISC-IV and WIAT-II Interpretive Report

EXAMINEE:	Haley Keller	REPORT DATE:	12/4/03
AGE:	11 years 9 months	GRADE:	Not Specified
DATE OF BIRTH:	2/18/92	ETHNICITY:	<Not Specified>
EXAMINEE ID:	Not Specified	EXAMINER:	Emily Martinez
GENDER:	Female		

Tests Administered: WISC-IV (6/12/03)   **Age at Testing:**   WISC-IV (11 years 3 months)
                          WIAT-II (6/12/03)   WIAT-II (11 years 3 months)

Is this a retest?   No

SCORES SUMMARY

WISC-IV COMPOSITE	SCORE	WIAT-II COMPOSITE	SCORE
Verbal Comprehension Index (VCI)	112	Reading	75
Perceptual Reasoning Index (PRI)	92	Mathematics	96
Working Memory Index (WMI)	102	Written Language	82
Processing Speed Index (PSI)	91	Oral Language	81
Full Scale IQ (FSIQ)	101		

Summary of student's scores

Reason for Referral
Referral information for Haley is unknown at this time.

Home
There is no data available regarding Haley's parent(s), guardian(s), living arrangements, or family stressors.

Language
There is no data available regarding Haley's language.

Development
There is no data available regarding Haley's pregnancy, birth, and developmental history.

Health
There is no information available regarding Haley's sensory/motor status. There is no information or behavioral observations available regarding Haley's medical, psychiatric, and neurological status. There is no data available regarding Haley's use of medication and substances.

School
There is no information provided regarding Haley's early educational history. Haley's school performance with regard to her attendance, conduct, and academics are unknown at this time. Haley's past and recent performance on standardized achievement tests is unknown at this time.

Behavior Observation
There are no additional behavioral observations regarding Haley's appearance, affect, test-taking attitude, and behavior.

Figure 4.4 (Continued)

WISC-IV and WIAT-II Interpretive Report

Interpretation of WISC-IV Results

Haley's unique set of thinking and reasoning abilities make her overall intellectual functioning difficult to summarize by a single score on the Wechsler Intelligence Scale for Children – Fourth Edition (WISC-IV). Her verbal reasoning abilities are much better developed than her nonverbal reasoning abilities. Making sense of complex verbal information and using verbal abilities to solve novel problems are a strength for Haley. Processing complex visual information by forming spatial images of part-whole relationships and/or by manipulating the parts to solve novel problems without using words is a less well-developed ability.

Haley's verbal reasoning abilities as measured by the Verbal Comprehension Index are in the High Average range and above those of approximately 79% of her peers (VCI = 112; 95% confidence interval = 105-118). The Verbal Comprehension Index is designed to measure verbal reasoning and concept formation. Haley performed comparably on the verbal subtests contributing to the VCI, suggesting that these verbal cognitive abilities are similarly developed.

Some norm-referenced performance information

Haley's nonverbal reasoning abilities as measured by the Perceptual Reasoning Index are in the Average range and above those of approximately 30% of her peers (PRI = 92; 95% confidence interval = 85-100). The Perceptual Reasoning Index is designed to measure fluid reasoning in the perceptual domain with tasks that assess nonverbal concept formation, visual perception and organization, simultaneous processing, visual-motor coordination, learning, and the ability to separate figure and ground in visual stimuli. Haley performed comparably on the perceptual reasoning subtests contributing to the PRI, suggesting that her visual-spatial reasoning and perceptual-organizational skills are similarly developed. Haley performed much better on abstract concept formation and categorical reasoning tasks that did not require verbal expression (Similarities = 12) than on abstract concept formation and categorical reasoning tasks that required verbal expression (Picture Concepts= 8).

Haley's ability to sustain attention, concentrate, and exert mental control is in the Average range. She performed better than approximately 55% of her age-mates in this area (Working Memory Index = 102; 95% confidence interval 94-109).

Haley's ability to sustain attention, concentrate, and exert mental control is in the Average range. She performed better than approximately 55% of her age-mates in this area (Working Memory Index = 102; 95% confidence interval 94-109).

Haley's ability in processing simple or routine visual material without making errors is in the Average range when compared to her peers. She performed better than approximately 27% of her peers on the processing speed tasks (Processing Speed Index = 91; 95% confidence interval 83-101). Processing visual material quickly is an ability that Haley performs less well than her verbal reasoning ability. Processing speed is an indication of the rapidity with which Haley can mentally process simple or routine information without making errors. Because learning often involves a combination of routine information processing (such as reading) and complex information processing (such as reasoning), a relative weakness in the speed of processing routine information may make the task of comprehending novel information more time-consuming and difficult for Haley. Thus, this relative weakness in simple visual scanning and

(Continued)

Figure 4.4 (Continued)

WISC-IV and WIAT-II Interpretive Report

tracking may leave her less time and mental energy for the complex task of understanding new material. The noticed by Haley's referral source may be related to this weakness in processing speed. Although much less developed than her verbal and nonverbal reasoning abilities Haley's speed of information processing abilities are still within the Average range and better than those of approximately 27% of her age-mates (Processing Speed Index = 91; 95% confidence interval 85-100).

Personal Strengths and Weakness

Haley achieved her best performance among the verbal reasoning tasks on the Vocabulary subtest. Her strong performance on the Vocabulary subtest was better than that of most students her age. The Vocabulary subtest required Haley to explain the meaning of words presented in isolation. As a direct assessment of word knowledge, the subtest is one indication of her overall verbal comprehension. Performance on this subtest also requires abilities to verbalize meaningful concepts as well as to retrieve information from long-term memory; (Vocabulary scaled score = 13).

Interpretation of WIAT-II Results

Reading

Haley presents a diverse set of skills on different aspects of reading. She performed much better on tasks that assessed her capability to read sentences and paragraphs and answer questions about what was read (Reading Comprehension standard score = 83) than on tasks that required her to correctly read a series of printed words (Word Reading standard score = 72). A relative strength in comprehension skills as compared to reading words in isolation may indicate that Haley is able to derive meaning from text using context clues but may not have learned vocabulary words to automaticity. For this reason, the Reading Composite score may not be the most accurate manner in which to summarize her reading skills. Her Reading Comprehension subtest score is higher than only approximately 13% of her peers, placing these skills in the Low Average range. Haley's performance on Word Reading is within the Borderline range and exceeds that of approximately 3% of students her age.

> Interpretations of student's scores in terms of identifying strengths and weaknesses

Mathematics

In overall mathematics skills Haley performed in the Average range, as indicated by her Mathematics Composite standard score (96). However, her skills in this area exceed that of only approximately 39% of students her age. Haley's performance on tasks that required her to add, subtract, multiple, and divide one- to three-digit numbers (Numerical Operations standard score = 103) is comparable to her performance on tasks that requires her to understand number, consumer math concepts, geometric measurement, basic graphs, and solve one-step word problems (Math Reasoning standard score = 91).

Oral Language

Haley performed in the Low Average range in overall language skills, as indicated by her standard score on the Oral Language Composite (81). Her skills in this area exceed those of only approximately 10% of students her age. Haley performed comparably on tasks that required her to identify the picture that best represents an orally presented descriptor or generate

Figure 4.4 (Continued)

WISC-IV and WIAT-II Interpretive Report

WISC-IV Composite Scores

Composite Score Profile

Vertical bar represents the Standard Error of Measurement.

Composite	Score	SEM	Composite	Score	SEM
VCI	112	3.97	PSI	91	4.74
PRI	92	3.97	FSIQ	101	2.6
WMI	102	4.24			

in Figure 4.5. This particular example provides one very small section of norm-referenced score information. However, the majority of the contents of this one-page report, separated by content area, gives the parents a summary of what is measured by each content subtest as well as a summary of Darcie's performance and provides suggestions for home activities that can support learning and instruction in the classroom. A nice feature of this report is the "Learning Snapshot," which summarizes in one sentence the student's strengths and needs.

Although many test publishers customize their individual student reports to meet their needs—as well as the needs of the schools that use their tests—these reports are basically variations of the four types presented here.

CLASS REPORTS

The second category of test score reports contains those reports that give the details of standardized test performance for an entire group of students, usually a class of students for the same teacher. There are two basic types of class reports—those that summarize test performance across an entire class and those that report individual student performance by listing all students in the class on one report. In addition, there are variations of each of these two types, which will be discussed and shown next.

Sample Class Reports

The first type of class report does not list all students by name, but rather summarizes test performance for the class as a whole, treating it as a single entity. The Group Report from the SAT10 (see Figure 4.6) looks essentially the same as its Student Report: it includes the same sections and provides the same scores for the same sub-tests, but it does so across all students in Smith's fourth-grade class in the example shown. A teacher can see the performance of his or her group of students in comparison to the national norm group. They can also see the specific skill areas where the class as a whole is achieving or is experiencing trouble. Therefore, this type of report is helpful at identifying a particular class's academic strengths and weaknesses.

A variation of this report in shown in Figure 4.7. The Group List Report from the TerraNova also summarizes the performance for the entire tenth-grade class taught by Jones, by providing norm-referenced scores in the upper half of the report and somewhat of a narrative interpretation in the lower half. In this test report, the content areas are not broken down into subtests, nor is the performance of various criterion-referenced skills provided. The purpose of this type of report is to provide for the teacher a quick means of determining the relative comparison of a group of students to the national norm group.

Figure 4.5 Sample Student Test Score Report for Parents

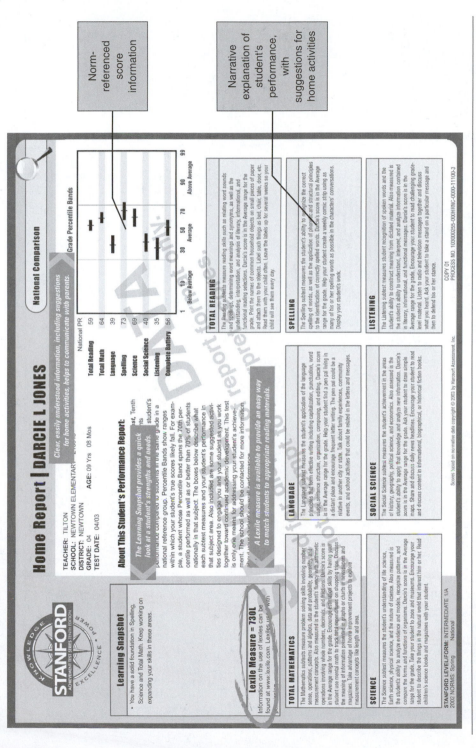

Figure 4.6   Sample Class Test Score Report

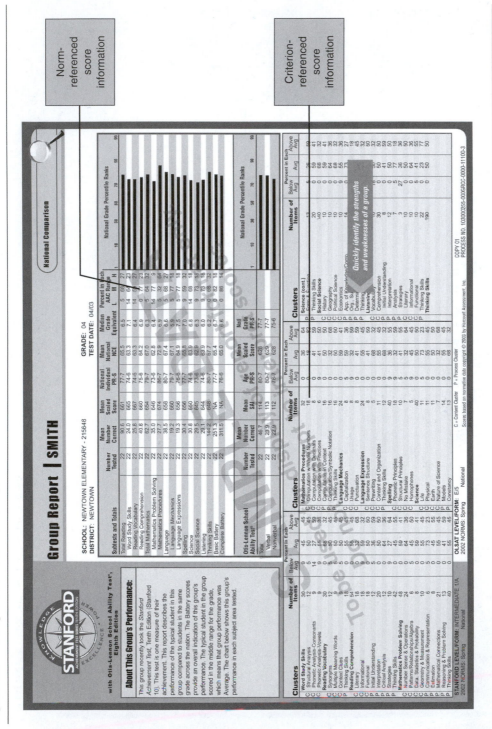

Another example of a report of overall class test performance is the Class Narrative Summary from the Iowa Tests of Basic Skills (ITBS). As shown in Figure 4.8, this sample report also supplies only norm-referenced information, in this case for Clark's fifth-grade class only on the reading portion of the ITBS. Information is provided for the vocabulary and reading comprehension subtests, as well as the total scores for reading. Scores are provided and also shown graphically, with the line plot representing the performance of the norm group and the bars representing the performance of the students in Clark's class. These graphs offer a nice visual aid in helping the teacher see how his or her students performed in relation to the norm group. In addition, for each of the three sections of the report, the publisher has included a brief narrative description of the performance of this class.

A final example of this type of class report, shown in Figure 4.9, comes from the Ohio Department of Education's state-mandated Ohio Achievement Test in Mathematics. The Class Score Report gives the average score (419, in this sample report) and classifies the performance of a class into one of five levels of mathematics proficiency—advanced, accelerated, proficient, basic, and limited. Also included on the bar at the top of the report is the average score for the school (414), the entire school district (414), as well as the average score across the entire state (418). The state has also defined each of these levels of proficiency with respect to third-grade math skills and provides "Recommended Next Steps" based on the average performance level of the class. On the second page, similar information is provided, but for each subtest appearing on the Mathematics Achievement Test, including class performance on both multiple-choice and constructed-response test items.

The second type of class report does not examine the overall average class performance, but rather provides a listing of each individual student in the class and summarizes his or her performance on the test. This type of information allows the teacher not only to gain an overall sense of class performance, but also to identify areas where individual students may be struggling. Two examples of this type of report are shown in Figure 4.10 (List of Student Scores from the ITBS) and Figure 4.11 (List Report of Student Scores from the GMRT). In this type of report, norm-referenced score information, similar to that which we saw in the various individual student test reports (for example, see Figure 4.2 for the GMRT report), is provided.

Reports in the form of student lists can also be supplied for indication of standard or objective mastery. Recall, using Figure 4.3 as an example, that test publishers may provide a test report for an individual student showing the appropriate level of mastery for content standards. Class results showing the same information can also be provided. Figures 4.12 and 4.13 are both reports from the TerraNova test depicting objective mastery across individual students in a given class. Figure 4.12 shows the attained level of mastery for each student in the class on each subtest of the overall battery. Figure 4.13 is essentially a variation of the one shown in Figure 4.12; very similar information is being provided, but in a different format. Students have been categorized into the five proficiency levels across all five subtests of the battery. In other words, each student's name appears on this report

Figure 4.7 Sample Class Test Score Report

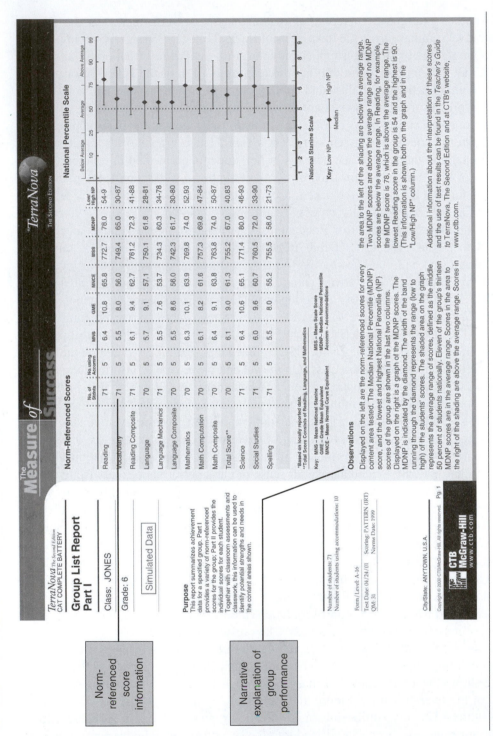

SOURCE: Copyright © 2001 by CTB/McGraw-Hill Companies, Inc. Sample "Group List Report" from TerraNova (2nd ed.). Reproduced with permission of the publisher. All rights reserved.

Figure 4.8 Sample Class Test Score Report

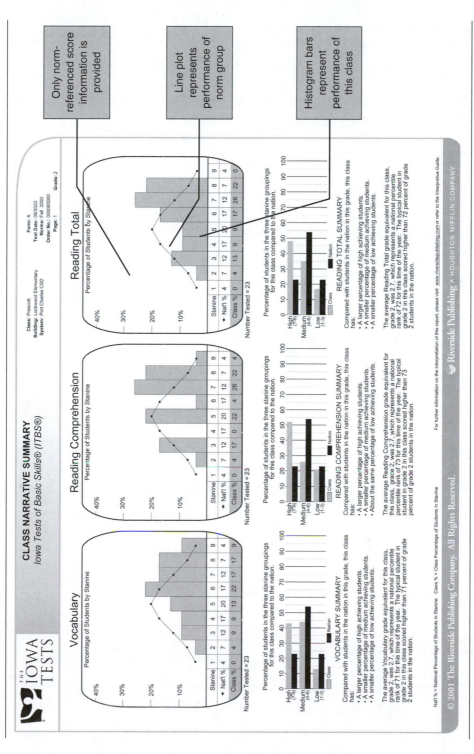

Figure 4.9   Sample Class Test Score Report

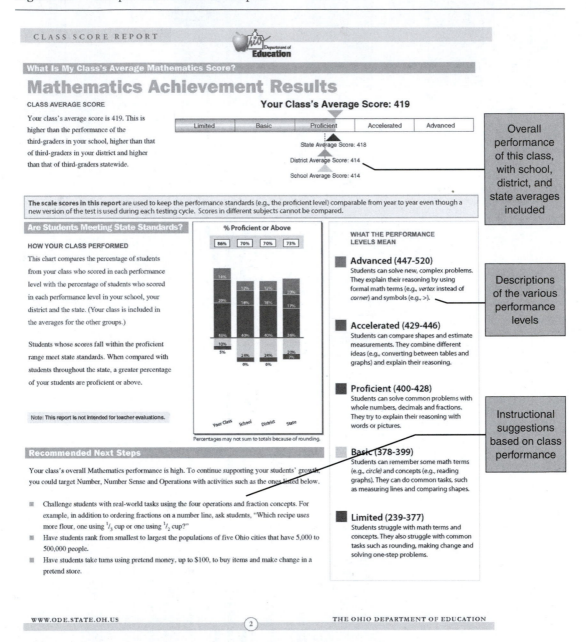

Figure 4.9 (Continued)

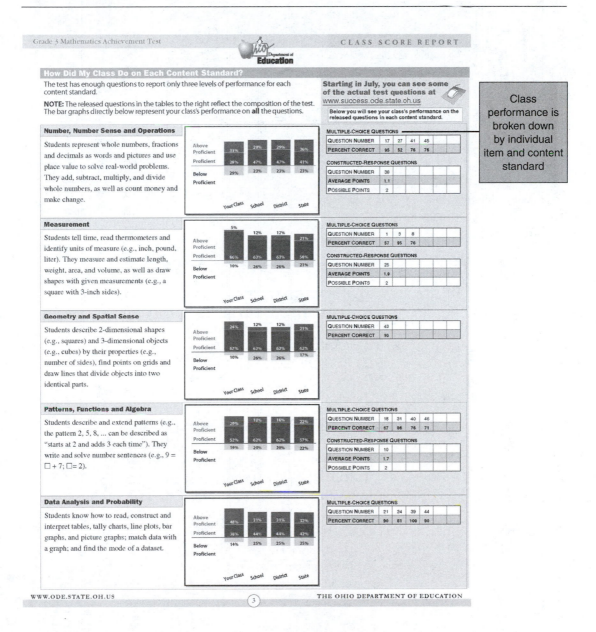

Class performance is broken down by individual item and content standard

Figure 4.10 Sample Class Test Score Report

SOURCE: Copyright © 2001 by The Riverside Publishing Company. Sample "List of Student Scores" from the Iowa Tests of Basic Skills (ITBS). Reproduced with permission of the publisher. All rights reserved.

Figure 4.11 Sample Class Test Score Report for Objectives

FOURTH EDITION
Gates-MacGinitie
R E A D I N G   T E S T S

Class/Group: CHAVEZ
Building: RIVERSIDE
Bldg. Code: PORT CHARLES
System:
Order No.: 000-A91001133-00-001 =

Grades: 6
Test Date: 09/99
Norms: Fall
Level: 5
Form: S
Page: 70

Service 9:
List Report of Student Scores

STUDENT NAME (ID Number / Other Information)	Birth Date / Age	Level / Gender	Form / Title I	Vocabulary					Comprehension					TOTAL				
				NCE	National PR	S	GE	ESS	NCE	National PR	S	GE	ESS	NCE	National PR	S	GE	ESS
BOWER, BRUCE	05/88 / 11-04	M	S	42	35	4	5.1	499	34	22	3	4.4	487	36	26	4	4.7	492
BUCK, DENIS	01/88 / 11-08	M	S	34	23	4	4.5	486	40	31	4	4.9	496	36	25	4	4.6	491
BYRD, ANDREA	09/87 / 12-00	F	S	87	96	9	PHS	585	69	82	7	9.9	550	80	92	8	PHS	564
CARLOS, LEONARD	06/88 / 11-03	M	S	62	71	6	8.2	535	54	57	5	6.7	521	58	64	6	7.3	527
CHAMBERS, SEAN	11/87 / 11-10	M	S	72	85	7	11.5	554	51	52	5	6.4	517	61	70	6	7.9	533
HOLMES, ANTHONY	04/88 / 11-05	M	S	46	42	5	5.6	505	48	46	5	5.9	511	46	43	5	5.8	508
JENSEN, DONNA	10/87 / 11-11	F	S	7*	2*	1*	2.7*	444*	30	17	3	4.1	481	17*	6*	2*	3.4*	465*
JONES, XAVIER	07/88 / 11-02	M	S	44	38	4	5.4	502	32	20	3	4.2	484	36	26	4	4.7	492
KIRKLIN, ELINA	12/87 / 11-09	F	S	46	42	5	5.6	505	48	46	5	5.9	511	46	43	5	5.8	508
LEAL, ERIKA	03/88 / 11-06	F	S	15	5	2	3.1	457	32	20	3	4.2	484	23	10	2	3.7	472
NORMAN, MAGGIE	08/87 / 12-01	F	S	20	8	2	3.5	465	20	8	2	3.4	465	17	6	2	3.4	465
PISCOPO, TIFFANEY	09/87 / 12-00	F	S	52	53	5	6.4	516	41	34	4	5.1	499	45	41	5	5.6	506
ROLF, LEANN	07/88 / 11-02	F	S	68	81	7	10.0	548	62	71	6	8.2	536	67	79	7	8.9	542
SINGER, LEONARD	09/87 / 12-00	M	S	62	71	6	8.2	535	59	67	6	7.8	532	61	70	6	7.9	533
STARKY, ARTHUR	01/88 / 11-08	M	S	42	35	4	5.1	499	59	67	6	7.8	532	51	51	5	6.3	515
STRAUBE, ROSE	09/87 / 12-00	F	S	75	88	7	PHS	560	66	78	7	9.3	545	73	86	7	10.5	552
WILLIAMS, JORDAN	08/88 / 11-01	F	S	20	8	2	3.5	465	24	11	3	3.6	471	19	7	2	3.5	468
WOODALL, RENO	09/87 / 12-00	M	S	36	26	4	4.6	489	19	7	2	3.3	462	24	11	3	3.8	475
WYSE, RICHARD	08/88 / 11-01	M	S	48	46	5	5.9	509	45	40	5	5.5	505	45	41	5	5.6	506
ZARS, SALLY	06/88 / 11-03	F	S	44	38	4	5.4	502	36	25	4	4.5	490	38	29	4	4.9	495
CLASS SUMMARY N TESTED = 20 — AVERAGE ESS — NCE, PR, S, AND GE OBTAINED FROM AVERAGE ESS				20					20					20				
				47	45	5	5.8	508	44	39	4	5.4	504	45	40	5	5.6	505

The performance of each student in the class is summarized across all subtests five times, indicating the proficiency level of each student in the five content areas (i.e., reading, language, mathematics, science, and social studies).

A final example of a student list report is provided in Figure 4.14. This page from the Ohio Reading Achievement Test lists each student in the class according to his or her overall level of reading proficiency (advanced, accelerated, proficient, basic, or limited), which is based on his or her overall reading score, and then further categorizes the proficiency level of each student on each of the subtests of the reading achievement test battery. For the subtests areas, proficiency is denoted by the following symbols: + ("above the minimally proficient level"), = ("at the minimally proficient level"), or ■ ("below the minimally proficient level").

BUILDING- AND DISTRICT-LEVEL REPORTS

Our final category of test report includes those that summarize test performance across an even larger scope, typically for an entire building or even an entire school district. For the most part, these reports will closely resemble the class-level reports we have previously examined, simply reporting test performance across a larger number of students.

Sample Building- and District-Level Reports

Shown in Figure 4.15 is the System Narrative Summary of the ITBS. This particular report looks quite similar to previous reports we have examined in that numerous types of scores across subtests are presented. The scores provided in this report, however, are norm-referenced scores. One should notice that they are both tables and different types of bar graphs to visually display the results. The bottom displays interpretive summaries of the norm-referenced performances of the students in this particular school district.

A second, much simpler, example of a district report is shown in Figure 4.16. The Building Averages report of the GMRT provides only a few norm-referenced scores and bar graphs to visually display the results. In this example, results are being reported for one school building. However, one can gain a very quick sense of how this school's students performed in relation to the norm group from across the nation.

The next two figures come from the Otis-Lennon School Abilities Test (OLSAT). The Summary Charts report (see Figure 4.17) summarizes, with only one norm-referenced score (i.e., national percentile rank) and in graphical format, the performance of each elementary school in the district on the total battery and on its two subtests (verbal and nonverbal). This type of report gives teachers and administrators a quick and straightforward mechanism to evaluate the performance of all schools across a district. Figure 4.18, the Summary Results report,

Figure 4.12 Sample Class Test Score Report

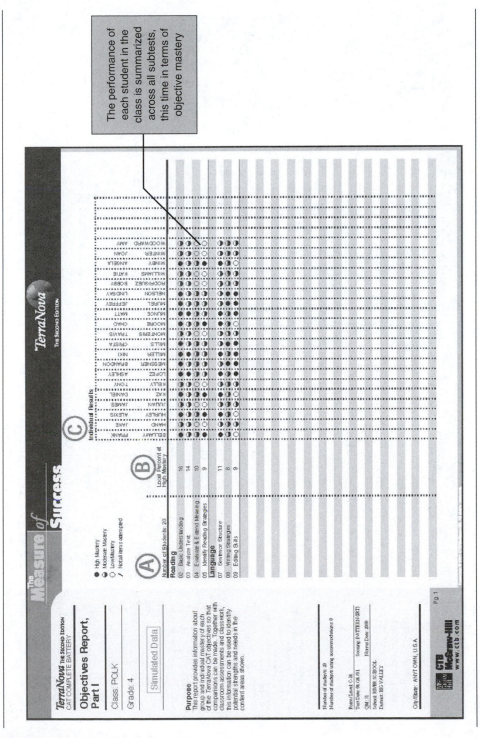

The performance of each student in the class is summarized across all subtests, this time in terms of objective mastery

Figure 4.13 Sample Class Test Score Report for Objectives

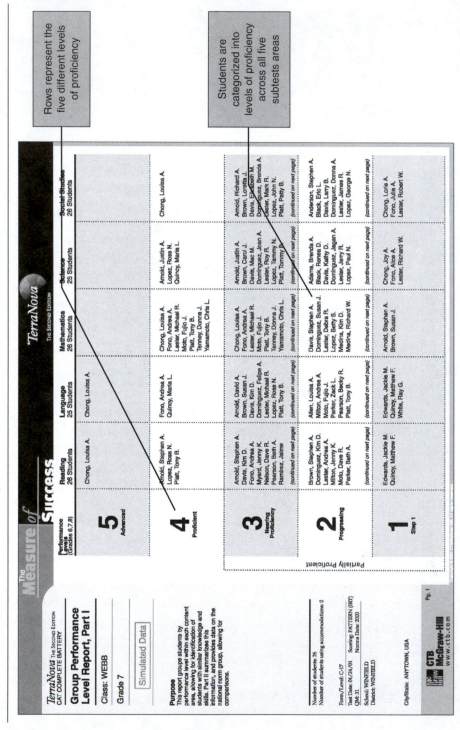

Figure 4.14   Sample Class Test Score Report

CLASS SCORE REPORT

Ohio Department of Education

Class Roster: Content Standard Performance

This roster shows each student's proficiency on each content standard. The symbols indicate if a student performed above, below or at the proficient level for each content standard. This roster also groups students by their overall performance level by placing the student in one of the five performance level categories (i.e., Advanced, Accelerated, Proficient, Basic, Limited).

LEGEND: + Above Proficient   = Proficient   ▪ Below Proficient

Student Name	Spring Reading Scale Score	Proficiency on Content Standards			
		Acquisition of Vocabulary	Reading Process	Informational Text	Literary Text
Advanced (451-548)					
Quraishi Sabir, Tarina	494	+	+	+	+
Knoechelman, Ariel	485	+	+	+	+
Fitzgerald, Krysti	478	+	+	+	+
Kitchen, Brooklyn	468	=	+	+	+
Muncy, Sarah	457	+	+	+	+
Wheeler, Tabitha	457	=	+	+	+
Daniels, Nicholas	451	+	+	+	+
Accelerated (428-450)					
Conaway, Jesse	447	=	+	+	+
Countryman, Katherine	444	+	+	+	+
Dunlap, Christopher	444	=	+	+	+
Peyton, Julia	441	=	=	+	+
Page, Mariah	438	+	=	+	=
Proficient (400-427)					
Staggs, Paige	425	=	=	+	+
Stephens, Nathan	425	=	+	+	=
Crothers, Travis	419	=	+	=	=
Pertuset, Levi	419	=	+	=	=
Sims, Courtney	416	=	=	=	+
Wheeler, Roxanne	416	=	+	=	=
Johnson, Robert	414	+	+	=	▪
Warner, Stephanie	414	=	=	=	=
Free, Cheyenne	405	=	▪	▪	=
Schuller, Nicole	405	=	▪	=	=
Swayne, Aaron	405	=	▪	=	=
Basic (378-399)					
Eldridge, Mary	386	=	▪	▪	=
Vincent, Devon	379	▪	=	▪	▪
Limited (267-377)					
Schutte, Aundrea	368	▪	▪	▪	▪

Proficiency for each student across all subtests indicated by +, =, or ▪

Figure 4.15 Sample District Test Score Report

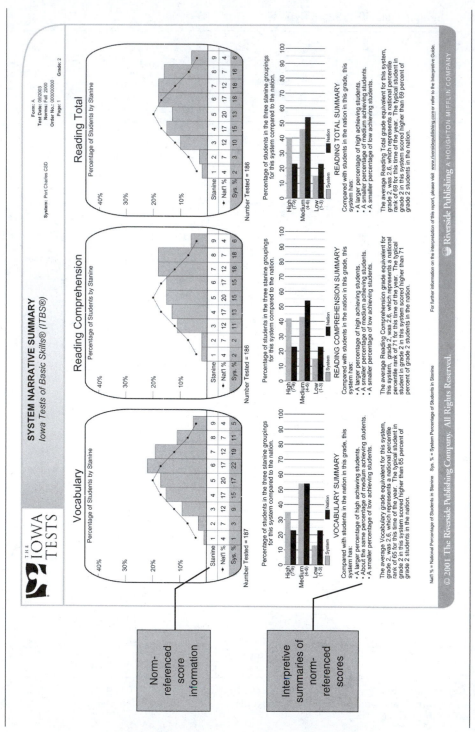

provides similar information to the Summary Charts report, but reports some additional scores in addition to disaggregating the performance on the total test and subtests by gender and ethnicity.

A final set of sample district-level reports again come from the Ohio Achievement Tests. The first page is quite similar to Figure 4.9, which showed the performance of a class in terms of proficiency. The report shown in Figure 4.19 gives the district's average score, as well as the average score across the entire state. Additionally, the percentages of students across the district who were categorized into each of the five levels of proficiency is provided. The second page, also analogous to its class-level counterpart, provides performance summaries for each subtest appearing on the Mathematics Achievement Test, including class performance on both multiple-choice and constructed-response test items. In addition to showing the performance of the district in the bar charts, the performance of similar districts and the state as a whole are included. Finally, on the third page in Figure 4.19, the performance of each individual school in the district, the district as a whole, and the entire state are shown and are disaggregated by "students with limited English proficiency," by "students with disabilities," and by ethnicity.

"It's fine to have building principals leading the charge, but if the people in central office have no clue about what this is all about, it's not going to fly in the long run because it has to be a district effort."

—Kathy Zachel,
District Assistant Superintendent

Summary

There are many types of reports that are produced from standardized tests by testing companies. Essentially, there are three types of reports—those for individual students, those for intact groups such as classes, and those for larger groups, such as school buildings or entire school districts. There are also versions of the individual student report designed specifically for parents. Designed to convey a great deal of information, most test reports do so in a very limited amount of space.

One of the keys to standardized test score interpretation is basically understanding what is being provided on a given test report. This includes familiarity with the general format of various types of test reports. Individual test reports will typically provide either norm-referenced score or criterion-referenced scores, or perhaps even both types of scores. Depending on the purpose of the test and the nature of the test report itself, the student report may also contain a brief narrative interpretation. There exists numerous variations of individual student test score reports.

Often, group reports will also provide the same types of score, especially if the group is as small as a single classroom. In this case, scores are summarized across all

Figure 4.16   Sample Building Test Score Report

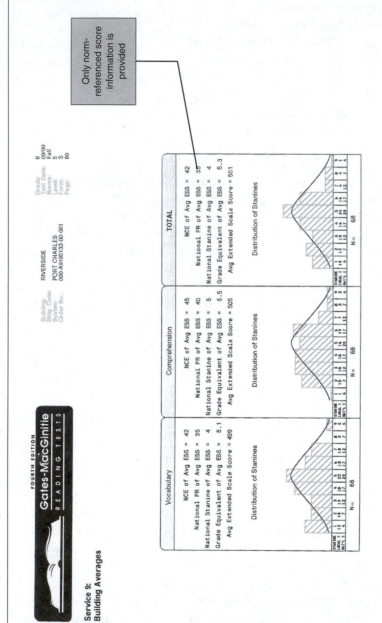

Figure 4.17   Sample District Test Score Report

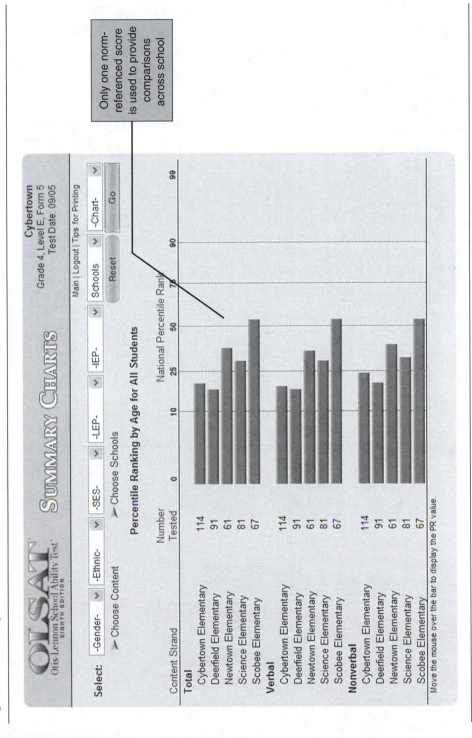

Figure 4.18 , Sample District Test Score Report

OLSAT®
Otis-Lennon School Ability Test
EIGHTH EDITION

SUMMARY RESULTS

Grade 4 Level E Form 5
Test Date 09/05

Get Text | Transpose | Statistic Help | Back | Main | Logout

Students Selected: All

Group	Total							Verbal								Nonverbal							
	N	Mean Raw Score	Mean Scale Score	Mean SAI	APR	GNCE	NPR	N	Mean Raw Score	Mean Scale Score	Mean SAI	Mean ANCE	APR	Mean GNCE	NPR	N	Mean Raw Score	Mean Scale Score	Mean SAI	Mean ANCE	APR	Mean GNCE	NPR
Cybertown	414	26.5	575	91	28	37.6	28	414	12.9	571	90	37.3	27	37.2	27	414	13.6	579	92	39.4	31	39.5	31
Male	195	26.6	575	90	28	37.7	28	195	12.8	570	89	36.4	26	36.7	26	195	13.8	580	92	39.6	31	39.9	32
Female	218	26.4	575	91	29	37.5	28	218	13.1	572	91	38.1	29	37.7	28	218	13.4	578	92	39.0	30	38.9	30
Asian/P.I.	22	34.0	594	100	49	50.0	50	22	16.9	592	99	49.0	48	48.9	48	22	17.1	596	99	49.9	50	50.5	51
African Am.	160	27.9	580	93	32	40.3	32	160	13.7	576	92	39.9	32	40.0	32	160	14.2	583	94	41.4	34	41.7	35
Hispanic	70	25.5	573	90	26	35.8	26	70	12.4	569	89	35.9	25	35.6	25	70	13.1	576	91	38.0	28	37.9	28
Am. Indian	15	28.0	579	93	33	39.9	32	15	12.7	569	90	36.6	26	35.9	25	15	15.3	588	96	44.9	40	44.8	40
White	135	23.2	566	86	20	32.0	20	86	11.3	561	86	32.0	20	31.9	19	135	12.0	561	86	34.1	22	34.1	22
Other	12	34.9	599	102	52	51.3	52	12	17.3	594	100	50.6	51	49.6	49	12	17.7	605	102	51.6	53	52.2	54
Cybertown Elementary	114	23.4	567	86	20	32.1	20	114	11.1	561	85	30.9	18	31.2	19	114	12.3	571	88	34.6	23	35.0	24
Male	55	25.1	571	88	23	35.1	24	55	11.6	564	86	31.9	19	32.6	20	55	13.5	578	91	38.3	29	39.1	30
Female	59	21.9	562	84	17	29.3	16	59	10.7	559	84	29.9	17	30.0	17	59	11.1	565	85	31.1	18	31.2	19
Asian/P.I.	5	35.8	598	101	52	52.1	54	5	18.2	597	101	51.8	53	50.8	51	5	17.6	598	100	50.4	51	50.9	52
African Am.	48	25.5	573	89	25	36.1	25	48	12.2	567	88	34.3	23	34.8	24	48	13.3	577	91	38.0	22	38.8	30
Hispanic	17	23.8	568	87	21	32.4	21	17	11.8	567	87	33.0	21	33.2	21	17	12.0	589	87	33.7	22	33.7	22
Am. Indian	3	18.3	554	81	12	23.4	10	3	7.7	543	78	23.5	9	19.6	7	3	10.7	585	85	28.6	18	30.5	18
White	39	19.3	556	81	12	25.4	12	39	8.9	548	79	22.1	11	24.1	11	39	10.4	561	83	26.6	15	28.9	16
Other	2	26.5	577	92	30	38.7	30	2	12.5	570	90	36.5	26	36.0	25	2	14.0	583	94	42.2	35	41.9	35
Deerfield Elementary	91	21.8	562	84	18	30.4	18	91	10.5	557	84	29.7	17	29.6	17	91	11.3	565	86	32.3	20	32.3	20
Male	44	23.1	565	86	20	32.3	20	44	11.1	560	85	31.3	19	31.4	19	44	12.0	569	88	34.3	23	34.3	23
Female	47	20.5	559	83	15	28.6	15	47	9.9	554	83	28.2	15	27.8	15	47	10.6	582	85	30.5	18	30.4	18
Asian/P.I.	5	31.4	589	98	44	47.0	44	5	14.4	580	94	42.6	36	42.7	36	5	17.0	597	100	50.5	51	51.3	52
African Am.	29	23.6	569	88	22	33.8	22	29	11.5	565	87	33.6	22	33.7	22	29	12.0	572	89	35.1	24	35.1	24
Hispanic	19	21.2	561	84	17	29.6	17	19	9.6	552	82	26.7	13	26.0	13	19	11.6	568	87	33.4	21	33.2	21
Am. Indian	4	25.5	572	88	23	34.6	23	4	12.3	567	87	32.9	21	34.5	23	4	13.3	578	90	37.4	27	38.7	30
White	32	18.6	550	79	12	24.3	11	32	9.3	548	81	26.0	13	25.6	12	32	9.3	551	81	25.9	13	25.2	12
Other	2	21.5	560	80	11	24.2	11	2	9.5	548	76	22.3	9	23.1	10	2	12.0	570	85	30.2	17	34.7	23
Newtown Elementary	61	29.2	583	95	37	43.1	37	61	14.3	580	94	42.2	35	42.1	35	61	14.9	587	96	44.1	39	44.2	39
Male	32	28.8	582	94	35	41.9	35	32	14.2	579	94	41.6	34	41.6	34	32	14.6	585	95	43.0	37	43.0	37
Female	29	29.7	585	95	39	43.8	38	29	14.4	580	95	42.8	37	42.6	36	29	15.2	589	97	45.4	41	45.5	41
Asian/P.I.	3	37.7	606	104	61	56.4	62	3	18.7	603	103	54.5	58	54.9	59	3	19.0	610	105	56.4	62	56.9	63
African Am.	25	29.7	585	95	38	43.8	38	25	14.8	582	95	43.3	37	43.6	38	25	14.9	587	96	44.3	39	44.6	40

Performance in each school, and across district, is broken down by gender and ethnicity

Figure 4.19   Sample District Test Score Report

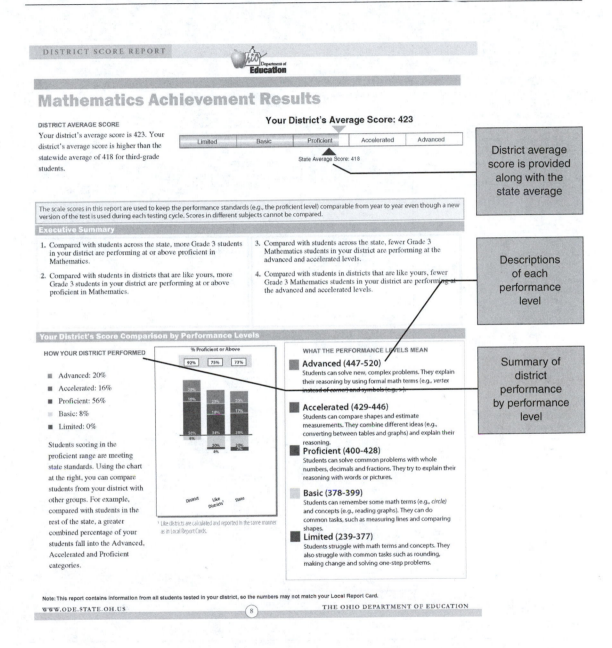

(Continued)

Figure 4.19 (Continued)

Department of
Education

DISTRICT SCORE REPORT

Your District's Mathematics Performance by Content Standards

The test has enough questions to report only three levels of performance for each content standard.

NOTE: The released questions in the tables to the right reflect the composition of the test. The bar graphs directly below represent your district's performance on **all** the questions.

Starting in July, you can see some of the actual test questions at www.success.ode.state.oh.us

Below you will see your district's performance on the released questions in each content standard.

Number, Number Sense and Operations

Students represent whole numbers, fractions and decimals as words and pictures and use place value to solve real-world problems. They add, subtract, multiply, and divide whole numbers, as well as count money and make change.

MULTIPLE-CHOICE QUESTIONS

QUESTION NUMBER	17	27	41	45		
PERCENT CORRECT	96	72	100	96		

CONSTRUCTED-RESPONSE QUESTIONS

QUESTION NUMBER	38					
AVERAGE POINTS	1.0					
POSSIBLE POINTS	2					

District performance by standard and by items

Measurement

Students tell time, read thermometers and identify units of measure (e.g., inch, pound, liter). They measure and estimate length, weight, area, and volume, as well as draw shapes with given measurements (e.g., a square with 3-inch sides).

MULTIPLE-CHOICE QUESTIONS

QUESTION NUMBER	1	3	8			
PERCENT CORRECT	88	96	92			

CONSTRUCTED-RESPONSE QUESTIONS

QUESTION NUMBER	25					
AVERAGE POINTS	1.8					
POSSIBLE POINTS	2					

Geometry and Spatial Sense

Students describe 2-dimensional shapes (e.g., squares) and 3-dimensional objects (e.g., cubes) by their properties (e.g., number of sides), find points on grids and draw lines that divide objects into two identical parts.

MULTIPLE-CHOICE QUESTIONS

QUESTION NUMBER	43					
PERCENT CORRECT	84					

Patterns, Functions and Algebra

Students describe and extend patterns (e.g., the pattern 2, 5, 8, ... can be described as "starts at 2 and adds 3 each time"). They write and solve number sentences (e.g., 9 = □ + 7; □= 2).

MULTIPLE-CHOICE QUESTIONS

QUESTION NUMBER	18	31	40	46		
PERCENT CORRECT	80	68	84	72		

CONSTRUCTED-RESPONSE QUESTIONS

QUESTION NUMBER	10					
AVERAGE POINTS	1.5					
POSSIBLE POINTS	2					

Data Analysis and Probability

Students know how to read, construct and interpret tables, tally charts, line plots, bar graphs, and picture graphs; match data with a graph; and find the mode of a dataset.

MULTIPLE-CHOICE QUESTIONS

QUESTION NUMBER	21	24	30	44		
PERCENT CORRECT	52	84	96	96		

Figure 4.19 (Continued)

DISTRICT SCORE REPORT

School Mathematics Performance by Group

This roster presents the percentage of students from each group who are proficient or above.

	# Tested	Average Mathematics Scale Score	Limited English Proficient	Students with Disabilities	African-American	American Indian	Asian/ Pacific Islander	Hispanic	Multi-Racial	White
Washington Ele	25	423	N/A*	N/A*	N/A*	N/A*	N/A*	N/A*	N/A*	92%
Total # of Students†			N/A	N/A	N/A	N/A	N/A	N/A	N/A	25
Total # of Males			N/A	N/A	N/A	N/A	N/A	N/A	N/A	15
Total # of Females			N/A	N/A	N/A	N/A	N/A	N/A	N/A	10
District	25	423	N/A*	N/A*	N/A*	N/A*	N/A*	N/A*	N/A*	92%
Total # of Students†			N/A	N/A	N/A	N/A	N/A	N/A	N/A	25
Total # of Males			N/A	N/A	N/A	N/A	N/A	N/A	N/A	15
Total # of Females			N/A	N/A	N/A	N/A	N/A	N/A	N/A	10
State	14625	418	41%	63%	47%	83%	83%	63%	67%	80%
Total # of Students†			1078	154	2518	12	204	320	447	10935
Total # of Males			729	77	1240	N/A	114	170	244	5547
Total # of Females			345	77	1276	N/A	90	150	203	5383

> Summary of performance for each school, district, and state disaggregated by LEP, disabilities, and ethnicity

* This table does not display data when there are fewer than 10 students in any given category.
† The sum of male and female students may not equal the total for each category because gender is not reported for every student.

Note: This report contains information from all students tested in your district, so the numbers may not match your Local Report Card.

WWW.ODE.STATE.OH.US   (12)   THE OHIO DEPARTMENT OF EDUCATION students in the given class. Norm-referenced and/or criterion-referenced scores may be included, as well as some narrative interpretation. Larger group reports—typically across an entire school district—can provide similar types of test performance information. However, several types of unique information may also be provided, such as disaggregated data (which is possible due to the inclusion of much larger groups of student results being reported). As with individual student reports, numerous variations of group reports also exist.

Activities for Application and Reflection

1. Locate a test report from a standardized test other than the ones discussed in this module. (This may be a test used in your school, or one that you find online.) Based on the schemes used in Table 4.1 to classify tests, try to classify the test and its report that you have located.

2. Using the report(s) you have located, summarize the information provided on the report. Do not be concerned with the actual scores themselves (at least, not yet!); rather, focus on the basic types of information (as discussed in this module) that are provided on the report.

3. Based on your relative needs as an educator, which type or level of standardized test report—individual student, class, or building/district—do you believe is, or will be, most beneficial to you? Explain why you selected this type of report. Do you think that you could find beneficial educational uses for those types you did not select?

4. In her interview transcript which appears in Section IV, Kathy Zachel, assistant superintendent, discussed her belief that administrators, along with teachers, need to understand and commit to the process of critically examining test reports. Do you believe this to be true? Discuss the pros and cons of administrator involvement in this process.

CRITERION-REFERENCED TEST SCORES AND THEIR INTERPRETATIONS

Recall from Module 1 that there are two general categories of test scores that are reported on standardized test score reports: criterion-referenced and norm-referenced scores. Criterion-referenced and norm-referenced tests—or more specifically, criterion- and norm-referenced test scores—serve very different purposes in terms of reporting student performance. The types of scores reported reflect these fundamental differences. Figure 5.1 summarizes the various scores used for each type of test. You will notice that there are only a few types of criterion-referenced scores, but numerous types of norm-referenced scores. We will discuss criterion-referenced scores and their interpretations in this module and norm-referenced scores in Module 6.

WHAT DO CRITERION-REFERENCED TEST SCORES TELL US?

Criterion-referenced test scores typically compare a student's performance to some preestablished criteria or objectives. The resulting scores are essentially interpreted as the degree of accuracy with which a student has mastered specific content. In examining the results of criterion-referenced tests, the level of student performance—whether for an individual student, a class, or an entire district—is not dependent on the performance of others. Standardized tests that report only criterion-referenced test scores may also be called objectives-based, absolute,

Figure 5.1   Summary of Methods of Reporting Scores on Standardized Tests, Highlighting Types of Criterion-Referenced Scores

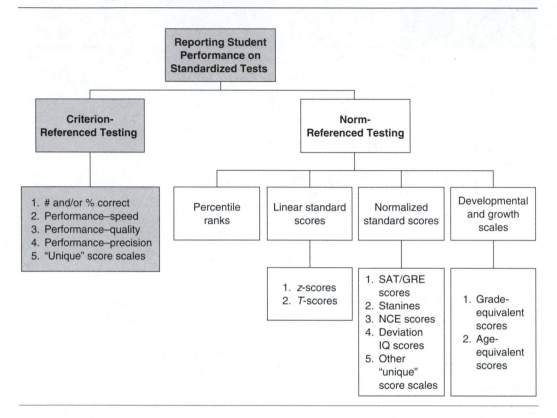

domain-referenced, standards-referenced, or content-referenced tests (McMillan, 2004). For the most part, criterion-referenced achievement tests are essentially variations of existing norm-referenced achievement tests on which objectives or standards are simply associated with or connected to items that already appear on the norm-referenced tests (Thorndike, 2005).

These tests may or may not include some sort of cut score for determining passage, depending on the purpose of the test. For example, on a typical nationally administered achievement test, a cut score is routinely not used because the purpose of the criterion-referenced scores on this type of test is simply to describe the current level of achievement for a particular student, class, or district. However, on a state-mandated graduation test, for example, there would be a cut score to determine whether or not an individual student has passed the required test and is permitted to graduate from high school. Similarly, cut scores may be used in order to place students into categories of mastery or proficiency, as you saw in some of the sample test reports provided in Module 4 (e.g., see Figures 4.3, 4.9, 4.13, and 4.14).

The results from the administration of a criterion-referenced test enable teachers and administrators to draw inferences about the level of student performance relative to a large domain (Nitko, 2004). Individual student scores are not compared with—nor are they dependent upon—the performance of others. Criterion-referenced tests provide evidence that essentially helps educators answer the following questions:

- What does this student (or do students in this class or in this district) know?
- What can this student (or these students in this class or in this district) do?
- What content and skills has this student (or these students in this class or in this district) mastered?

Most of the scores resulting from criterion-referenced tests are relatively simple to interpret. They do not have well-derived, complex, statistically based scoring systems as do norm-referenced tests (Nitko, 2004). The predominant way that the results of criterion-referenced tests are reported is in terms of raw scores, although several other methods also exist. A discussion of each of these types of criterion-referenced scores follows.

SELECTED-RESPONSE TEST ITEMS

As you will recall from Module 1, selected-response items have only a single correct answer; and that correct answer is part of the question provided to students. The task is to simply select the correct option. Predominantly, multiple-choice and true-false items—or any of their numerous variations—make up the majority of selected-response items that appear on standardized tests. Since there is only one correct answer to these types of items, student responses are quite easy to score—they are either right or they are wrong. It follows, logically then, that the criterion-referenced scores resulting from the administration of selected-response items are fairly straightforward. They consist primarily of a summary of the number of items that an individual student (or class of students depending on the type of report) answered correctly.

Types of Criterion-Referenced Scores

There are four basic types of criterion-referenced scores that may be reported as the result of the administration of a given standardized test. These types include the *raw score* (usually the number and/or percent of items answered correctly), which is the most commonly used type, as well as scores representing the speed of performance, the quality of performance, and the precision of performance.

Number and/or Percent Correct

The most common type of criterion-referenced score used on standardized test reports is the raw score, typically presented as the number or percentage of items answered correctly. Typically, a percentage of items answered correctly is provided for each subtest appearing on the test. This allows students, teachers, and parents to see the percentage of the sampled content domain the student has mastered. An educator's decision concerning the degree of mastery that a particular student has demonstrated on a standardized test is usually based on the percentage of items answered correctly that measure a specific target or content area or on the judgment of an expert scorer who reviews samples of student work such as a writing sample (McMillan, 2001). However, the raw score itself is not very meaningful without further information (Linn & Miller, 2005). For example, if Susan answers 64 items correctly on a test, she would receive a raw score of 64. But what does that score of 64 really mean? Is it a good, bad, or average score? We would certainly want (perhaps even need) further information to interpret its meaning. At a minimum, we would want to know how many items were on the test. Was her score of 64 out of a total of 70 items or out of 120 items? This piece of information certainly makes a difference when interpreting the meaning behind a given raw score.

The meaning that is given to the percentage of items answered correctly is typically a subjective one based on the test publisher's definition of the target, the difficulty of the items, the number of items appearing on the test or subtest, the extent to which the items match the district's curriculum, and so on (McMillan, 2004). This involves professional judgment on the part of the individual teacher, or perhaps teams of educators who must determine just what those scores mean. In other instances, especially those where criterion-based test performance results in important decisions (e.g., graduation from high school), content area experts typically determine the number of items to be answered correctly to pass the test or to be classified within some other classification scheme.

That being said, most publishers of criterion-referenced tests or publishers of tests that report criterion-referenced scores (usually along with norm-referenced scores) will also report student performance in comparison to some specified, predetermined standard of performance. This is done by placing student performance into one of several preestablished categories based on the scores received. For example, these might include such classification systems of performance standards as the following:

- pass—fail,
- below mastery—at mastery—above mastery,
- below average—average—above average,
- not proficient—proficient—advanced, or
- novice—basic—proficient—advanced.

Often, test publishers will report performance along these standards not only for an entire test, but also for clusters of items (Gronlund, 2006). Each cluster of items represents a specific content area, skill, or objective with an indication of the level of performance.

Examine closely the sample test reports provided in Figures 5.2–5.5, focusing your attention on these types of commonly used criterion-referenced scores. Figures 5.2, 5.3, and 5.4 come from the Stanford Achievement Test (SAT10). The Individual Student Report, as shown in Figure 5.2, provides both criterion- and norm-referenced score information for Darcie L. Jones, a fourth-grade student. The criterion-referenced score information is provided in the bottom-half of the report. First, you should notice that the scores are provided by content clusters. Immediately to the left of each content area and its respective clusters is a letter code indicating the type of skill being tested within that particular cluster, where *C* represents a content cluster and *P* represents a process cluster. Content clusters would include knowledge-based types of performance, such as knowledge of "Synonyms" and "Context Clues" under the Reading Vocabulary subtest and knowledge of "History," "Geography," and "Economics" under the Social Studies subtest. Process clusters include areas that are more skill-based; in other words, students must demonstrate that they can do something as opposed to the demonstration of knowing something. On the SAT10, process cluster items include "Critical Analysis" and "Thinking Skills" on the Reading Comprehension subtest and "Estimation" and "Reasoning and Problem Solving" on the Mathematics Problem Solving subtest. Often, individual items are classified as both a content item as well as a process item, provided both types of skills are being tested by that item. Analysis of content cluster scores are very useful in identifying students' strengths and weaknesses on specific objectives or standards within a content area. Additional analysis of process cluster scores can help in further understanding these strengths and weaknesses.

To the right of each cluster are three numerical scores, which appear under the headings of NP, NA, and NC. The values under the NP column provide the "Number Possible" (i.e., the total number of possible items or points within that cluster). Those values beneath NA give the "Number Attempted" by the student within that cluster. Finally, NC is the number of items the student answered correctly (i.e., "Number Correct"). For example, you will notice that the entire Science subtest contained 40 items, all of which were attempted by Darcie—meaning that she did not omit any items. She correctly answered 30 of the total number. Within the content clusters of the Science subtest, she correctly answered 9 of 11 items on "Life," 6 of 11 on "Physical," 10 of 11 on "Earth," and 5 of 7 on "Nature of Science."

The final component of the criterion-referenced score section of this report is the classification of Darcie's performance into performance categories (in this case, "Below Average," "Average," and "Above Average"). On this particular test report, this is accomplished by the placement of a dot (i.e., "•") into one of those three columns for each of the clusters tested. For example, correctly answering eight of nine items on the "Phonemic Analysis–Consonants" cluster of the Word Study Skills subtest placed Darcie's performance in the above average category. Similarly, correctly answering only 2 of 10 items on the economics cluster of the social studies subtest placed her in the below average category. This information is highly useful in quickly scanning the report to identify the student's areas of strength and areas of weakness.

The Student Performance Standards Report, shown in Figure 5.3, provides similar criterion-referenced information about Darcie's performance. However, in this case the focus of her performance report is the classification of her performance into performance standard categories. There are four such categories—"Below Basic," "Basic," "Proficient," and "Advanced"—provided on this report. A generic (i.e., not subtest- or content-specific) description of these four performance standards are provided in the box labeled, "Standards Connection." Furthermore, Darcie's performance is classified for each of the seven subtests contained within the entire test battery. For example, based on Darcie's performance she is classified as proficient in reading, spelling, and social studies. Additionally, a narrative is provided for each of the seven subtests describing the student's performance on academic standards that represent the skills and concepts a student should know and be able to do in the given subtest areas.

The SAT10 Group Report, shown in Figure 5.4 provides very similar information to that discussed in the Student Report (Figure 5.2). The difference between the two reports is how the criterion-referenced performance is reported. Summarizing performance across an entire group does not lend itself to reporting raw score values such as the number of items attempted and answered correctly, for what should be obvious reasons. Therefore, only the total number of items is provided for each cluster. To the right of this value is the percentage of students in the class who were classified into each of the three performance categories (i.e., "Below Average," "Average," and "Above Average"). For example, the students in Smith's class performed fairly well across the test battery, as evidenced by the low percentage of students in the below average category across all clusters. The poorest performance for this class was on the "Comprehension Strategies" cluster of the Listening subtest, where 27% of the class performed below average. However, the scores on this cluster raise an important issue, something that teachers should always keep in mind when examining test reports. Notice that this cluster contained a total of only three items. Most of us would probably agree that performance on three items across an entire class is likely not sufficient information to make decisions about future instruction on this set of process skills. Although examining these types of test results can be very informative, it is important to look at all of the information provided and weigh it accordingly in any decision-making process.

The next example of a criterion-referenced test report is the Family Score Report from the Ohio Mathematics and Reading Achievement Tests (see Figure 5.5). The

Figure 5.2   Sample Individual Student Test Score Report

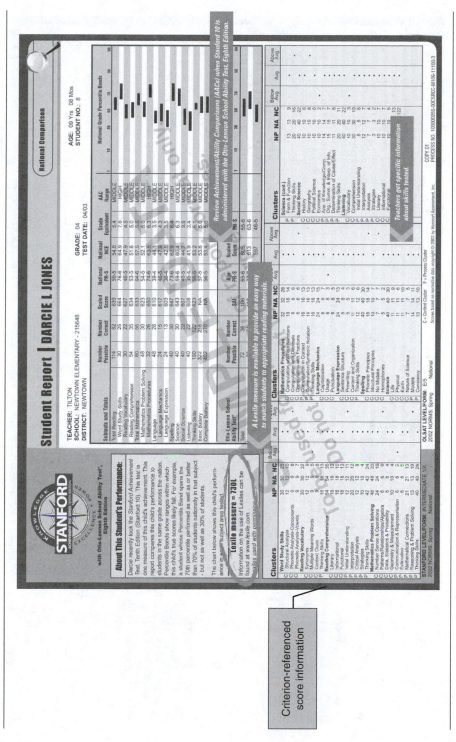

Figure 5.3 Sample Standards Score Report

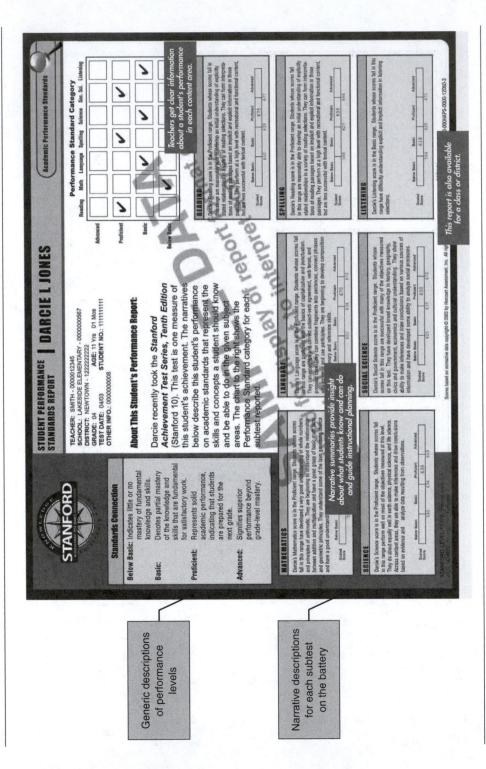

first sample page from this report summarizes Alexandra's performance in both reading (the upper portion) and mathematics (the lower portion). For each test, the student's overall score is indicated (in this case, 454 for reading and 397 for mathematics) and is visually placed on the scale of proficiency, ranging from "Limited" to "Advance." You should notice that each point on the two scales is described in terms of that particular content area. Alexandra's reading score of 454 placed her in the advanced category, where a score of 451 was the lowest score possible (i.e., the cut score) to be placed in this category. Also indicated on this scale are the district, school, and state average scores. Although these achievement tests are criterion-referenced, these averages provide an indication of the student's performance relative to other students across the school, district, and state (i.e., they provide a sort of informal norm-referenced type of information). Based on these averages, in the case of reading, Alexandra outperformed her school, her district, and the rest of the state. The opposite level of performance was attained for mathematics, as her performance was classified in the basic category and the school, district, and state averages were all higher than her scores.

On the right side of this sample page are the student's strengths and weaknesses for each subtest area, or standard, of the reading test (four standards) and mathematics test (five standards). The student's overall level of performance (i.e., "Below Proficient," "Proficient," or "Above Proficient") is determined by her collective performance across these individual standards. Alexandra performed above proficient in all four reading standards, which ultimately placed her in the advanced level for overall performance. She performed at the proficient level on three of the five mathematics standards and below proficient on the other two, placing her overall performance in the basic category.

The second and third pages of this sample report further explain the student's performance on these individual standards. For example, on the second page each of the four reading standards is described in the left column. The middle column contains the student's level of performance, which is the same from the preceding page (i.e., "Below Proficient," "Proficient," or "Above Proficient"), and an explanation or interpretation of what these results mean. The column on the right provides suggestions for activities that can be done to support and encourage growth within this standard. Similar information is provided on the third page for the mathematics standards.

A final set of sample criterion-referenced test reports come from the Dynamic Indicators of Basic Literacy Skills (DIBELS), published by the University of Oregon's Center on Teaching and Learning. DIBELS consists of a set of standardized, individually administered measures of early literacy development. They are designed to be quick fluency measures done at regular intervals to monitor the development of prereading and early reading skills. Figure 5.6 is an Individual Student Performance Profile for John Smith, a first-grade student. In this report, John's early literacy skills are being described against preestablished criteria in the

Figure 5.4   Sample Group Test Score Report

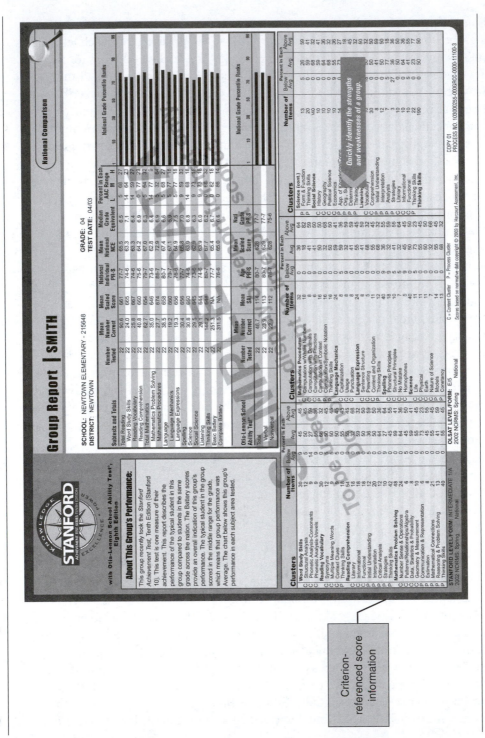

92

areas of phonemic awareness, alphabetic principles, vocabulary, and fluency and comprehension. DIBELS measures are intended to be longitudinal in nature (i.e., they are designed to be repeated at specific intervals) to monitor growth and development. Notice that the graphs in the report are essentially timelines showing levels of performance across time. Scores resulting from initial assessments (called benchmarks) are noted on the graphs by a darkened circle (i.e., "•"). Scores from progress monitoring, or periodic follow-up assessments, are noted with open circles (i.e., "o"). The predetermined criteria for each area is defined as the "Target Goal" and is noted on the timelines by the shaded horizontal bars.

For example, notice that in the area of "Phoneme Segmentation Fluency" under phonemic awareness, John's performance throughout his Kindergarten year hovered right around the target goal. However, in August of first grade he scored at the upper level of the target (roughly 45 correct phonemes); and by December of that school year, he had surpassed the goal (approximately 58 correct phonemes). He continued to improve throughout first grade by scoring more than 60 correct phonemes at the April testing. You will also notice that he continued to improve, relative to the target goal, in the area of alphabetic principle. However, it appears that John needs to work on his oral reading fluency since his score in April of first grade was further below the goal than it was in December.

The two pages shown in Figure 5.7 are also from DIBELS, but instead of individual students they report performance across groups. The first sample page from this group report summarizes student performance on the test across an entire school district on the Nonsense Word Fluency subtest. This report shows the percentage of students who were classified into one of three performance level categories—"Low Risk," "Some Risk," and "At Risk." The specific criterion, or benchmark goal, is clearly stated along with what students should be able to do with respect to letter-sound correspondence in January of their Kindergarten year (which was the time when this particular measure was taken). Of the 89 students tested, 56 (or 63%)—as indicated by the darkened bars in the graph (i.e., ■)—were at low risk for not achieving the stated goal. Twenty-four students (or 27%)—as shown by the diagonally-marked bars in the graph (i.e., ▨)—were at some risk. Finally, nine students were at risk, as indicated by the clear bar (i.e., ▯). This information is, of course, also shown graphically at the top of the page.

The final page of this DIBELS group report is a class-level report summarizing the performance of each individual child in the particular class. Each student is listed, followed at the right by his or her scores on each of the four subtests. Accompanying the score for each subtest is the performance level classification (under the column labeled "Status") and suggestions for future instruction and/or intervention. These suggestions (which are located under the column labeled "Instructional Recommendations") include "Benchmark—At Grade Level," "Strategic—Additional Intervention," and "Intensive—Needs Substantial Intervention."

Figure 5.5 Sample Student Test Score Report

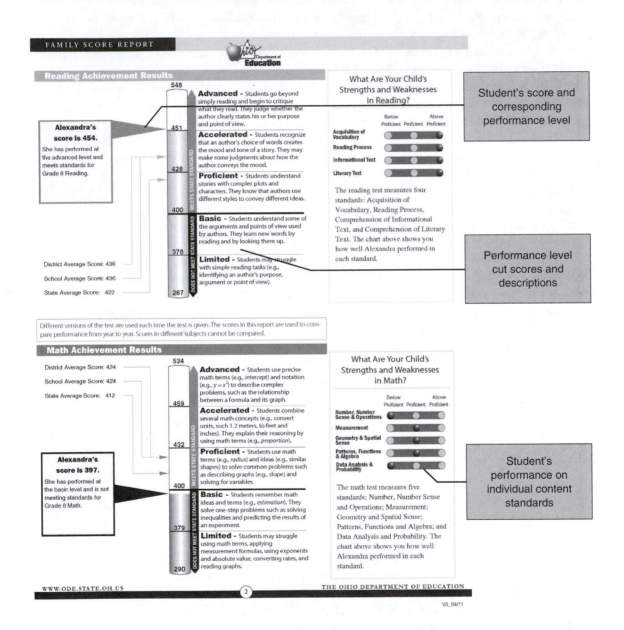

Figure 5.5 (Continued)

Ohio Department of Education

FAMILY SCORE REPORT

Starting in July, you can see some of the actual test questions at www.success.ode.state.oh.us

What Are Your Child's Strengths and Weaknesses in Reading?

→ Description of each Reading standard

Acquisition of Vocabulary

Students learn new words by knowing how words relate to each other (e.g., *ample* and *plenty* are synonyms; *detain* and *release* are antonyms). They understand figurative language (e.g., metaphors and idioms) and discuss why it is used.

Alexandra Scored Above Proficient

WHAT THESE RESULTS MEAN

Your child can discuss the ways that different events (cultural, political, technological, scientific) impact and add to the English language (e.g., *laptop, blog, spam*). She can also understand new words used in other subjects, including science and math.

NEXT STEPS

Have your child read different texts. Discuss how authors are influenced by different things. For example, some authors use words from other languages (e.g., croissant from the French language), and others might use words reflecting a social trend (e.g., inbox, bytes, and blog from technology).

→ Interpretation of the student's score

Reading Process

Students practice and use reading strategies learned in earlier grades (summarizing, predicting, comparing, contrasting) to help them understand complex texts (history or science articles) and difficult literary material (novels, plays, poems).

Alexandra Scored Above Proficient

WHAT THESE RESULTS MEAN

Your child can form her own arguments and find materials to support these arguments. She can also research a topic and use many resources to provide a complete picture (public documents, including speeches; consumer materials, such as product information).

NEXT STEPS

Have your child select an article of interest. Discuss the article and then have a debate with your child about the topic.

→ Suggestions for activities that support and encourage growth

Informational Text

Students judge how well authors organize their ideas (e.g., order of events, problem-solution). They also judge whether an author effectively supports his or her argument with details.

Alexandra Scored Above Proficient

WHAT THESE RESULTS MEAN

Your child can identify whether an author has slanted his or her information to convey a certain opinion. She is able to read an article or a speech and decide what bias it shows. She can tell if an author's information develops a strong argument.

NEXT STEPS

Read a newspaper editorial together. Ask your child if the author's argument is convincing. Why is the argument strong? What could make it stronger?

Literary Text

Students evaluate the elements of a story (e.g., subplots, foreshadowing, universal themes, symbolism) and describe how these elements work together (e.g., how setting affects the plot). They judge the different ways authors make their stories interesting.

Alexandra Scored Above Proficient

WHAT THESE RESULTS MEAN

Your child can analyze and compare how authors choose different words to create a faster or slower pace of action. She knows that authors can tell the same story by using different techniques (fantasy, factual reporting).

NEXT STEPS

Choose a book that you and your child can read independently. Discuss what each of you likes about the book and how it compares with other books read. Have your child describe examples of foreshadowing and flashback that might have occurred in the story.

(Continued)

Figure 5.5 (Continued)

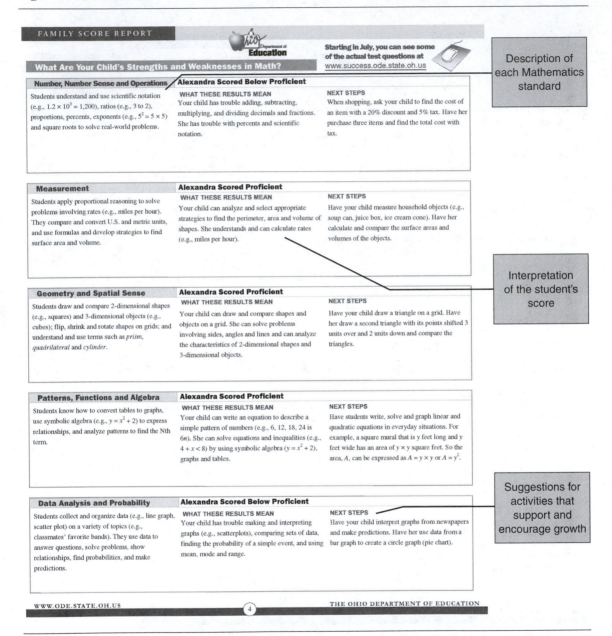

FAMILY SCORE REPORT

Ohio Department of Education

Starting in July, you can see some of the actual test questions at www.success.ode.state.oh.us

What Are Your Child's Strengths and Weaknesses in Math?

Number, Number Sense and Operations

Students understand and use scientific notation (e.g., $1.2 \times 10^3 = 1,200$), ratios (e.g., 3 to 2), proportions, percents, exponents (e.g., $5^2 = 5 \times 5$) and square roots to solve real-world problems.

Alexandra Scored Below Proficient

WHAT THESE RESULTS MEAN
Your child has trouble adding, subtracting, multiplying, and dividing decimals and fractions. She has trouble with percents and scientific notation.

NEXT STEPS
When shopping, ask your child to find the cost of an item with a 20% discount and 5% tax. Have her purchase three items and find the total cost with tax.

Description of each Mathematics standard

Measurement

Students apply proportional reasoning to solve problems involving rates (e.g., miles per hour). They compare and convert U.S. and metric units, and use formulas and develop strategies to find surface area and volume.

Alexandra Scored Proficient

WHAT THESE RESULTS MEAN
Your child can analyze and select appropriate strategies to find the perimeter, area and volume of shapes. She understands and can calculate rates (e.g., miles per hour).

NEXT STEPS
Have your child measure household objects (e.g., soup can, juice box, ice cream cone). Have her calculate and compare the surface areas and volumes of the objects.

Geometry and Spatial Sense

Students draw and compare 2-dimensional shapes (e.g., squares) and 3-dimensional objects (e.g., cubes); flip, shrink and rotate shapes on grids; and understand and use terms such as *prism*, *quadrilateral* and *cylinder*.

Alexandra Scored Proficient

WHAT THESE RESULTS MEAN
Your child can draw and compare shapes and objects on a grid. She can solve problems involving sides, angles and lines and can analyze the characteristics of 2-dimensional shapes and 3-dimensional objects.

NEXT STEPS
Have your child draw a triangle on a grid. Have her draw a second triangle with its points shifted 3 units over and 2 units down and compare the triangles.

Interpretation of the student's score

Patterns, Functions and Algebra

Students know how to convert tables to graphs, use symbolic algebra (e.g., $y = x^2 + 2$) to express relationships, and analyze patterns to find the Nth term.

Alexandra Scored Proficient

WHAT THESE RESULTS MEAN
Your child can write an equation to describe a simple pattern of numbers (e.g., 6, 12, 18, 24 is $6n$). She can solve equations and inequalities (e.g., $4 + x < 8$) by using symbolic algebra ($y = x^2 + 2$), graphs and tables.

NEXT STEPS
Have students write, solve and graph linear and quadratic equations in everyday situations. For example, a square mural that is y feet long and y feet wide has an area of y × y square feet. So the area, A, can be expressed as $A = y \times y$ or $A = y^2$.

Data Analysis and Probability

Students collect and organize data (e.g., line graph, scatter plot) on a variety of topics (e.g., classmates' favorite bands). They use data to answer questions, solve problems, show relationships, find probabilities, and make predictions.

Alexandra Scored Below Proficient

WHAT THESE RESULTS MEAN
Your child has trouble making and interpreting graphs (e.g., scatterplots), comparing sets of data, finding the probability of a simple event, and using mean, mode and range.

NEXT STEPS
Have your child interpret graphs from newspapers and make predictions. Have her use data from a bar graph to create a circle graph (pie chart).

Suggestions for activities that support and encourage growth

Figure 5.6   Sample Student Test Score Report

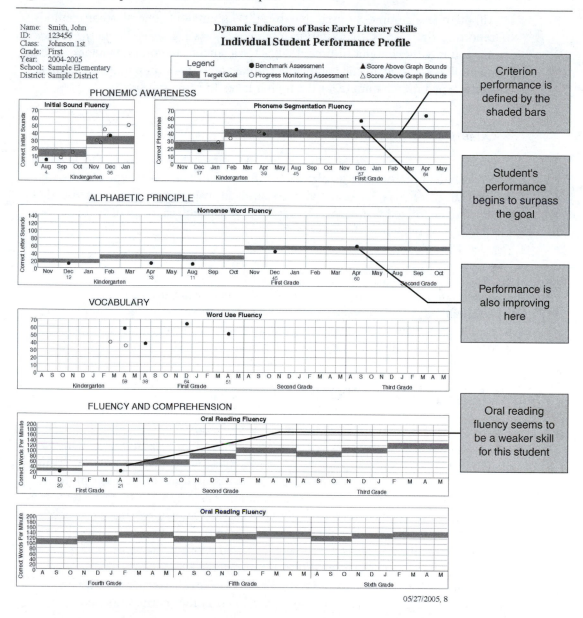

Speed of Performance

Although less commonly used, Nitko (2004) points out several other methods of reporting the results for criterion-referenced tests. A *speed of performance score* is simply the amount of time it takes for a student to complete a task or the number of tasks a student can complete in a fixed amount of time (e.g., the number of words typed in one minute, or the time it takes to run a mile).

Quality of Performance

Quality of performance scores consist of ratings that indicates the level at which a student performs (e.g., *excellent* or *four out of five*). This type of criterion-referenced score may be used with constructed-response or more open-ended types of standardized test items. Quality of performance scores will be discussed more extensively later in this module.

Precision of Performance

A *precision of performance score* involves measuring the degree of accuracy with which a student completes a task (e.g., accurately weighing a sample to the nearest gram). These last three types of scores are typically used for classroom assessments, but are rarely measured by standardized tests.

CONSTRUCTED-RESPONSE TEST ITEMS

Recall from Module 1 that a constructed-response test item requires students to recall from their own memories, or otherwise create, their response to an item on a standardized test. Examples of constructed-response items include tests of writing as well as open-ended or performance-type items that are being used more frequently on standardized achievement and aptitude tests. Scoring a student's response to a constructed-response item is much more subjective than scoring a response to its selected-response counterpart. Since the student is creating and supplying the answer, it cannot be subjected to computer-based scoring. Because there may be more than one correct answer to a constructed-response item—or perhaps only one correct answer, but different ways to arrive at that answer or to explain it—judgment on the part of the scorer does play a part in the scoring process.

Scoring of Constructed-Response Test Items

The most important aspect to the criterion-based scoring of a constructed-response item is the reduction of scorer bias. Test publishers accomplish this by clearly specifying the desired criteria that they expect to see in a student's response.

Figure 5.7   Sample Group Test Score Report

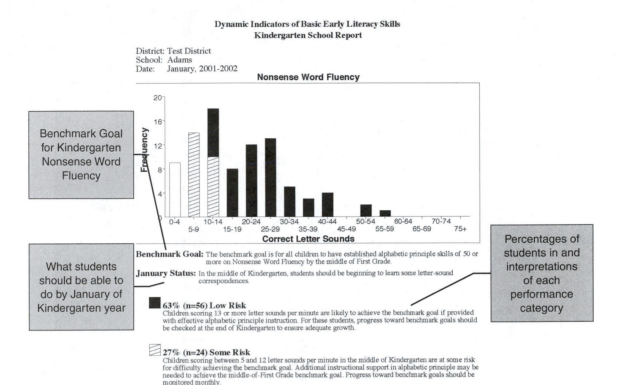

Dynamic Indicators of Basic Early Literacy Skills
Kindergarten School Report

District: Test District
School: Adams
Date: January, 2001-2002

Nonsense Word Fluency

Benchmark Goal
for Kindergarten
Nonsense Word
Fluency

What students
should be able to
do by January of
Kindergarten year

Percentages of
students in and
interpretations
of each
performance
category

Benchmark Goal: The benchmark goal is for all children to have established alphabetic principle skills of 50 or
more on Nonsense Word Fluency by the middle of First Grade.

January Status: In the middle of Kindergarten, students should be beginning to learn some letter-sound
correspondences.

■ 63% (n=56) Low Risk
Children scoring 13 or more letter sounds per minute are likely to achieve the benchmark goal if provided
with effective alphabetic principle instruction. For these students, progress toward benchmark goals should
be checked at the end of Kindergarten to ensure adequate growth.

▧ 27% (n=24) Some Risk
Children scoring between 5 and 12 letter sounds per minute in the middle of Kindergarten are at some risk
for difficulty achieving the benchmark goal. Additional instructional support in alphabetic principle may be
needed to achieve the middle-of-First Grade benchmark goal. Progress toward benchmark goals should be
monitored monthly.

□ 10% (n=9) At Risk
Students scoring below 5 letter sounds per minute in the middle of Kindergarten are at risk for difficulty
achieving the alphabetic principle goal. For students in this range, intensive intervention in alphabetic
principle may be needed to achieve the benchmark goal. Progress toward benchmark goals should be
monitored at least every 2 weeks.

Note: Split bars where the bottom part indicates "at risk" and the top part indicates "some risk" or where the
bottom part indicates "some risk" and the top part indicates "low risk" are used when the cutoff scores for "at
risk" or "some risk" occur in the middle of a score range. The number of students is indicated by the size of the
part.

School Report, 11/27/2002, 4

(Continued)

Figure 5.7 (Continued)

Dynamic Indicators of Basic Early Literacy Skills
Kindergarten Class List Report

District: Test District
School: Adams
Date: January 2001-2002
Class: Adams K #4

Note: Scores provide an indication of performance only. If there is any concern about the accuracy of scores for an individual student, performance should be verified by retesting to validate need for support.

Student	Initial Sound Fluency Score	Percentile	Status	Letter Naming Fluency Score	Percentile	Status	Phoneme Segmentation Fluency Score	Percentile	Status	Nonsense Word Fluency Score	Percentile	Status	Instructional Recommendations
B. JUDY	5	2	Deficit	6	10	At risk	3	7	At Risk	6	16	Some Risk	Intensive - Needs Substantial Intervention
R. CHRISTIAN	9	6	Deficit	20	41	Some risk	7	11	Some Risk	12	34	Some Risk	Strategic - Additional Intervention
Y. SAMANTHA	14	14	Emerging	7	12	At risk	9	14	Some Risk	6	16	Some Risk	Intensive - Needs Substantial Intervention
W. KATHLEEN	15	17	Emerging	11	20	At risk	10	15	Some Risk	5	14	Some Risk	Intensive - Needs Substantial Intervention
M. AUSTINE	17	22	Emerging	15	29	Some risk	25	32	Low Risk	20	55	Low Risk	Strategic - Additional Intervention
H. ADRIAN	20	32	Emerging	64	98	Low risk	41	61	Low Risk	44	95	Low Risk	Benchmark - At Grade Level
P. NYSHEL	23	41	Emerging	49	89	Low risk	38	55	Low Risk	14	40	Low Risk	Benchmark - At Grade Level
R. MICHAEL	24	47	Emerging	19	39	Some risk	23	30	Low Risk	0	3	At Risk	Strategic - Additional Intervention
B. CHELSEA	25	51	Established	29	60	Low risk	29	38	Low Risk	21	58	Low Risk	Benchmark - At Grade Level
M. CLAY	27	57	Established	11	20	At risk	27	35	Low Risk	10	28	Some Risk	Strategic - Additional Intervention
W. NICHOLAS	28	60	Established	10	17	At risk	2	6	At Risk	11	31	Some Risk	Strategic - Additional Intervention
V. IRIS	30	66	Established	23	49	Some risk	29	38	Low Risk	9	25	Some Risk	Strategic - Additional Intervention
J. AUSTIN	31	69	Established	41	80	Low risk	31	41	Low Risk	6	16	Some Risk	Benchmark - At Grade Level
D. KAYLEE	32	72	Established	21	43	Some risk	40	59	Low Risk	32	81	Low Risk	Benchmark - At Grade Level
D. KAI	40	88	Established	19	39	Some risk	39	57	Low Risk	9	25	Some Risk	Benchmark - At Grade Level
G. WILLIAM	42	90	Established	28	58	Low risk	48	74	Low Risk	4	11	At Risk	Benchmark - At Grade Level
C. BRIANNA	43	91	Established	41	80	Low risk	51	82	Low Risk	24	64	Low Risk	Benchmark - At Grade Level
M. JUSTIN	48	94	Established	61	96	Low risk	46	71	Low Risk	23	61	Low Risk	Benchmark - At Grade Level
C. LEXINGTON	50	94	Established	14	27	At risk	43	65	Low Risk	37	88	Low Risk	Strategic - Additional Intervention
D. MARIAH	51	95	Established	27	56	Low risk	38	55	Low Risk	18	50	Low Risk	Benchmark - At Grade Level
B. EMERALD	60	98	Established	27	56	Low risk	42	63	Low Risk	19	52	Low Risk	Benchmark - At Grade Level
E. CALEM	70	>99	Established	47	87	Low risk	55	90	Low Risk	25	66	Low Risk	Benchmark - At Grade Level
	32 Mean			25.9 Mean			30.7 Mean			16.1 Mean			

Individual student scores for each of the four subtests

Performance level classifications

Class averages appear at the bottom of each column

Instructional recommendations for each student

Class List Report, 11/27/2002, 9

Presented in Figure 5.8 is an example of a holistic scoring rubric used to score student responses to writing prompts on the Ohio Grade 4 Writing Achievement Test. Notice that each of the four scores levels (i.e., 4–3–2–1–0) are clearly described. These "Score Point Descriptions" provide the specific criteria for scoring the written responses. In essence, these descriptions delineate the five performance levels in quite similar fashion to descriptions we have previously examined on various test reports.

THE NATURE OF CUT SCORES

At this point, you may be asking yourself questions about these various schemes of categorizing levels of criterion-referenced performance, such as "How is the minimum score for a certain category such as proficient or low risk determined?" and "Why are these values set there and who determines them?" These scores are generally referred to as cut scores—that is, they serve as the cutoff points between adjacent categories along some performance continuum. The process used to determine various cut scores is known as *standard setting*.

There are both opponents and advocates of standard setting, particularly when the cut scores are used to determine classification of student competence on high-stakes tests, such as those mandated by many states (Payne, 2003). Those individuals who oppose this process argue that virtually all methods of establishing cut scores are arbitrary and that it is extremely difficult to get judges to agree on a particular set of standards. Advocates of the process typically rely on the abundant research which supports the consistency in specifying standards, especially when training of judges and test data are available to help guide these cut score decisions (Payne, 2003).

Common Methods of Deriving Cut Scores

Early standard setting techniques often used norm-referenced approaches (typically referred to as relative methods); however, these techniques are not used as extensively today (Cizek, 1996). For example, a relative method of standard setting might establish a passing score at one standard deviation below the mean score for a given group of examinees. With the increase in the development and use of criterion-referenced tests, relative methods of setting standards were replaced with absolute methods (Cizek, 1996). These criterion-based models have been classified as either state or continuum models. State models—which have not been widely used in testing programs—assume that competency or proficiency is a truly dichotomous entity (i.e., a student is either proficient or is not proficient). Continuum models—which can focus either on judgments of individual test items or on judgments about individual examinees—assume that competency is a continuous variable (i.e., there exist degrees of proficiency). These latter models have seen broader uses in educational contexts (Cizek, 1996).

Figure 5.8   Ohio Grade 4 Writing Achievement Holistic Rubric From the Ohio Achievement Tests

Ohio Grade 4 Writing Achievement Holistic Rubric for Writing Prompt Items

Score Point	Score Point Description
4	The written response: • Fully addresses the prompt and purpose for writing • Focuses on the topic with ample supporting details and little or no extraneous information • Includes all components of the mode of writing • Displays a sense of wholeness (cohesiveness) including a logical order of ideas • Contains a beginning, middle and end appropriate for the mode of writing (introduction, body, conclusion-Expository) (Date, Salutation, Body, Closing, Signature-Letter) • Contains appropriate paragraphing with clear transitions and topic sentences • Uses language effectively by varying vocabulary and sentence patterns • Contains correct grammatical structures with few or no errors • Uses correct spelling of high-frequency and grade-level words; few or no minor errors in punctuation and capitalization
3	The written response: • Adequately addresses the prompt and purpose for writing • Relates to the topic with adequate supporting details but may have some extraneous information • Includes most of the components of the mode of writing • Contains a logical order of ideas • Contains an apparent beginning, middle and end appropriate for the mode of writing • (introduction, body, conclusion-Expository) (Date, Salutation, Body, Closing, Signature-Letter) • Contains paragraphing with some transitions and topic sentences • Varies vocabulary and sentence patterns • Contains grammatical structures that are mostly correct • Uses correct spelling of high-frequency and grade-level words; few errors in punctuation and capitalization
2	The written response: • Partially addresses the prompt and purpose for writing • Demonstrates an awareness of the topic, with some supporting detail, but may contain extraneous information • Includes some of the components of the mode of writing • Contains fragmented ideas and is hard to understand • Attempts a beginning, middle and end appropriate for the mode of writing • (introduction, body, conclusion-Expository) (Date, Salutation, Body, Closing, Signature-Letter) • Contains some paragraphing with few transitions of ideas, topic sentences and/or details • Contains limited vocabulary and simple or incorrect sentences • Contains grammatical errors that interfere with meaning • Contains frequent errors in spelling, capitalization and punctuation that interfere with meaning
1	The written response: • Attempts to address prompt and purpose for writing • Relates slightly to topic, has little or no supporting detail and may contain much • extraneous information • Includes few of the components of the mode of writing • Contains no logical order of ideas • Contains little or no evidence of beginning, middle or end appropriate for the mode of writing (introduction, body, conclusion-Expository) (Date, Salutation, Body, Closing, Signature-Letter) • Contains little evidence of paragraphing, lacks topic sentences • Contains limited vocabulary and sentence patterns, and errors in language usage • Contains serious grammatical errors that impede meaning • Contains many errors in spelling, punctuation, and capitalization that impede meaning
0	The written response: • Does not meet the criteria required to earn one point. • May only repeat or restate information given in the writing prompt. • May only provide information completely irrelevant to the writing prompt. • May have addressed a different topic or simply contain "I don't know"

According to Payne (2003), there exist approximately 38 different methods for standard setting. Most of these techniques can be organized nicely into one of three major categories (Crocker & Algina, 1986), all of which would be considered absolute methods. These categories are as follows:

1. judgments based on holistic impressions of the examination or item pool (a holistic absolute model),

2. judgments based on the content of individual test items (a test-centered absolute model), and

3. judgments based on examinee's test performance (an examinee-centered absolute model).

You will notice that all standard setting is determined by judgments made by experts in the content areas being tested (McMillan, 2001).

In the first group of techniques where judgments are based on the holistic impressions of the overall test, a panel of experts first closely examines the test content. These experts then suggest the percentage of items that should be correctly answered by an examinee who has achieved a minimum level of competency to perform at the given level of interest (Crocker & Algina, 1986). Individual judges typically set their own recommended standard, and then those recommendations are averaged in order to arrive at the final standard. Although this notion of holistic judgment is arguably the most widely used method of setting standards and establishing cut scores, it is often difficult to defend. A common criticism of these methods is that a test publisher can never be sure that a different sample of judges or content experts might not have established the standard at a different point (Crocker & Algina, 1986).

The second category of absolute models focuses on judgments based on item content. There are three basic techniques in this group, as originally proposed by Nedelsky, Angoff, and Ebel (as cited in Crocker & Algina, 1986). Although each of these techniques is slightly different from the others, each involves the examination of individual items appearing on a given test. As an example, the Angoff method is briefly described here. Using a hypothetical group of minimally competent persons, judges must estimate the proportion of this minimally competent group who would likely answer each item correctly. This proportion can also be interpreted as the probability that a minimally competent person will answer a given item correctly. These probabilities are summed across all items in order to obtain the minimum passing score as recommended by that particular judge. Consensus techniques are then used across all judges to obtain the final minimum passing score for the test.

The final category of absolute standard setting models focuses on the anticipated performance of a particular group of examinees. As a general example, a test could be administered to a particular group of students who, based on knowledge of their past academic performance, should be expected to score lower on the test than the ultimate target population. The resulting minimum competency standard, or cut score, is then based on the mean or median for this lower-achieving group of students (Crocker & Algina, 1986).

As an example of this standard setting procedure let us examine the process used to set the performance standards for the Metropolitan Achievement Test, 8th edition (MAT8). The test publisher recruited approximately 300 teachers representing school districts from around the country to participate in an online administered standard setting. Teachers were assigned to groups on the basis of grade levels and subject area expertise. There were 24 groups of approximately 10 to 15 teachers. Following training sessions, teachers were asked to take the tests for which they would be setting performance level standards. Using a modified Angoff procedure, teachers were required to make three independent judgments about each item in their respective subtests and to decide how students at various performance levels should perform on the item. At the conclusion of the three sets of judgments, the raw-score cut point for each performance level for each subtest was obtained by summing the ratings for all items in that subtest and averaging the sums across all teachers (Harcourt Assessment, 2002).

An inspection of the Ohio Graduation Test standard setting process will serve as a second example. Read the following passage taken directly from the Statistical Summary of the Ohio Graduation Tests (Ohio Department of Education, 2006):

> In August of 2003, House Bill 3 was signed into law. The most significant impact of this law on the Ohio Graduation Tests was the use of five categories for performance, instead of four. Intended to better show progress that schools were making both in moving students toward proficient and to the higher levels above proficient, the new categories included: Limited, Basic, Proficient, Accelerated, and Advanced. In spring of 2004, groups of Ohio educators met to recommend cut scores for the Reading and Mathematics tests. Those recommendations were adopted by the State Board of Education in June of 2004. Similarly, groups of Ohio educations met in June 2005 to recommend cut scores for Writing, Science and Social Studies; those recommendations were adopted by the State Board of education in June 2005. (pp. 1–2)

The resulting cut scores for each level of proficiency across each of the five subtests are shown in Figure 5.9. You will also notice in this figure a column labeled "Scaled Score." These are values obtained by taking the raw scores and transforming them into some other type of scale. Mathematical transformations are commonly used for the derivation of many norm-referenced scores, and there are common, standard ways to obtain those scores. However, with respect to

Figure 5.9   Performance Levels and Associated Cut Scores for Ohio Graduation Test

Subject	Performance Level	Raw Score	Scaled Score
Reading	Advanced	40.0 – 48.0	448 – 545
	Accelerated	32.0 – 39.5	429 – 447
	Proficient	18.0 – 31.5	400 – 428
	Basic	12.0 – 17.5	383 – 399
	Limited	0.0 – 11.5	268 – 382
Mathematics	Advanced	34.5 – 46.0	444 – 568
	Accelerated	27.5 – 34.0	425 – 443
	Proficient	18.0 – 27.0	400 – 424
	Basic	12.5 – 17.5	384 – 399
	Limited	0.0 – 12.0	260 – 383
Writing	Advanced	41.0 – 48.0	476 – 611
	Accelerated	34.0 – 40.5	430 – 475
	Proficient	25.5 – 33.5	400 – 429
	Basic	18.0 – 25.0	378 – 399
	Limited	0.0 – 17.5	258 – 377
Science	Advanced	37.5 – 48.0	445 – 591
	Accelerated	32.0 – 37.0	425 – 444
	Proficient	23.5 – 31.5	400 – 424
	Basic	14.5 – 23.0	371 – 399
	Limited	0.0 – 14.0	211 – 370
Social Studies	Advanced	39.0 – 48.0	446 – 565
	Accelerated	33.0 – 38.5	429 – 445
	Proficient	21.5 – 32.5	400 – 428
	Basic	15.0 – 21.0	382 – 399
	Limited	0.0 – 14.5	231 – 381

Figure 5.10 Raw Score to Scaled Score Conversion Table, March 2005 OGT Administration

RAW SCORE	READING		MATHEMATICS		WRITING		SCIENCE		SOCIAL STUDIES	
	Status	Scaled Score	Status	Scaled Score	Status	Scaled Score	Status	Scaled Score	Status	Scaled Score
11.5	Limited	382	Limited	381	Limited	358	Limited	360	Limited	370
12	Basic	384	Limited	383	Limited	360	Limited	362	Limited	371
12.5	Basic	385	Basic	384	Limited	362	Limited	364	Limited	373
13	Basic	387	Basic	386	Limited	363	Limited	366	Limited	375
13.5	Basic	388	Basic	388	Limited	365	Limited	368	Limited	377
14	Basic	390	Basic	389	Limited	366	Limited	370	Limited	378
14.5	Basic	391	Basic	390	Limited	368	Basic	372	Limited	380
15	Basic	392	Basic	392	Limited	369	Basic	374	Basic	382
15.5	Basic	394	Basic	393	Limited	371	Basic	375	Basic	383
16	Basic	395	Basic	395	Limited	372	Basic	377	Basic	385
16.5	Basic	396	Basic	396	Limited	374	Basic	379	Basic	386
17	Basic	398	Basic	397	Limited	375	Basic	380	Basic	388
17.5	Basic	399	Basic	399	Limited	376	Basic	382	Basic	389
18	Proficient	400	Proficient	400	Basic	378	Basic	384	Basic	391
18.5	Proficient	401	Proficient	401	Basic	379	Basic	385	Basic	392
19	Proficient	402	Proficient	403	Basic	381	Basic	387	Basic	393
19.5	Proficient	404	Proficient	404	Basic	382	Basic	388	Basic	395
20	Proficient	405	Proficient	405	Basic	384	Basic	390	Basic	396
20.5	Proficient	406	Proficient	407	Basic	385	Basic	391	Basic	398
21	Proficient	407	Proficient	408	Basic	387	Basic	393	Basic	399
21.5	Proficient	408	Proficient	409	Basic	388	Basic	394	Proficient	400
22	Proficient	409	Proficient	410	Basic	390	Basic	396	Proficient	402
22.5	Proficient	410	Proficient	412	Basic	391	Basic	397	Proficient	403

criterion-referenced scores, these scales tend to be unique to a particular standardized test. For example, the Ohio Department of Education (ODE) has developed its own unique formula for transforming raw test scores into the scaled scores that also appear on the Ohio Achievement Tests and Ohio Graduation Tests reports. Additionally, ODE provides a table showing the conversion of scores along the continuum (see Figure 5.10).

Summary

Criterion-referenced test scores compare a student's performance or the performance of a group of students to some preestablished criteria or standards. The interpretation of these scores typically reflects the degree of accuracy with which specific content has been mastered. The overall purpose of criterion-referenced tests or criterion-referenced scores is simply to describe the current level of achievement. These types of tests may or may not include some sort of cut scores. Criterion-referenced test results can be effectively used to enable educators to draw inferences about the level of student performance relative to some larger content domain. They help educators gain a better understanding of what students know, what they are able to do, and what they have mastered.

There are four basic types of criterion-referenced test scores: raw scores (typically presented as the number or percentage of items answered correctly), speed of performance, quality of performance, and precision of performance. The reporting of raw scores is clearly the most commonly used type of criterion-referenced score. It is important to note that a raw score is essentially meaningless without further information. It is crucial to know the total number of items appearing on the test, the difficulty of the items, and the extent to which the items match the curriculum. Only then can some meaning be attached to a particular score. However, even then, the interpretation of a score and subsequent meaning associated with it are subjective.

Criterion-referenced levels of performance, or cut scores, are determined through a process known as standard setting. These absolute methods of setting performance standards are classified either as state models (assuming that proficiency is a dichotomy) or continuum models (assuming that there exist degrees of proficiency). All standard setting is based on professional, expert judgment. These judgments can be based on the holistic impressions of the examination or item pool (the most widely used set of techniques), on the content of individual test items, or on the individual examinee's test performance.

Activities for Application and Reflection

1. Obtain an actual student test report from any test you may use in your school or district that includes some criterion-referenced score information. Closely examine the criterion-referenced scores and briefly summarize the student's performance. What would you describe as the student's strengths and weaknesses?

2. Obtain a similar report for the performance of a group (i.e., a class, school, or entire district) for a test used in your district. Closely examine the criterion-referenced scores and summarize the group's performance. What do you see as the strengths and weaknesses of this particular group?

3. Using one of the reports and your interpretations from the previous two activities, write a narrative paragraph or two summarizing the resulting scores as detailed on the test report you have selected.

4. In your opinion as either a current or future educator, what are your opinions of cut scores as well as perhaps the processes used for standard setting? What do you see as their advantages and limitations?

Norm-Referenced Test Scores and Their Interpretations

Compared to the number of different criterion-referenced scores used on standardized test reports, the various types of norm-referenced scores substantially outnumber those that we examined in the previous module. Figure 6.1 summarizes the various scores used for each type of test, this time highlighting those that are norm-referenced. In this module, we will explore the information that is reported by norm-referenced test scores, the various types of norm-referenced scores, and the importance of understanding what is meant by the standard error of measurement, as well as how to apply this knowledge when interpreting student test performance. Information specific to how these scores can be used to help guide or revise instruction will be discussed in Modules 7, 8, and 9.

WHAT DO NORM-REFERENCED SCORES TELL US?

When norm-referenced standardized tests are administered to students, the results are reported in a way that permits comparisons with a well-defined group of other students who have taken the same assessment (Nitko, 2004). The primary difference between criterion- and norm-referenced scores is that with norm-referenced test scores, individual student scores are entirely dependent upon the performance of other students. Norm-referenced tests and their resulting scores provide evidence that assists educators in answering the following questions:

Figure 6.1   Summary of Methods of Reporting Scores on Standardized Tests, Highlighting
Types of Norm-Referenced Scores

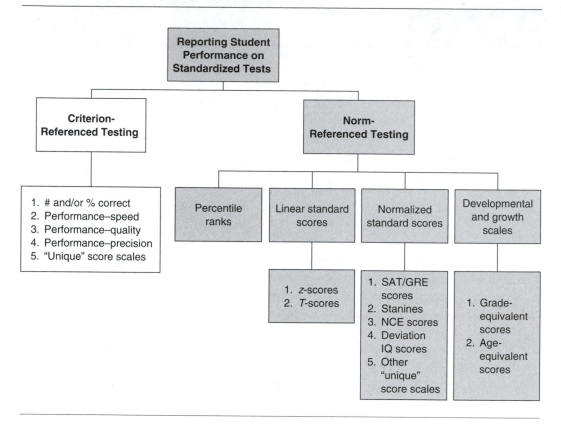

- What is the relative standing of this student (or the students in this class or district) across this broad domain of content?
- How does the student (or do these students) compare to other similar students?

As you read earlier in Module 1, the makeup of the group functioning as the comparison students forms the basis for interpreting scores resulting from norm-referenced tests. This well defined group of students, known as a norm group, is given the same assessment under the same conditions (e.g., same time limits, same materials, same directions). Comparisons to norm groups enable teachers and administrators to describe achievement levels of students across different subject areas, to identify strengths and weaknesses across the curriculum, and to identify areas of deficiency—as well as subsequent intervention strategies—within each subject area (Nitko, 2004).

THE NATURE OF NORM GROUPS

Descriptions of norm groups are typically provided in the test manuals that accompany the actual tests. It is important to realize that the average performance of the norm group does not represent a standard to be attained or exceeded by all students in every school across the country. In contrast, the performance of the norm group on a particular standardized test is intended to represent the current level of achievement for a specific group of students, usually at a certain grade level (Nitko, 2004). Therefore, comparisons to the norm group can assist educators in making decisions about the general range or level of performance to expect from their students.

There are several types of norms that can be reported in norm-referenced tests. These include local norm groups (e.g., composed of student within a particular school district), special norm groups (e.g., composed of students who are blind or deaf), and school average norms. However, most norm-referenced tests rely on national norms (Airasian, 2005; Nitko, 2004). National norm groups are selected in order to be representative of the entire country. This representation is based on such characteristics as gender, race, ethnicity, culture, and socioeconomic status. The purpose of obtaining a representative norm group is to reduce any potential bias when comparing students from diverse backgrounds around the country. In addition to being representative, norm groups must also be current (Nitko, 2004). Test publishers work very hard at ensuring representativeness, although perfect representation can never be achieved. If the norm group for a given test is not representative and current, the resulting test scores will likely lead to misinterpretation and ultimately inappropriate educational decisions.

Publishers of norm-referenced tests have found it advantageous to sometimes transform scores so that they can be placed in some common distribution. This common distribution is called a *normal distribution*, also known as a *normal curve* or a *bell-shaped curve*. Normal distributions have three main characteristics (Mertler, 2003). These characteristics are as follows:

- The distribution is symmetrical (i.e., the left and right halves are mirror images of each other).
- The mean (or arithmetic average), median (the score that separates the upper 50% of scores from the lower 50% of scores), and the mode (the most frequently occurring score) are the same score and are located at the exact center of the distribution.
- The percentage of cases in each standard deviation (or the average distance of individual scores away from the mean) is known precisely.

The normal distribution was derived over 250 years ago (Nitko, 2004). When first originated, it was based on the belief that nearly all physical characteristics in humans were, by nature, distributed randomly around an average value. Furthermore, the vast majority of cases were located in the middle of the distribution (indicating that most people were, roughly speaking, average). A very small proportion of individuals can be found at the extreme ends of the distribution. This serves as an indication that, with respect to most characteristics, the majority of people are relatively similar to one another (e.g., approximately average height), with a minority of people at the high (i.e., very tall) and low (i.e., very short) ends. The concept of randomly and normally distributed physical characteristics has since carried over into the realm of mental measurement.

As shown in Figure 6.2, each standard deviation in a normal distribution contains a fixed percentage of cases (Nitko, 2004). The mean score plus and minus 1 standard deviation contains approximately 68% of the individuals making up the distribution; 95% of the cases are within 2 standard deviations of the mean; and over 99% of the cases are within 3 standard deviations. From the figure, it should be clear that 50% of the cases, or scores, are located above the mean (i.e., the right half of the distribution) and 50% are located below the mean (i.e., the left half); this should also make intuitive sense because in a normal distribution, the mean and median are located at the same score. Moreover, nearly 16% of the scores are greater than one standard deviation above the mean.

This information about the percentage of cases in the various segments of the distribution is key to the interpretation of scores resulting from norm-referenced standardized tests. A main purpose of the normal distribution is to help educators get a sense of how high or low a given score is in relation to an entire distribution of scores (Mertler, 2003). This serves as the basis for many of the scores we will discuss next.

TYPES OF NORM-REFERENCED SCORES

As you saw in Figure 6.1, there are numerous types of norm-referenced scores. Most of them are based on mathematical transformations. In other words, the raw scores are changed or converted to some other scale. These new scales then conform to the characteristics of the normal distribution as were previously discussed. It is important to bear in mind that norm-referenced test scores are all based on the notion of how an individual student performs as compared to a large group of similar students. Most of these students will be average, with their performance being located near the middle of the distribution.

Raw Scores

In the previous module on criterion-referenced test scores, you read about the use of raw scores. Raw scores are the main method of reporting results of

Figure 6.2   Characteristics of the Normal Distribution

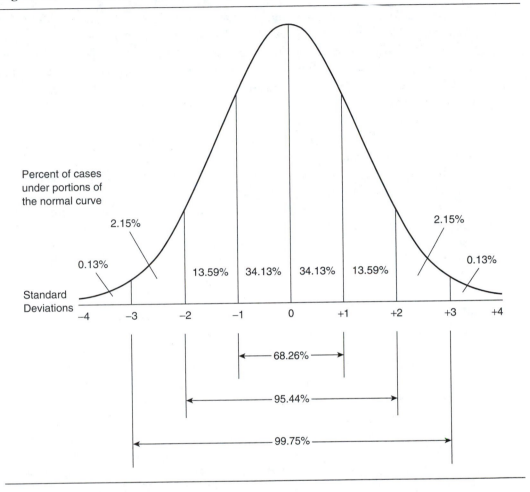

criterion-referenced tests. However, norm-referenced test reports also typically provide the raw scores (i.e., the number of items answered correctly) obtained by students on various tests and subtests. However, these scores are not very useful when interpreting the results of achievement or aptitude tests for purposes of norm-referenced comparisons, for their distributions would likely not be symmetrical or normal in nature. More importantly, teachers need to know how a particular student's raw score compares to the specific norm group. To make these types of comparisons, raw scores must first be converted to some other score scale. These new scales are referred to as *transformed* or *derived scores* and include such scores as percentile ranks, z-scores, T-scores, normal curve equivalent scores, deviation IQ scores, and stanines, among others.

Percentile Ranks

A *percentile rank* is a single number that indicates the percentage of the norm group that scored below a given raw score. Possible values for percentile ranks range from 1 to 99. However, since percentile ranks indicate various percentages of individuals above and below scores that are normally distributed, they do not represent equal units (Mertler, 2003). Percentile ranks are much more compactly arranged in the middle of the normal distribution since that is where the majority of individuals fall.

Let us consider a hypothetical example for a student, Annie, who recently took a norm-referenced achievement test. Annie's test report includes a percentile rank for all subtests appearing on the report. Let us assume that Annie correctly answered 34 out of a possible 45 items on the reading subtest of the total test battery. When converted, this raw score of 34 converts to a percentile rank equal to 86. This means that based on her raw score Annie scored higher than 86% of the other students (in the norm group) who took the test. In other words, 86% of the students who made up the norm group answered fewer than 34 items correctly.

Percentile ranks are among the most frequently reported derived scores, yet they are also among the most frequently misunderstood (Mertler, 2003). A common misinterpretation of these test scores is that they are equivalent to the percentages of items answered correctly. In our example above, Annie correctly answered 76% (i.e., 34 out of 45) of the items—clearly not the same as the 86th percentile. It is important to realize that making the assumption that a percentile rank should be interpreted in the same manner as a percentage of items answered correctly implies a criterion-referenced (i.e., the score that she actually received) rather than a norm-referenced (i.e., her score in relation to others) interpretation.

Percentile ranks indicate relative standing, but have some limitations when compared to other types of derived scores we will discuss shortly. Percentile ranks are expressed in ordinal units, which means that the distance between adjacent units on a percentile scale are not equal (Payne, 2003). The distance between the 49th and 50th percentiles is much smaller—due to the substantially large number of individuals clustered at the center of the distribution—than the distance between the 1st and 2nd percentiles. In fact, the distance between the 1st and 3rd percentiles is exactly the same as the distance between the 16th and 50th percentiles. Since units are not equal, a difference in student performance for two students located at the extreme right end of the distribution (e.g., a one-unit difference) will appear less important on a percentile rank scale than the same difference for two students located in the middle of the distribution. For example, a one raw-score unit difference for students scoring near the mean (i.e., near the middle of the distribution) may differ by several percentile ranks while two students located in the tail of the distribution with a one raw-score unit difference might both have the same percentile rank (Mertler, 2003).

There is sometimes a dangerous temptation for teachers to average percentile ranks to find a student's typical performance or to subtract them to find the difference between two scores. Since percentiles do not represent equal units, they should not be mathematically manipulated in such a manner. In other words, they cannot be added, subtracted, multiplied, or divided as a means of further comparing students' relative standings or comparing student gains or losses (Oosterhof, 2001).

Developmental/Growth Scores

Developmental scales seek to identify a student's development across various levels (e.g., grade or age) of growth (Airasian, 2005). The purpose of these scores is to compare a student's performance to a series of reference groups that vary developmentally.

Grade-Equivalent Scores

A common type of developmental score that frequently appears on norm-referenced test reports is the *grade-equivalent score*. A grade-equivalent score indicates the grade in the norm group for which a certain raw score was the median performance (Oosterhof, 2001) and is intended to estimate a student's developmental level (Airasian, 2005). Grade-equivalent scores are expressed in years and 10th of years (Spinelli, 2006); they consist of two numerical components separated by a period. The first number indicates the grade level, and the second indicates the month during that particular school year, which ranges from zero (equivalent to September) to nine (equivalent to June). For example, if a student receives a raw score of 67 on the mathematics portion of an achievement test, this score might be transformed to a grade-equivalent score of 4.2. This means that this student's performance corresponds to the performance of a typical student taking the same test in November (i.e., the 2nd month) of fourth grade.

Grade-equivalent scores are often misinterpreted as standards that all students should be expected to achieve (Oosterhof, 2001). It is again important to remember that a criterion-referenced interpretation such as this is an inappropriate use of a grade-equivalent score, which is a norm-referenced score. Similarly, grade-equivalent scores are not intended to indicate appropriate grade-level placement. If a student receives a score of 5.1 on a mathematics subtest, we should not assume that he is ready for fifth-grade math, an assumption which is again a criterion-referenced interpretation and an inappropriate use of the score. We could not possibly know where this student stands with respect to fourth-grade material since he was tested on third-grade content. An additional limitation of grade-equivalent scores is that although the scores represent months, they do not, in reality, represent equal units. For example, gains made in reading achievement between grade 1.0 and grade 1.5 are very likely greater than reading achievement gains made between grade 6.0 and grade 6.5. Because these scores can be misleading and can lead to inaccurate generalizations, they should be interpreted and used for instructional decisions with substantial caution (Spinelli, 2006). Finally, with respect to grade-equivalent scores, it is important to remember that the scores represent what is considered typical or average. If the scores for the norm group result in a normal distribution, half of the total group of students who take the test will score below the average for the group (Tanner, 2001).

Age-Equivalent Scores

Very similar to grade-equivalent scores, *age-equivalent scores* are based on the average test performances of students at various age levels as opposed to various grade levels as we saw previously (Payne, 2003). Their units are also unequal, meaning that equal age units (e.g., 6 months or 1 year) do not correspond to equal age-equivalent score units. As with grade-equivalent scores, age-equivalent scores are useful for measuring and describing growth in mental ability, reading ability, and other types of characteristics that exhibit fairly consistent growth patterns within an instructional program (Payne, 2003). They are very useful in monitoring development and growth. Age-equivalent scores are expressed in a similar fashion to their grade-equivalent counterparts.

Figure 6.3 is a sample Individual Performance Profile from the Iowa Tests of Basic Skills (ITBS). On this report, the norm-referenced score information appears in the upper portion of the report. Labeled on this sample are the grade-equivalent scores and national percentile ranks.

Standardized Scores

You have seen that both percentile ranks and grade-equivalent or age-equivalent scores exist on scales with unequal units. This characteristic seriously limits the interpretability and utility of each type of score. *Standardized scores* (also known as standard scores) are obtained when raw scores are transformed to fit a distribution whose characteristics are known and fixed (Tanner, 2001). Specifically, this known distribution is the normal distribution; and the scores are reported in standard deviation units, which are equal across the entire continuum. As a result of these transformations, scores can be interpreted in a way that is unaffected by the characteristics of a particular test. Regardless of the test, standardized scores efficiently indicate whether a particular score is typical, above average, or below average as compared to others who took the test and also clearly indicate the magnitude of the variation away from the mean score (Tanner, 2001).

Moreover, standardized scores allow for comparisons of test performance across two different measures (Mertler, 2003). For example, suppose you want to compare

Figure 6.3   Sample Individual Student Test Score Report

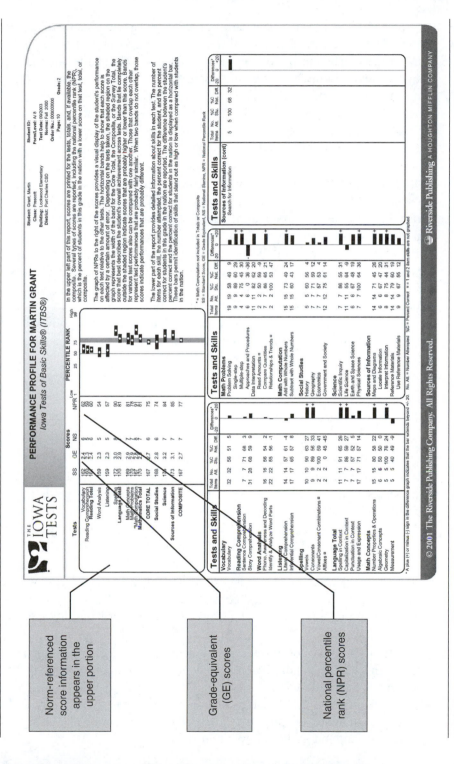

students' performances on a standardized reading test and a standardized mathematics test. However, the reading test is composed of 65 items and the math test contains 34 items. The mean score on the reading test is 45 and on the math test is 24. Simply comparing raw scores would not tell you very much about a student's relative standing as compared to the norm group. If Katherine received a raw score of 40 (i.e., 40 out of 65) on the reading test and a raw score of 30 (i.e., 30 out of 45) on the math test, it would be incorrect to say that she performed better on the reading test, even though she answered more items correctly. (Remember, in this case we are examining test performance from a norm-referenced perspective.) You might notice on the score report that her score of 40 on the reading test is below the average while her score of 30 on mathematics is above average. This type of norm-referenced comparison is possible only through the use of standardized scores because scores from two different subtests are essentially put on the same score scale.

Standardized scores simply report performance on various scales in terms of how many standard deviations the score is away from the mean. There are several types of standardized scores. The main types of scores we will examine next include *z*-scores, *T*-scores, stanines, normal curve equivalent (NCE) scores, and deviation IQ scores. These various types of standard scores and their relation to the normal distribution are depicted in Figure 6.4. As you can see in this figure, these scores are essentially analogous to one another; they are simply being reported on different scales.

Linear Standard Scores

A *linear standard score* tells how far a raw score is located from the mean of the norm group with the distance being expressed in standard deviation units (Nitko, 2004). Generally speaking, a distribution of linear standard scores will have the same shape as the distribution of raw scores from which the standard scores were derived. This is not the case for percentile ranks, grade- or age-equivalent scores, or nonlinear standard scores (which we will examine shortly). These types of scores are often used to make two distributions (e.g., scores from a science test and those from a mathematics test) more comparable by placing them on the same numerical scale (Nitko, 2004). These standard scores are called linear because if you were to plot in a graph each raw score against its corresponding linear standard score and then connect the resulting points, it would always form a straight line (Nitko, 2004).

Z-scores. This type of norm-referenced, linear standard score is typically referred to as the most basic standard score (Gredler, 1999). *Z-scores* exist on a continuum, where more than 99% of the scores range from −3.00 to +3.00. The sign indicates whether the raw score is above or below the mean; the numerical value indicates how many standard deviations it is located away from the mean. A student's *z*-score is calculated in the following manner:

Figure 6.4   Comparison of Various Types of Standard Scores and Their Relation to the Normal Distribution

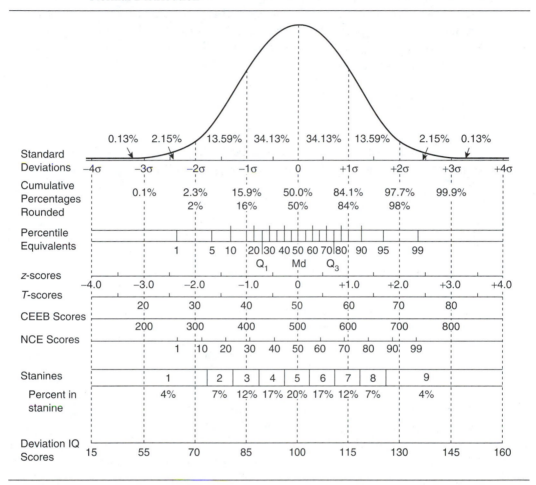

(1) The mean of the set of scores is subtracted from the student's raw score.

(2) The resulting value is then divided by the standard deviation for the set of scores.

Assume that the administration of a standardized test resulted in a mean score equal to 75 and a standard deviation equal to 8. A student whose raw score is 75 would receive a z-score equal to zero (i.e., her score is zero standard deviation units away from the mean). Another student whose raw score is 91 receives a z-score of +2.00 (i.e., 2 standard deviation units above the mean). Finally, a student who earns a raw score of 63 would receive a z-score of −1.50 (i.e., 1.5 standard deviation units below the mean).

One distinct disadvantage of z-scores is that by definition half the students will receive scores below the mean (see Figure 6.4). In other words, they will receive z-scores with negative values. It is very difficult to explain to students—and to parents—how a student could receive a score equal to –2.50 on a standardized test (Nitko, 2004). Receiving negative scores on an academic achievement test can also have adverse effects on a student's level of motivation. Understanding the proper interpretation requires knowledge of the mean, standard deviation, and norm-referencing in general.

T-scores. One way that this problematic characteristic of half of the students receiving negative scores can be overcome is through the use of *T-scores*. A *T*-score—also sometimes referred to as an *SS-score*—provides the location of a raw score in a distribution that has a mean of 50 and a standard deviation of 10 (Chase, 1999; Gredler, 1999). In addition to eliminating the possibility of having negative scores, the fractional portion of the score is also removed through the use of *T*-scores. Using the z-score scale as our guide, more than 99% of the *T*-scores on a standardized test will range from 20 (3 standard deviations below the mean) to 80 (3 standard deviations above the mean). A student's *T*-score is calculated in the following manner:

(1) A z-score is first calculated and then multiplied by 10 (this becomes the value for a standard deviation on the new scale).

(2) The resulting value is added to 50 (the new value for the mean) to obtain the *T*-score.

If we examine the hypothetical example from our previous discussion of z-scores, the first student's z-score of zero would equate to a *T*-score of 50; the second student (z-score = +2.00) would have a *T*-score of 70; and the third (z-score = –1.50) would have a *T*-score of 35. Furthermore, a student who obtains a z-score equal to +0.80 would have an equivalent *T*-score equal to 58. Thus, you can see how both negative and fractional scores have been eliminated. This comparison of z-scores and *T*-scores can be seen in Figure 6.4.

Although *T*-scores offer an improvement over z-scores, they too can be misinterpreted. Since they range from approximately 20 to 80 (i.e., the mean plus or minus 3 standard deviations), they are often confused for percentages. A *T*-score of 60 (i.e., one standard deviation above the mean) can be misinterpreted as meaning that a student answered 60% of the items correctly. Once again, this is essentially a criterion-referenced interpretation; *T*-scores provide norm-referenced information.

Normalized Standard Scores

Test publishers will also transform raw scores to a new set of scores that is distributed normally (or very close to a normal distribution) regardless of the shape of the distribution of the original set of raw scores. This type of transformation actually changes the shape of the distribution by making it conform to a normal distribution. Once the shape has been altered, various types of standard scores can be derived. Each of these types of scores will then have appropriate normal, bell-shaped curve interpretations (Nitko, 2004). These derived scores are collectively known as *normalized standard scores*, also sometimes called area transformations as opposed to linear transformations. Area transformations are so-called because the goal of the transformation is to obtain the same area beneath a curve representing the same distribution of scores as is found in a normal distribution. Following are discussions of several commonly used types of normalized standard scores.

Stanines. *Stanines* comprise a very common type of score scale on which to report norm-referenced performance, but do so by representing a band of scores as opposed in precise score values (Chase, 1999). A stanine (short for *sta*ndard *nine*) provides the location of a raw score in a specific segment of the normal distribution (Nitko, 2004). Furthermore, stanines range in value from 1 (i.e., the extreme low end) to 9 (i.e., the extreme high end), where the mean is equal to 5 and the standard deviation is equal to 2 (see Figure 6.4). Each band actually spans one half of a standard deviation (Chase, 1999).

All individuals falling in a specific interval are assigned the stanine number of that interval (Nitko, 2004). For example, individuals with percentile ranks ranging from 40 to 59 fall into stanine 5; those with percentile ranks from 60 to 76 would be assigned to stanine 6; and so on. This relationship between stanines and percentile ranks can be seen in Figure 6.4. Stanines can typically be interpreted in the following manner: stanine scores of 1, 2, and 3 indicate below average performance; scores of 4, 5, and 6 indicate average performance; and scores of 7, 8, and 9 indicate above average performance (Airasian, 2005).

The main disadvantage of stanines is that they represent more coarse groupings of scores, especially when compared to percentile ranks (Nitko, 2004). However, a stanine is likely a more accurate estimate of the student's achievement because it represents a band or range within which the student's test performance truly belongs (Gredler, 1999), as opposed to a precise estimate of the student's performance. An individual's stanine score is calculated in the following manner:

(1) A *z*-score is first calculated and then multiplied by 2 (this is the value for a standard deviation on the new scale).

(2) The resulting value is then added to 5 (the new value for the mean) to obtain the stanine score.

SAT/GRE Scores. The scores resulting from both the Scholastic Assessment Test (SAT) and Graduate Record Examination (GRE) are reported on yet a different type of scale, although the scores convey the same basic information. The *SAT/GRE scores* (also known as CEEB scores, for the College Entrance Examination Board, which originally developed them) are reported on a scale that has a mean of 500 and a standard deviation of 100 (see Figure 6.4). Once again, possible scores on the SAT and GRE range from a low of 200 (i.e., 3 standard deviations below the mean) to a high of 800 (i.e., 3 standard deviations above the mean). A student's SAT or GRE score is calculated in the following manner:

(1) A z-score is first calculated and then multiplied by 100 (this becomes the value for a standard deviation on the new scale).

(2) The resulting value is added to 500 (the new value for the mean) to obtain the SAT or GRE score.

Normal Curve Equivalent Scores. These normalized standard scores, also known as normal curve equivalent scores (NCE scores), have a mean of 50 and a standard deviation of 21.06. Similar to percentile ranks, NCE scores range from 1 to 99. The somewhat odd value for the standard deviation has been established so that NCE scores will precisely match percentile ranks at 3 specific points: 1, 50, and 99 (Chase, 1999; Oosterhof, 2001), as can be seen in Figure 6.4. The basic advantage of NCE scores is that they represent equal units across the entire continuum (i.e., 1 to 99), unlike percentile ranks (Chase, 1999; Oosterhof, 2001). NCE scores are calculated in a similar fashion to the scores previously discussed:

(1) A z-score is calculated and multiplied by 21.06 (the new value for a standard deviation).

(2) The value of 50 (the new value for the mean) is added to the resulting value in order to obtain the NCE score.

Deviation IQ Scores. A final type of standardized score, used primarily with assessments of mental ability, is a deviation IQ score (Nitko, 2004). *Deviation IQ scores* provide the location of a raw score in a normal distribution having a mean of 100 and a standard deviation equal to 15 or 16 (depending on the specific test). For a test with a standard deviation set at 15, an individual's deviation IQ score is calculated in the following manner:

(1) A z-score is first calculated and then multiplied by 15.

(2) The value of 100 is added to the resulting value to obtain the deviation IQ score.

Other "Unique" Scales. The basic advantage of all of these standard scores is that raw scores can be converted directly to scores related to the normal curve and to percentile ranks (McMillan, 2004). However, this advantage also tends to make things difficult for those of us who try to interpret these various test scores from the standpoint that there are so many of them to consider. In addition, many test publishers use their own unique standard score scales. Once you understand the nature of those scores, you should be able, with relative ease, to interpret those scores. You may have to examine the technical manual or norms books to find out what the publisher has used as the mean and standard deviation for a given type of scaled score (McMillan, 2004).

Shown in Figure 6.5 is a sample Group Report from the Stanford Achievement Test (SAT10). Note the inclusion of several norm-referenced scores for this group including a unique scaled score, national percentile ranks, national stanines, normal curve equivalent scores, and grade-equivalent scores.

A Final Note About Interpreting Norm-Referenced Scores

Figure 6.4 shows the relative correspondence between the normal distribution and the various standard score scales we have discussed. From this figure, it should be somewhat clear that all norm-referenced scores provide essentially identical information concerning the location of an individual raw score within a distribution; they simply do so on different scales. In this figure, it is also important to notice the unequal nature of percentile ranks, as well as the 1st and 9th stanines, which represent much larger bands than the other stanines. It really does not matter which specific norm-referenced score you choose to interpret, for they all provide the same information about a particular student's test performance.

Two final sample test reports are provided in Figures 6.6 and 6.7. The ITBS List of Student Scores (see Figure 6.6) provides norm-referenced information for each student in a class. Specifically, a scaled score, grade-equivalent score, stanine, and percentile rank are listed for each subtest taken by the student. Similar information is provided in the List Report of Student Scores from the Gates-MacGinite Reading Tests (GMRT), as shown in Figure 6.7.

STANDARD ERROR OF MEASUREMENT AND CONFIDENCE INTERVALS

When interpreting student performance on norm-referenced measures, it is important to remember that no educational assessment is perfect. Error exists in all test scores (Airasian, 2005). A test is given at a specific moment in time, and a variety of factors can affect—both positively and negatively—students' test scores. For example, these factors might include that a student was ill on the day of the test or recently experienced a traumatic event, such as a death in the family. These types of events would likely result in lowered student performance. In contrast, a student might be exceptionally good at guessing, which would result in performance

Figure 6.5 Sample Group Test Score Report

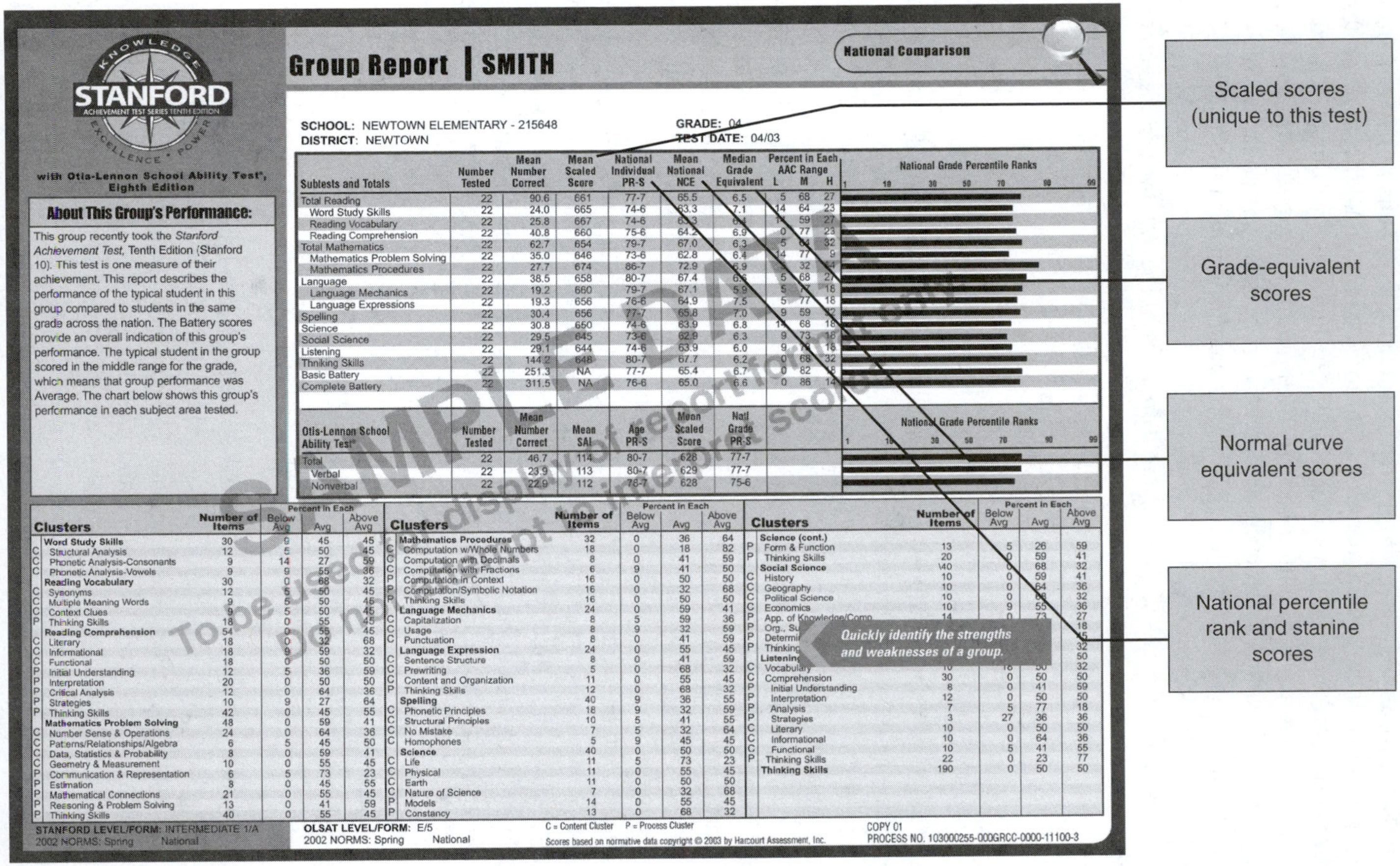

SOURCE: Copyright © 2003 by Harcourt Assessment, Inc. Sample "Group Report" from the Stanford Achievement Test (SAT10). Reproduced with permission of the publisher. All rights reserved.

above the true ability or achievement level of the student. Norm-referenced test scores, which factor in this measurement error, are also often included on test reports. The concepts of *standard error of measurement (SEM)* and *confidence intervals* are important in understanding how to interpret these scores.

A SEM, also known simply as a *standard error,* is the average amount of measurement error across students in the norm group. It is basically interpreted as the standard deviation of all errors in measurement. If the standard error is both added to and subtracted from the score a student receives on a standardized test, a range of student performance can be defined. This range serves as an estimate within which the student's true performance most likely lies. In other words,

True Score Range = Scaled Score +/– (i.e., plus and minus) Standard Error

This true score range is known as a *confidence interval* or confidence band. The purpose of confidence intervals is to establish a range of scores that we are *reasonably* confident includes the student's true ability or achievement score (Gredler, 1999). Recall from Figure 6.2 that the mean plus and minus one standard deviation contains approximately 68% of the individuals in a normal distribution of test scores. A somewhat related interpretation can be made for confidence intervals. For example, assume that the standard error for a given standardized test is calculated to be equal to 3.5—in other words, this is the average of all errors in measurement across all students in the norm group. Further assume that a student receives a score of 64 on the test. The resulting confidence interval (based on the addition and subtraction of one standard error; i.e., 64 +/– 3.5) for that student would be 60.5 to 67.5. This confidence interval is appropriately interpreted in the following manner: If it were possible to test the student repeatedly under ideal conditions, 68% of this student's scores would fall within this interval (Gredler, 1999). In other words, 68% of the student's possible scores would be located between 60.5 and 67.5. A student's obtained score plus and minus one standard error is sometimes referred to as the 68% confidence interval. An alternative interpretation is to say that *we* are 68% confident that the student's true ability score lies between 60.5 and 67.5.

Since the interpretation of standard errors and the resulting confidence intervals are based on a normal distribution, we can generalize our example to provide various statements regarding the precision of the student's test scores. Again, using Figure 6.2 as a reference, we could conclude the following:

(1) We can be approximately 68% confident that the student's true scores lie in the range of 60.5 to 67.5 (i.e., within one standard error, or 64 +/– 3.5).

(2) We can be approximately 96% confident that the student's true scores lie in the range of 57 to 71 [i.e., within two standard errors, or 64 +/– (2)(3.5)].

(3) We can be approximately 99% confident that the student's true scores lie in the range of 53.5 to 74.5 [i.e., within three standard errors, or 64 +/– (3)(3.5)].

Figure 6.6 Sample Group Test Score Report

Each student is listed along with her or his scaled score, grade-equivalent score, national percentile rank, and national stanine

SOURCE: Copyright © 2001 by Riverside Publishing. Sample "List of Student Scores" from the Iowa Tests of Basic Skills (ITBS). Reproduced with permission of the publisher. All rights reserved.

Figure 6.7 Sample Group Test Score Report

Gates-MacGinitie READING TESTS — FOURTH EDITION

Service 9:
List Report of Student Scores

Class/Group: CHAVEZ
Building: RIVERSIDE
Bldg. Code:
System: PORT CHARLES
Order No.: 000-A9100133-00-001 =

Grade: 6
Test Date: 09/99
Norms: Fall
Level: 5
Form: S
Page: 70

STUDENT NAME (ID Number / Other Information)	Birth Date / Age	Level	Form (Title I)	Gender	Vocabulary					Comprehension					TOTAL				
					NCE	National PR	S	GE	ESS	NCE	National PR	S	GE	ESS	NCE	National PR	S	GE	ESS
BOWER, BRUCE	05/88 11-04	5	S	M	42	35	4	5.1	499	34	22	3	4.4	487	36	26	4	4.7	492
BUCK, DENIS	01/88 11-08	5	S	M	34	23	4	4.5	486	40	31	4	4.9	496	36	25	4	4.6	491
BYRD, ANDREA	09/87 12-00	5	S	F	87	96	9	PHS	585	69	82	7	9.9	550	80	92	8	PHS	564
CARLOS, LEONARD	06/88 11-03	5	S	M	62	71	6	8.2	535	54	57	5	6.7	521	58	64	6	7.3	527
CHAMBERS, SEAN	11/87 11-10	5	S	M	72	85	7	11.5	554	51	52	5	6.4	517	61	70	6	7.9	533
HOLMES, ANTHONY	04/88 11-05	5	S	M	46	42	5	5.6	505	48	46	5	5.9	511	46	43	5	5.8	508
JENSEN, DONNA	10/87 11-11	5	S	F	7*	2*	1*	2.7*	444*	30	17	3	4.*	481	17*	6*	2*	3.4*	465*
JONES, XAVIER	07/88 11-02	5	S	M	44	38	4	5.4	502	32	20	3	4.2	49.	36	26	4	4.7	492
KIRKLIN, ELINA	12/87 11-09	5	S	F	46	42	5	5.6	505	48	46	5	5.9	511	46	43	5	5.8	508
LEAL, ERIKA	03/88 11-06	5	S	F	15	5	2	3.1	457	32	20	3	4.2	484	23	10	2	3.7	472
NORMAN, MAGGIE	08/87 12-01	5	S	F	20	8	2	3.5	465	20	8	2	3.4	465	20	6	2	3.4	465
PISCOPO, TIFFANEY	09/87 12-00	5	S	F	52	53	5	6.4	516	41	34	4	5.1	499	45	41	5	5.6	506
ROLF, LEANN	07/88 11-02	5	S	F	68	81	7	10.0	548	62	71	6	8.2	536	67	79	7	8.9	542
SINGER, LEONARD	09/87 12-00	5	S	M	62	71	6	8.2	535	59	67	6	7.8	532	61	70	6	7.9	533
STARKY, ARTHUR	01/88 11-08	5	S	M	42	35	4	5.1	499	59	67	6	7.8	532	51	51	5	6.3	515
STRAUBE, ROSE	09/87 12-00	5	S	F	75	88	7	PHS	560	66	78	7	9.3	545	73	86	7	10.5	552
WILLIAMS, JORDAN	08/88 11-01	5	S	F	20	8	2	3.5	465	24	11	3	3.6	471	19	7	2	3.5	468
WOODALL, RENO	09/87 12-00	5	S	M	36	26	4	4.6	489	19	7	2	3.3	462	24	11	3	3.8	475
WYSE, RICHARD	08/88 11-01	5	S	M	48	46	5	5.9	509	45	40	5	5.5	505	45	41	5	5.6	506
ZARS, SALLY	06/88 11-03	5	S	F	44	38	4	5.4	502	36	25	4	4.5	490	38	29	4	4.9	495
CLASS SUMMARY — N TESTED = 20 — AVERAGE ESS				N	20				508	20				504	20				505
NCE, PR, S, AND GE OBTAINED FROM AVERAGE ESS					47	45	5	5.8		44	39	4	5.4		45	40	5	5.6	

LEGEND: NCE = Normal curve Equivalent; PR = Percentile Rank; S = Stanine; GE = Grade Equivalent; ESS = Extended Scale Score; * = Chance level score

Each student is listed with normal curve equivalent scores, percentile ranks, stanines, grade-equivalent scores, and scaled score

SOURCE: Copyright © 2000 by Riverside Publishing Co. Sample "List Report of Student Scores" from the Gates-MacGinitie Reading Tests (GMRT). Reproduced with permission of the publisher. All rights reserved.

Although we would typically like to be as confident as possible when interpreting test results, confidence and precision have an inverse relationship. In other words, notice that as confidence increases (a good thing), precision decreases (a not-so-good thing). It is not very informative to say that we are 99% sure that a student's true achievement spans a more-than-20-unit range on the scale. The 68% confidence interval is typically seen as a meaningful compromise between confidence and precision.

On norm-referenced test reports, confidence intervals are typically presented around a student's obtained percentile rank scores. These are often referred to as *national percentile bands*. Figure 6.8 shows a hypothetical example of three students' scores, including their respective confidence bands. For each student, notice that the obtained score is located in the middle of the band, although this will not always be the case since, as you know, percentile ranks do not represent equal units. It is further important to note that Annette's performance is clearly better than that of Collette. However, Bob and Annette could actually be performing at nearly the same level, or Bob's performance could even be above that of

Figure 6.8　　Examples of Percentile Rank Confidence Bands (Standard Error = 4)

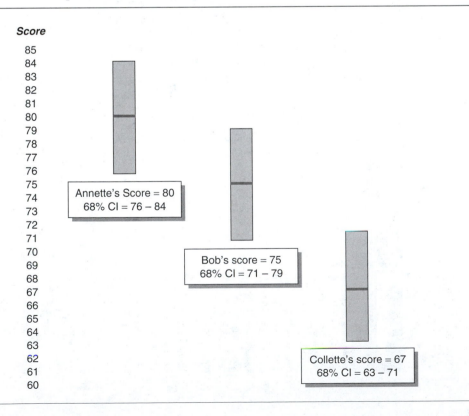

Annette because their bands overlap. In other words, when the bands overlap, there is no real difference between estimates of the true achievement levels for students. This is true both across students and across subtests for a given student.

This interpretation can be extended to comparisons of the relative performances on various subtest scores for an individual student. For example, the national percentile rank bands for the ITBS are provided for an individual student, as shown in Figure 6.3. When examining the national percentile bands for an individual student, it is important to examine the overlap of subtest bands. If the bands for two subtests do not overlap, there is a significant difference in the performance in those areas. In this example, there is a significant difference in test performance between the Listening and Spelling subtests since the bands to not overlap.

Summary

Norm-referenced scores provide test performance information about individuals or groups of students as compared to a representative norm group. Norm groups must be selected such that they are current and representative of the larger population, whether it be a national population or a smaller, more specific one. Often, scores related to the performance of the norm group are based on the normal distribution, which has three consistent characteristics. Within the normal distribution, most individuals are average, with their performance falling roughly near the center of the distribution. Since the distribution is consistent, a fixed percentage of cases or scores can be defined within the distribution.

Norm-referenced scores are based on mathematical transformations of raw scores. Percentile ranks are defined as the percentage of the norm group that scored below a particular raw score. They do not represent equal units and are often misinterpreted as a percentage of items answered correctly (which is a criterion-referenced interpretation). Developmental scales, such as grade-equivalent and age-equivalent scores, seek to identify a student's development across various grade or age levels. Although they can be useful, they are often misinterpreted as standards that all students should be expected to achieve.

Standardized scores are obtained by transforming scores to fit some type of distribution. They allow for comparisons of test performance across two or more different measures. Linear standard scores, including z-scores and T-scores, maintain the same distributional shape as their corresponding raw scores. However, since they are on the same scale, they allow for comparisons between two distributions of test performance. Normalized standard scores are those that are transformed to convert their raw score distributions to a normal distribution. This permits interpretations based on knowledge of the characteristics of a normal distribution.

These types of scores include stanines, SAT/GRE scores, normal curve equivalent scores, deviation IQ scores, as well as others that may be unique to specific tests. It is important to note that norm-referenced scores all provide the same information about a particular student's test performance.

Also important to remember when interpreting norm-referenced test scores is that because no test is a perfect measure, all scores contain error. This error may serve to increase or decrease a student's true achievement or ability performance. The standard error of measure is the average amount of error across all students in the norm group. This value can be used to estimate the range within which a given student's true test performance probably falls. Furthermore, levels of confidence are attached to these ranges of scores, thus allowing an extension of the interpretation of test performance. Finally, these confidence levels permit the comparison across students or across subtests for a particular student.

Activities for Application and Reflection

1. Obtain an actual student test report from any test you may use in your school or district that includes some norm-referenced score information. Closely examine the norm-referenced scores and briefly summarize the student's performance. What would you describe as the student's strengths and weaknesses relative to those students in the norm group?

2. If you could use only one type of norm-referenced score as presented in this module to interpret a student's test performance, which one would you choose? Why did you choose that particular score?

3. Paulette receives both norm-referenced and criterion-referenced scores for her performance on a standardized test in science. The norm-referenced scores indicate that she scores at the 85th percentile in "Earth and Space Science," but the criterion-referenced information indicates that she is deficient (i.e., failed to meet the performance criteria) in this area. Is this possible? Why or why not?

4. Using the information provided in Figure 6.4, approximate the values on the scales below that correspond to a z-score of $+ .50$:

   a. percentile rank = ?
   b. T-score = ?
   c. stanine = ?
   d. NCE score = ?

National Percentile Bands

	10	20	30	40	50	60	70	80	90
Reading				----X----					
Vocabulary				---X---					
Language			--X--						
Math						---X---			
Science				---X---					
Social Studies							------X------		

5. Refer to the diagram above, which shows the 68% confidence intervals for a set of test scores:

   a. Which test has the largest standard error of measure? How do you know?
   b. Which pair(s) of test scores are significantly different from each other?
   c. The following interpretation of the percentile rank is incorrect; rewrite it so that it is accurate.
      The student correctly answered almost 80% of the social studies items.
   d. The following interpretation is incorrect; rewrite it so that it is accurate.
      The student's true reading achievement is at the 40th percentile.

6. Carefully read the interview transcript for Amy Kenyon, first- and second-grade teacher, paying particular attention to her discussion of using stanine scores for the identification of students for special services. Discuss the appropriateness (e.g., the pros and cons) of using stanine scores for this purpose.

SECTION III

Using Standardized Test Scores in Instructional Decision Making

Module 7: Group-Level Decision Making

Module 8: Student-Level Decision Making

Module 9: Value-Added Analysis and Interpretation

Module 7

GROUP-LEVEL DECISION MAKING

In this section of the book, we begin to take the information we have learned about standardized test reports and apply it to curricular and instructional decision making. Specifically, this module begins with a discussion of data-driven decision making and continues with an examination of a basic process for using standardized test results for making decisions. As you will see, the sequential, linear process (as shown in Figure 7.1) focuses on the identification of critical content or subtest areas, the determination of where and how these are taught within the curriculum, and the development of new or different methods of instruction, reinforcement, and so on. The explanation of this process is followed by some examples that demonstrate the application of this process through the use of several sample test reports previously examined in earlier modules.

DATA-DRIVEN DECISION MAKING

Since the beginning of formalized education in this country, teachers have used information about students to help inform decisions about their instruction. Quality teachers tend to gather information from a wide variety of sources. However, from a historical perspective, teachers typically have not incorporated data resulting from the administration of standardized tests into this process. As we have discussed in earlier modules, they admittedly do not like standardized tests (although who among us *really* does?). However, due to the advent of No Child Left Behind (NCLB) and its associated Adequate Yearly Progress (AYP) requirements, utilization of standardized test data has become an accountability requirement. It has

" . . . with No Child Left Behind, we don't have a choice. It's not a choice to change; there is no choice. You have to change. Your choice is how you want to change."

—Martha Fether,
Elementary School Principal

become crucial that classroom teachers and building-level administrators understand the importance of and how to make data-driven instructional decisions (Mertler & Zachel, 2006).

Data-driven instructional decision making is a process by which educators examine the results of standardized tests to identify student strengths and deficiencies. The ultimate goal of this process is for teachers to critically examine their curriculum and their instructional practices relative to their students' actual performance on standardized tests. This, in turn, provides teachers with another level or type of information to help them make instructional decisions that are more accurately informed; in other words, these decisions are, at least in part, driven by student performance on statewide as well as national assessments of learning (Mertler & Zachel, 2006).

" . . . if you really want to make your classroom as a teacher as effective as it possibly can be, and your teaching as effective as it can be, you have to accept the fact that we need to look at it from more of a scientific angle, analyze the data, make decisions based on that data."

—Hugh Caumartin,
District Superintendent

The notion of data-driven instructional decision making has gained importance over the past several years. With each passing year, there seems to be an increasing amount of accountability requirements being placed on school districts, their administrators, and their teachers. NCLB and AYP compliance have become critical focal points for school districts. In the state of Ohio, for example, state ratings for school districts and individual school buildings are based on 25 performance indicators—23 of which are based on standardized test performance. Nine of these occur at the elementary level (i.e., Grades 3 through 6) (Ohio Department of Education, 2004).

The concept of teachers using assessment information to make decisions about their instructional practices and intervention strategies is nothing new; teachers have been doing that forever. It is an integral part of being an educational professional.

" . . . teachers are going from what was considered the art of teaching to much more of a science of teaching."

—Hugh Caumartin,
District Superintendent

In the past, these types of decisions were based on instinct. However, the old tools of education—intuition, teaching philosophy, and personal experience—do not seem to be enough anymore (LaFee, 2002). What occurs less frequently in schools and individual classrooms is the use of standardized test results as an additional source of information about students and as a source upon which such curricular and instructional decisions can be based. There are two main ways that classroom teachers can make use of standardized test results. These results can be used to assist teachers in (1) revising instruction for entire classes or courses and (2) developing specific intervention strategies for individual students (Mertler, 2002, 2003).

This infrequent use typically occurs as a result of the seemingly overwhelming amount of information provided on test reports. I have heard teachers comment that "there is so much information here! I don't know where to start!" In addition, many educators believe that this idea of using test performance to help guide decision making reduces the educational process to something more business like. In business settings, data is absolutely essential. Information about aspects such as customers, inventory, and sales are crucial in determining a business's success or failure. In contrast, in education we tend to focus on the more human side of things, and rightfully so. Kids are real, living, breathing entities; data is abstract. For many educators, this truly makes data a four-letter word (LaFee, 2002). This idea of data-driven instructional decision making is not new, but it does take some practice on the part of the classroom teacher. Focusing on a few key pieces of information on test reports and essentially ignoring other data is one method of avoiding this overwhelming feeling.

> *"Don't try to do it all in one year. Pick either a subject area or a test. Start with 'baby stuff.' I mean you can't do it all. But if you can see the advantage of doing it with a subject area or with a particular test and really work to maximize that information and use it and really, really stay consistent to it for a year, then I think you can build on that, from year to year."*
>
> —Ellen Sharp,
> *First- and Second-Grade Teacher*

A PROCESS FOR FOCUSING ON GROUP INSTRUCTION

When examining test results for the purpose of revising instruction, the best—or, at least, most common—practice is to interpret results provided for an entire class or course (Mertler, 2002; Mertler & Zachel, 2006). As you have seen in numerous examples provided throughout this book, this type of test report is one of many that is typically provided to classroom teachers by test publishers. It allows the classroom teacher to see how students are performing across the curriculum as a whole. Areas in which students are deficient may be identified following the process shown in Figure 7.1.

The process itself is admittedly not an extremely difficult one. However, adherence to its steps is critical to clearly see the possible relationships between student test performance and the curriculum and/or instructional practices. The first step in this process is the identification of any content areas or subtests (as well as

Figure 7.1   Steps in a Generic Process for Identifying Curricular Areas in Which Students Are Deficient (Focusing on Group Instruction)

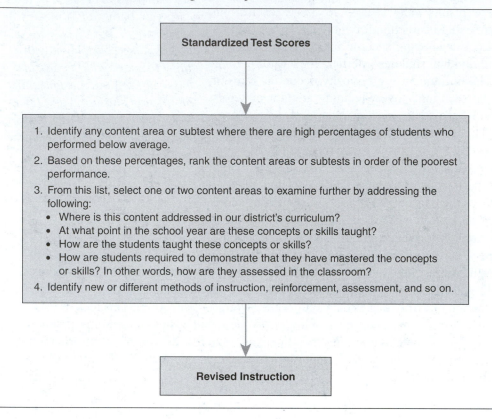

any specific types of skills) where there are high percentages of students who performed below average (in the case of criterion-referenced test scores) or where group performance is low in relation to the norm group (in the case of norm-referenced scores). Secondly, these identified content areas or subtests should then be ranked in order of performance with number 1 on the list being the area with the poorest student performance.

The third step is to flag one or two of these specific content areas (i.e., the areas with the poorest performances) for further examination and to ultimately serve as the focus for any curricular or instructional revisions. This closer scrutiny of any deficiencies, as identified by poor performance across a majority of students, should be targeted by the teacher for instructional revision. As part of this closer examination, it is strongly recommended that teachers consider addressing the following questions for those topic areas or skills identified as deficient:

(1) Where is this content addressed in our district's curriculum?

(2) At what point in the school year are these concepts/skills taught?

(3) How are the students taught these concepts or skills?

(4) How are students required to demonstrate that they have mastered the concepts/skills? In other words, how are they assessed in the classroom?

Answers to these questions, as well as others that are raised during the process, will often provide important information and will ultimately guide decisions regarding instructional revisions. The specification of these revisions—which might consist of the identification of new or different methods of instruction, the incorporation of new supplemental materials or activities, a reorganization of the sequence of instructional topics, or the development of different types of classroom assessments—constitutes the fourth and final step in the process. First, however, a word of caution is in order. It is important to remember that, generally speaking, achievement tests are intended to survey basic skills across a broad domain of content (Chase, 1999). On some subtests of most any standardized achievement test, a specific subtest may consist of as few as five or six items. Careless errors committed or lucky guesses by students may substantially alter the score on that subtest, especially if they are reported as percentages of items answered correctly or as percentile ranks. Therefore, it is important to examine not only the raw scores and percentile ranks, but also the total number of items possible on a given test prior to making any intervention decisions.

As you well know by this point, most publishers of standardized achievement tests provide both criterion- and norm-referenced results on individual student reports. Many results are reported in terms of average performance (i.e., below average, average, above average). It is again important to remember that average simply means that half of the norm group scored above and half scored below that particular score. Teachers should take great care to avoid the over interpretation of test scores (Airasian, 2005).

> "We sat together as a department last year and at the beginning of this year when the numbers came out. And we went item by item through each of the test questions and we looked at percentage [passing]. What we really looked at mostly was percentages of kids that passed each question. And then if there's over an abnormal percentage of kids that didn't pass it, then we asked questions. Why? Did we not get to this? Did we cover it differently? Was there an aspect of it that we left out? Do we even offer this at the high school? Do we offer it at the freshman and sophomore levels before they take this test? And what we ended up doing is . . . changing the entire sequence of our whole department. We got rid of a course. We moved world history from the sophomore year to the freshman year and American history from the junior year to the sophomore year."
>
> —Joe Hudok,
> *High School Social Studies Teacher*

Examples

Three examples of test reports and explanations of how teachers might engage in the process outlined in Figure 7.1 are presented next. These examples focus on instructional decisions resulting from group performance on standardized achievement tests. These three examples use the SAT10 and the third- and eighth-grade Ohio Achievement Tests (OAT), respectively.

Example 1: Fourth-Grade Achievement Test Battery

Ms. Smith's fourth-grade class, comprised of 22 students, was tested in April 2003 using the Stanford Achievement Test, version 10 (SAT10). The students were tested in the areas of reading, mathematics, language, spelling, science, social science, listening, and thinking skills. The class results are presented in Figure 7.2.

As Ms. Smith observed in the norm-referenced portion of the report, her students performed above average across all of the subtests on the total test battery. This is evidenced by the percentile rank scores (which range from 73 on "Social Science" to 86 on "Mathematics Procedures") and the stanine scores (all of which are equal to 6 or 7; this information is highlighted in boxed area #1 of Figure 7.2). She was pleased that, compared to the national norm group of fourth-grade students, her students performed relatively well.

She then turned her attention to the criterion-referenced portion of the test report. She quickly scanned the "Below Average" column for each of the clusters, making a list of those areas where higher percentages of her students were classified as performing below the average number of items answered correctly. She quickly noticed that 14% of her class scored below average on the nine items comprising the "Phonetic Analysis—Consonants" portion of the Word Study Skills cluster (shown in boxed area #2 of Figure 7.2). Although this is not a huge percentage of her students, she realized that it does represent an area where at least some of her students seemed to struggle.

She also noticed that 18% of her students were below average on the "Vocabulary" portion of the Listening cluster (highlighted in boxed area #3 of Figure 7.2). Finally, Ms. Smith noted that her students did not perform well on the "Comprehension—Strategies" portion of the Listening cluster, with 27% performing below average (shown in boxed area #4 of Figure 7.2). However, she realized that that score included only three items. Although she decided to add that cluster to her list of deficient areas, she also made a note to remind herself to keep her students' performance on this portion in perspective, so to speak, since it was based on such a small number of test items.

Based on the information provided on the test report and the relative importance in her district's curriculum, Ms. Smith decided to prioritize the deficient content areas/skills in the following manner:

Figure 7.2 Sample Class Test Score Report

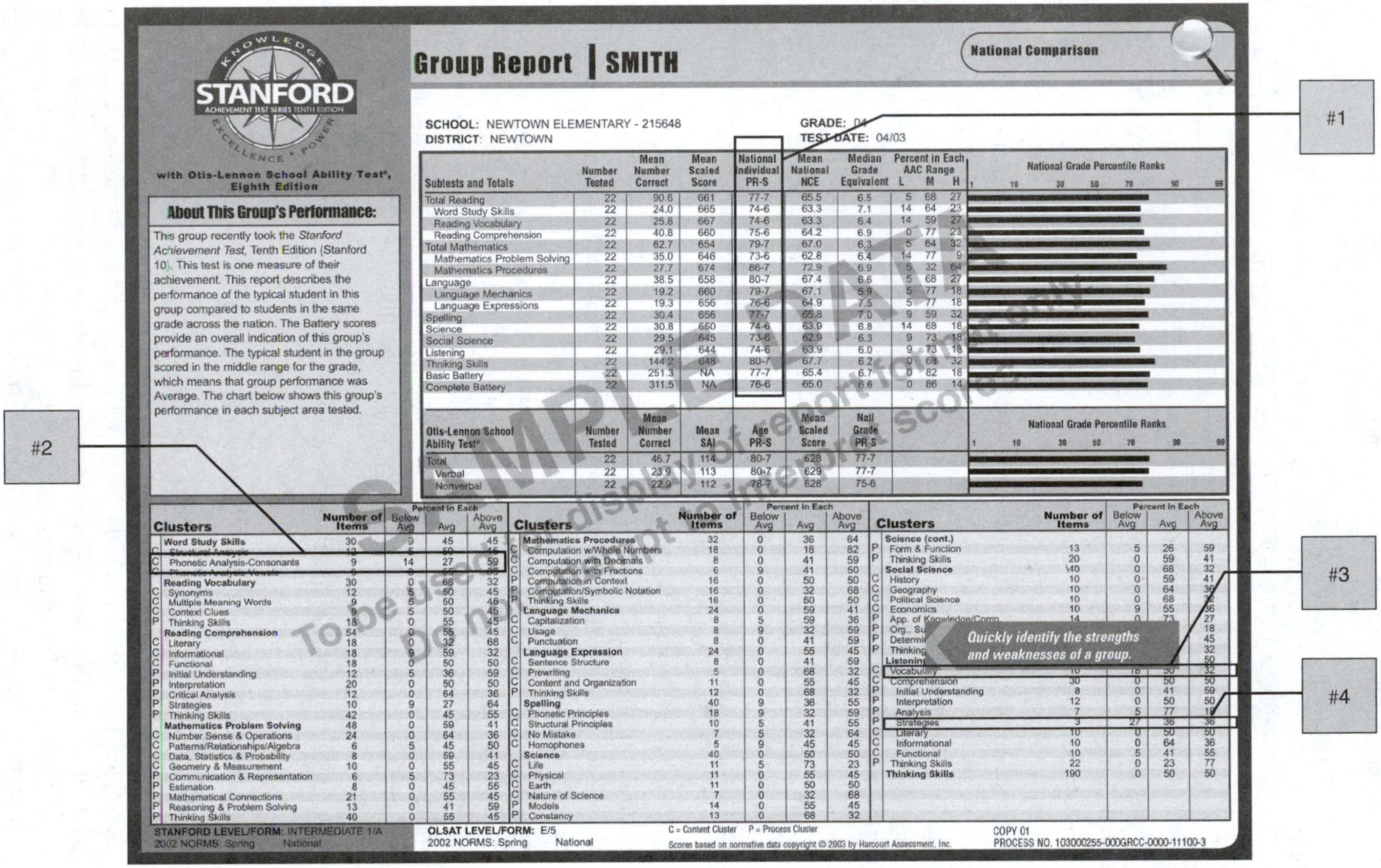

1. Phonetic Analysis—Consonants

2. Listening—Vocabulary

3. Listening—Comprehension Strategies

Furthermore, since her students seemed to be deficient in an area (i.e., phonetic analysis focusing on consonant sounds) that they should have previously mastered, she decided to focus her attention on revising how she teaches and assesses that content and skill.

Normally, Ms. Smith teaches consonant blends and digraphs early in the school year. In fourth grade, this typically involves some basic review of these letter and sound combinations. Students typically learn various consonant blends (e.g., *bl, fr, cl, sn, sk*) and digraphs (e.g., *sh, ch, th, wh, ng*) in the early elementary grades, but this year's students seemed to still be having difficulty with them. Therefore, she decided that it may be necessary for her to reinforce both consonant blends and digraphs through the use of word families with weekly spelling lists that contain these letter and sound combinations and to do so throughout the entire school year.

In addition to changing how and when she teaches these consonant sounds, Ms. Smith also concluded that she should revise how she assesses her students' learning of this material. Each week during the next school year, she plans to provide her students with random lists of words that they may not necessarily recognize from their weekly spelling lists, but that contain those various letter and sound combinations. The students will then be assessed by requiring them to sort these words according to blend or digraph family. The extent to which they are able to perform these sorts with unfamiliar words will serve as an indication to Ms. Smith of her students' competency with regard to phonetic consonant analysis.

In addition to the instructional and assessment changes she plans to make for her own classroom for next year, Ms. Smith is highly aware of the fact that some of her current students (who will soon be leaving her classroom for the fifth grade) are moving on with this deficiency intact. She planned to meet with the fifth-grade teachers in order to share these test results and her plan for revising her instruction, in the hopes that it will provide some guidance for their instruction, as well.

Example 2: Third-Grade Statewide Reading Achievement Test

Mr. Alvarez received his third-grade students' Ohio Reading Achievement Test results (see Figure 7.3) in the late spring with some degree of disappointment. He examined the scores not only from both norm- and criterion-referenced perspectives, but also in terms of the growth of his students over the course of this academic year since his students also took a similar version of this test earlier in the fall. Although the average scaled score (*SS* = 404) for students in his class was below the average performance of third graders in his school (*SS* = 411), in the district ($SS = 411$), and in the state ($SS = 416$), his students did demonstrate positive growth over the course of the year, based on the average score of his class in the fall ($SS = 392$) (this information is shown in boxed area #1 in Figure 7.3). This improvement raised his class's performance from the "Basic" level to the "Proficient" level. In the fall, 57% (i.e., 24% + 33%) of his class was classified as below proficient. However, following spring testing that percentage had fallen to 43% (highlighted in boxed area #2 in Figure 7.3).

For obvious reasons, Mr. Alvarez was still concerned with the substantial proportion of his students that were continuing not to meet the state standards in reading. He then decided to take a closer look at the specific strands in hopes of being able to identify the specific reading content and/or skills where his students may be struggling. Although 29% of his students were below proficient, students did not seem to struggle as much with "Acquisition of Vocabulary," relative to the other three strands. Performance on the five released multiple-choice items for this strand indicated that percentage of students answering items correctly ranged from 81% (question 26) to 100% (question 2). The second strand, "Reading Process," proved to be a bit more difficult for Mr. Alvarez's students, with 38% classified as being below proficient. There was a distinct problem with question 12, where only 62% of his students answered the item correctly (see boxed area #3 of Figure 7.3). Question 25, a constructed-response item, also posed a good deal of difficulty for them. On this item, where the total possible points was equal to 4, his students scored an average of 1.3 (shown in boxed area #4 of Figure 7.3).

Although there seemed to be two problematic multiple-choice test questions (questions 14 and 15) in the "Informational Text" strand (as highlighted in boxed area #5 of Figure 7.3), student performance was the highest on this strand. Only 19% were below proficient while 57% were classified as proficient and another 24% were above proficient. The final strand, "Literary Text," was the strand where Mr. Alvarez's students demonstrated their poorest performance. Nearly half (48%) of the students were below proficient. Students had difficulties with three of the released multiple-choice items (see boxed area #6 of Figure 7.3). In addition, the percentage of his class that was below proficient was markedly higher than the percentages of students across his school, the district, and the state.

Based on his interpretation of test results for his class and based on the indicated student weaknesses, Mr. Alvarez ranked the reading strands in the following order:

1. Literary Text

2. Reading Process

3. Acquisition of Vocabulary

4. Informational Text

Figure 7.3   Sample Class Test Score Report

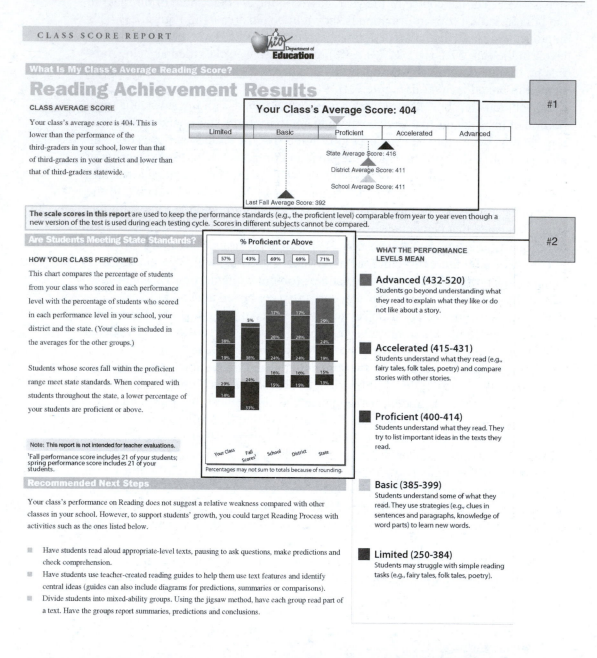

CLASS SCORE REPORT

Reading Achievement Results

CLASS AVERAGE SCORE

Your class's average score is 404. This is lower than the performance of the third-graders in your school, lower than that of third-graders in your district and lower than that of third-graders statewide.

Your Class's Average Score: 404

| Limited | Basic | Proficient | Accelerated | Advanced |

State Average Score: 416
District Average Score: 411
School Average Score: 411
Last Fall Average Score: 392

#1

The scale scores in this report are used to keep the performance standards (e.g., the proficient level) comparable from year to year even though a new version of the test is used during each testing cycle. Scores in different subjects cannot be compared.

Are Students Meeting State Standards?

HOW YOUR CLASS PERFORMED

This chart compares the percentage of students from your class who scored in each performance level with the percentage of students who scored in each performance level in your school, your district and the state. (Your class is included in the averages for the other groups.)

Students whose scores fall within the proficient range meet state standards. When compared with students throughout the state, a lower percentage of your students are proficient or above.

% Proficient or Above

| 57% | 43% | 69% | 69% | 71% |

#2

WHAT THE PERFORMANCE LEVELS MEAN

Advanced (432-520)
Students go beyond understanding what they read to explain what they like or do not like about a story.

Accelerated (415-431)
Students understand what they read (e.g., fairy tales, folk tales, poetry) and compare stories with other stories.

Proficient (400-414)
Students understand what they read. They try to list important ideas in the texts they read.

Note: This report is not intended for teacher evaluations.

[1]Fall performance score includes 21 of your students; spring performance score includes 21 of your students.

Percentages may not sum to totals because of rounding.

Basic (385-399)
Students understand some of what they read. They use strategies (e.g., clues in sentences and paragraphs, knowledge of word parts) to learn new words.

Recommended Next Steps

Your class's performance on Reading does not suggest a relative weakness compared with other classes in your school. However, to support students' growth, you could target Reading Process with activities such as the ones listed below.

Limited (250-384)
Students may struggle with simple reading tasks (e.g., fairy tales, folk tales, poetry).

- Have students read aloud appropriate-level texts, pausing to ask questions, make predictions and check comprehension.
- Have students use teacher-created reading guides to help them use text features and identify central ideas (guides can also include diagrams for predictions, summaries or comparisons).
- Divide students into mixed-ability groups. Using the jigsaw method, have each group read part of a text. Have the groups report summaries, predictions and conclusions.

Figure 7.3 (Continued)

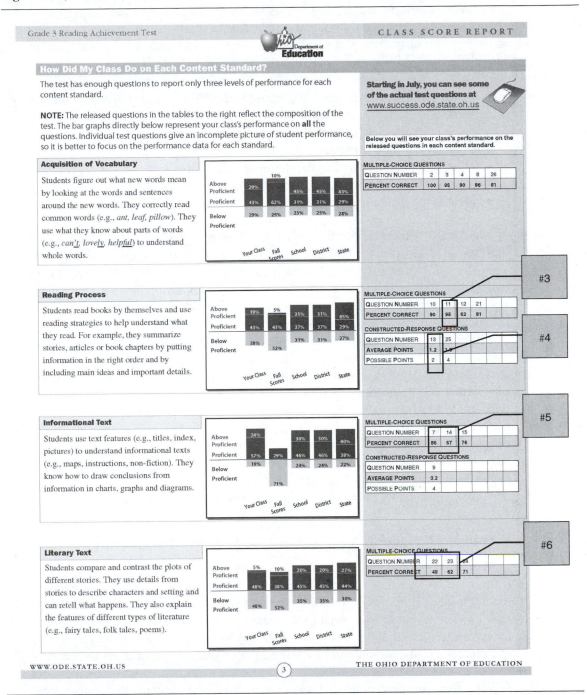

Due to the overall class performance being so low on Literary Text, he began by reflecting on how he taught these skills to his students during the course of the school year. He reviewed the contents of his district's curriculum guide with respect to literary text instruction just to refresh his memory and made a list of the types of knowledge and skills in this curricular strand. These included objectives such as

- recognizing and describing similarities and differences of plot across literary works;
- using concrete details from the text to describe characters and setting;
- retelling the plot sequence;
- identifying and explaining the defining characteristics of literary forms and genres including fairy tales, folk tales, poetry, fiction, and nonfiction; and
- identifying stated and implied themes.

Mr. Alvarez also reviewed the three released items from the test and discovered that they all addressed the students' abilities to retell, in detail, the plot of a given story, focusing primarily on the appropriate sequence of events. This seemed to make sense to him as he had also observed his students' struggling a bit with these skills earlier in the school year. Therefore, he decided that these skills would be the focus of his revised instruction.

Mr. Alvarez began searching for alternative lessons, activities, and reading passages to help support his new focus of helping his students become more competent at retelling the details of the plot of given reading passages. He searched a variety of instructional manuals as well as the Internet and consulted with several other third-grade teachers in his district. He also located several ideas for alternative methods of assessing his students' retelling skills including some ideas for developing multiple-choice items that would be similar in format to those appearing on the statewide achievement test. After a short period of time, he felt that he had really begun to put together a thorough series of materials, activities, and assessment formats that would really help support him in this new instructional endeavor.

Example 3: Eighth-Grade Statewide Mathematics Achievement Test

Mrs. Johnson was initially quite pleased as she looked over the score report from her class's most recent performance on the statewide mathematics achievement test (see Figure 7.4). Her class's average scaled score of 412 was well within the "Proficient" range and equal to the state average and only slightly below that for the entire school and district (this information is highlighted in boxed area #1 of Figure 7.4). In addition, only 21% (i.e., 17% + 4%) of the students in her class scored at a level below the proficient performance level, which was a smaller percentage than the percentages of students in her entire school, the district, and across the state (as shown in boxed area #2 of Figure 7.4). However, she knew that she needed to examine the results a little closer since it was apparent that there was still room for her students to improve.

The mathematics test is broken down into five strands, and Mrs. Johnson examined each of them next. Nearly one third (30%) of her students were below proficient on the "Numbers, Number Sense, and Operations" strand. Although this performance initially concerned her—especially in light of the students' performance on the released items, particularly question 5 (highlighted in boxed area #3 of Figure 7.4) and question 28 (shown in boxed area #4 of Figure 7.4)—she wanted to examine the results for all strands and put them in an appropriate context prior to making any decisions. Her students' performance on the "Measurement" strand was really quite good, with only 4% of her class being below proficient.

Over one fourth (26%) of her class did not meet the standard for "Geometry and Spatial Sense," which was partially demonstrated in the results for released items (highlighted in boxed areas #6 and #7 of Figure 7.4). However, she was not quite as concerned as she perhaps could have been since her class still outperformed students in the rest of the school, district, and the state. She felt that this might be an area on which to focus some instructional revisions, but at this point it may not be the most critical area. Similarly, although there was still room for improvement on the "Patterns, Functions, and Algebra" strand (see boxed area #8 of Figure 7.4), Mrs. Johnson's students performed better than the comparison groups. Again, she decided to hold off on making a decision about this strand.

The fifth strand, "Data Analysis and Probability," worried Mrs. Johnson even before she looked at her students' results. The reason for this uneasiness was that, although she taught a unit on these very topics each year, the data analysis and probability unit typically fell late in the year in terms of its place in the instructional sequence of topics. Often, she would teach it just prior to, and sometimes just following, the administration of the statewide achievement tests. Her students never seemed to do very well on it, and this really bothered her, especially in light of the fact that it was content that she really enjoyed teaching and with which she believed that she did a good job. She sometimes believed that she was not giving the students a fair opportunity to do well on this strand. When she examined the test results, Mrs. Johnson felt that her prior beliefs had been confirmed. Students seemed to have difficulties with all three of the released items (shown in boxed area #9 of Figure 7.4) and 22% scored below the proficient level.

"Some of the things that we [found with] our data analysis were very eye opening."

—Megan Newlove,
High School English Teacher

Although her class's performance on several of the strands indicated the need for some additional attention or instructional revisions, Mrs. Johnson decided to focus on making some changes to the "Data Analysis and Probability" unit, due not only to her students' test results, but also based on her prior beliefs and experiences over the past several years. Mrs. Johnson

Figure 7.4 Sample Class Test Score Report

CLASS SCORE REPORT — Ohio Department of Education

What Is My Class's Average Mathematics Score?

Mathematics Achievement Results

CLASS AVERAGE SCORE

Your class's average score is 412. This is similar to the performance of the eighth-graders in your school, similar to that of eighth-graders in your district and similar to that of eighth-graders statewide.

Your Class's Average Score: 412

| Limited | Basic | Proficient | Accelerated | Advanced |

State Average Score: 412
District Average Score: 414
School Average Score: 414

#1

The scale scores in this report are used to keep the performance standards (e.g., the proficient level) comparable from year to year even though a new version of the test is used during each testing cycle. Scores in different subjects cannot be compared.

#2

Are Students Meeting State Standards?

HOW YOUR CLASS PERFORMED

This chart compares the percentage of students from your class who scored in each performance level with the percentage of students who scored in each performance level in your school, your district and the state. (Your class is included in the averages for the other groups.)

Students whose scores fall within the proficient range meet state standards. When compared with students throughout the state, a greater percentage of your students are proficient or above.

Note: This report is not intended for teacher evaluations.

% Proficient or Above

| 78% | 73% | 73% | 69% |

4%
6%   6%
                5%
16%   16%
                19%
70%   51%   51%   45%
17%
4%   23%   23%   22%
      4%   4%   9%

Your Class   School   District   State

Percentages may not sum to totals because of rounding.

WHAT THE PERFORMANCE LEVELS MEAN

Advanced (459-534)
Students use precise math terms (e.g., *intercept*) and notation (e.g., $y = x^2$) to describe complex problems, such as the relationship between a formula and its graph.

Accelerated (432-458)
Students combine several math concepts (e.g., convert units, such 1.2 meters, to feet and inches). They explain their reasoning by using math terms (e.g., *proportion*).

Proficient (400-431)
Students use math terms (e.g., *radius*) and ideas (e.g., similar shapes) to solve common problems such as describing graphs (e.g., slope) and solving for variables.

Basic (379-399)
Students remember math ideas and terms (e.g., *estimation*). They solve one-step problems such as solving inequalities and predicting the results of an experiment.

Limited (290-378)
Students may struggle using math terms, applying measurement formulas, using exponents and absolute value, converting rates, and reading graphs.

Recommended Next Steps

Your class's overall Mathematics performance is high. To continue supporting your students' growth, you could target Patterns, Functions and Algebra with activities such as the ones listed below.

- Have students solve systems of linear equations, such as $x + 2y = 5$ and $x - 2y = 5$ ($x = 5, y = 0$), by using graphing, simple substitution and elimination.
- Have students solve quadratic equations both graphically and algebraically.
- Extend patterns using complex real-world situations that represent linear quadratic or exponential relationships. Measure students' heights. For 7 days, ask students to determine half their heights and then graph and analyze the data.

V3_04/18

Figure 7.4 (Continued)

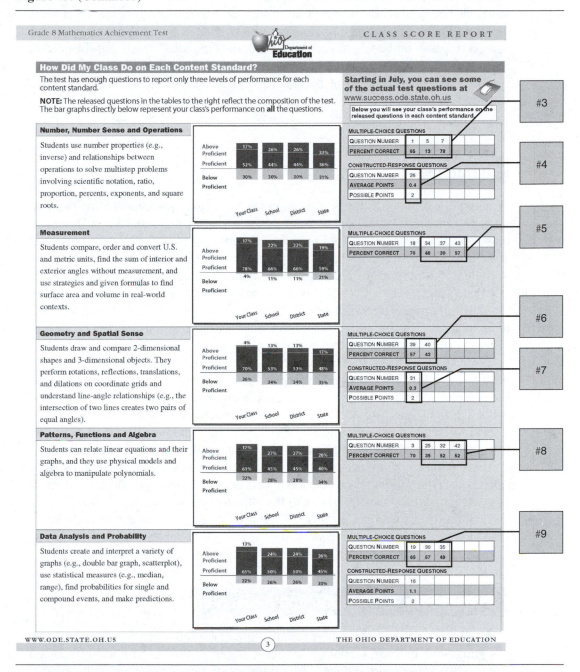

decided to revise the order in which she taught several of her units. First and foremost, she decided to move the "Data Analysis and Probability" unit up several weeks so that during the next school year, she would teach it as the first unit in the second semester of the school year. Of course, she reminded herself that she needed to be mindful of some other content being pushed back to a time in the spring, closer to the administration of the test. She knew that when she examined next spring's test results, she would have to take into consideration this fact.

Summary

Teachers have historically used whatever information was available to them to inform decisions they make about students, curriculum, and instruction. However, they typically have not utilized information resulting from the administration of standardized tests. NCLB has forced the use of this type of information for accountability purposes. In addition, more educators are making use of standardized test scores for their own classroom-based decisions. Data-driven decision making is a process by which educators examine the results of standardized tests to identify student strengths and weaknesses. This information can then be used in order to critically reflect on and revise curriculum and instructional practices.

Test results can be used in two ways: to revise instruction for entire classes and to develop intervention strategies for specific students. The most common practice is to use these results for reflecting on and revising group-level instruction. The process is not a difficult one, but it does require knowledge about the nature of standardized tests as well as a sound understanding about the proper interpretation of the resulting test scores. Teachers should first identify any areas indicated as weaknesses or deficiencies by students' test performance. Those areas are then rank ordered in terms of importance or severity of each deficiency. One or two of these specific areas are then targeted for further investigation, with the ultimate goal of making revisions to the curriculum or instructional practices. Several guiding questions can provide information vital to this step. The final step is to make and implement these revisions. Care should be taken to avoid the overinterpretation of standardized test scores.

Activities for Application and Reflection

1. Obtain an actual test report for an entire class you teach from any test you may use in your school or district. Closely examine the norm-referenced and/or criterion-referenced score information that is provided on the report. Briefly summarize the performance of your class. Follow the four-step

process as outlined in Figure 7.1 and make a list of possible revisions you could make to your instruction.

2. Closely examine the sample test report from the Gates-MacGinitie Reading Tests (GMRT) provided in Figure 7.5, focusing your attention on the overall class (highlighted in the boxed area). Follow the process discussed in this module and demonstrated in the three examples to develop a plan for addressing any student weaknesses you identify from these test results.

3. Carefully read the interview transcript with Joe Hudok, high school social studies teacher at Bowling Green High School, looking primarily at his description of the process his department used to address low student test scores on the statewide achievement test in social studies. Discuss this process with your classmates or colleagues. Are there ways you could adapt this process for your own classroom, academic department, or school?

Figure 7.5   Sample Class Test Score Report

FOURTH EDITION
Gates-MacGinitie
R E A D I N G   T E S T S

Service 9:
List Report of Student Scores

Class/Group:	CHAVEZ
Building:	RIVERSIDE
Bldg. Code:	
System	PORT CHARLES
Order No.:	000-A9100133-00-001 =

Grade:	6
Test Date:	09/99
Norms:	Fall
Level:	5
Form:	S
Pages:	70

STUDENT NAME ID Number Other Information	Birth Date Age	Level Gender	Form Title I	Vocabulary NCE	National PR	S	GE	ESS	Comprehension NCE	National PR	S	GE	ESS	TOTAL NCE	National PR	S	GE	ESS
BOWER, BRUCE	05/88 11-04	5 M	S	42	35	4	5.1	499	34	22	3	4.4	487	36	26	4	4.7	492
BUCK, DENIS	01/88 11-08	5 M	S	34	23	4	4.5	486	40	31	4	4.9	496	36	25	4	4.6	491
BYRD, ANDREA	09/87 12-00	5 F	S	87	96	9	PHS	585	69	82	7	9.9	550	80	92	8	PHS	564
CARLOS, LEONARD	06/88 11-03	5 M	S	62	71	6	8.2	535	54	57	5	6.7	521	58	64	6	7.3	527
CHAMBERS, SEAN	11/87 11-10	5 M	S	72	85	7	11.5	554	51	52	5	6.4	517	61	70	6	7.9	533
HOLMES, ANTHONY	04/88 11-05	5 M	S	46	42	5	5.6	505	48	46	5	5.9	511	46	43	5	5.8	508
JENSEN, DONNA	10/87 11-11	5 F	S	7*	2*	1*	2.7*	444*	30	17	3	4.1	481	17*	6*	2*	3.4*	465*
JONES, XAVIER	07/88 11-02	5 M	S	44	38	4	5.4	502	32	20	3	4.2	484	36	26	4	4.7	492
KIRKLIN, ELINA	12/87 11-09	5 F	S	46	42	5	5.6	505	48	46	5	5.9	511	46	43	5	5.8	508
LEAL, ERIKA	03/88 11-06	5 F	S	15	5	2	3.1	457	32	20	3	4.2	484	23	10	2	3.7	472
NORMAN, MAGGIE	08/87 12-01	5 F	S	20	8	2	3.5	465	20	8	2	3.4	465	17	6	2	3.4	465
PISCOPO, TIFFANEY	09/87 12-00	5 F	S	52	53	5	6.4	516	41	34	4	5.1	499	45	41	5	5.6	506
ROLF, LEANN	07/88 11-02	5 F	S	68	81	7	10.0	548	62	71	6	8.2	536	67	79	7	8.9	542
SINGER, LEONARD	09/87 12-00	5 M	S	62	71	6	8.2	535	59	67	6	7.8	532	61	70	6	7.9	533
STARKY, ARTHUR	01/88 11-08	5 M	S	42	35	4	5.1	499	59	67	6	7.8	532	51	51	5	6.3	515
STRAUBE, ROSE	09/87 12-00	5 F	S	75	88	7	PHS	560	66	78	7	9.3	545	73	86	7	10.5	552
WILLIAMS, JORDAN	08/88 11-01	5 F	S	20	8	2	3.5	465	24	11	3	3.6	471	19	7	2	3.5	468
WOODALL, RENO	09/87 12-00	5 M	S	36	26	4	4.6	489	19	7	2	3.3	462	24	11	3	3.8	475
WYSE, RICHARD	08/88 11-01	5 M	S	48	46	5	5.9	509	45	40	5	5.5	505	45	41	5	5.6	506
ZARS, SALLY	06/88 11-03	5 F	S	44	38	4	5.4	502	36	25	4	4.5	490	38	29	4	4.9	495

| CLASS SUMMARY N TESTED = 20 | AVERAGE ESS N = 20   NCE, PR, S, AND GE OBTAINED FROM AVERAGE ESS | | | 47 | 45 | 5 | 5.8 | 508 | 44 | 39 | 4 | 5.4 | 504 | 45 | 40 | 5 | 5.6 | 505 |

LEGEND: NCE = Normal curve Equivalent; PR = Percentile Rank; S = Stanine; GE = Grade Equivalent; ESS = Extended Scale Score; * = Chance level score

SOURCE: Copyright © 2000 by The Riverside Publishing Company. Sample "List Report of Student Scores" from the Gates-MacGinitie Reading Tests (GMRT). Reproduced with permission of the publisher. All rights reserved.

152

Module 8

STUDENT-LEVEL DECISION MAKING

The content of this module is a continuation of the process we examined in Module 7. However, the application—and adaptation—of that process in this module focuses on the revision of instruction to meet the needs of individual students. Similarly to the previous module, we will first examine the process, and then we will consider three examples.

A PROCESS FOR FOCUSING ON INDIVIDUAL INSTRUCTION (INTERVENTION)

Standardized test data may also be used very effectively to guide the development of individualized intervention strategies. However, I again offer the same cautionary advice that was provided in Module 7. Remember that, generally speaking, achievement tests are intended to survey basic skills across a broad domain of content. Student performance on any given subtest must be interpreted with a good deal of care because a given subtest may consist of only a handful of items. Educators must be aware that any careless errors committed by students or lucky guesses made by students may substantially alter the score on that subtest, especially if they are reported as percentages of items answered correctly, as percentile ranks, or if the number or items answered correctly are used to categorize student performance (e.g., into classes such as below average, average, and above average).

For example, as you have observed on many of the test reports provided in this book, test publishers often provide criterion-referenced scores in the form of the number of items answered correctly. One such portion of a test report is shown in Figure 8.1.

Figure 8.1   Portion of an Individual Student Test Report, Showing Criterion-Referenced Test Performance

Clusters	Number Correct/ Number of Items	Below Average	Average	Above Average
Verbal	13/30		✓	
Verbal Comprehension	6/12		✓	
Verbal Reasoning	7/18		✓	
Nonverbal	14/30		✓	
Pictorial Reasoning	2/7	✓		
Figural Reasoning	12/23		✓	
TOTAL	27/60		✓	

Notice the wide-ranging number of possible items (under the column labeled "Number Correct/Number of Items") for each of these four subtests on an aptitude test. They range from a low of 7 items (for the "Pictorial Reasoning" subtest) to a high of 21 (for the "Figural Reasoning" subtest). Someone who only quickly scans the performance categories (with the checkmarks) might spontaneously decide to focus any instructional interventions on "Pictorial Reasoning" since that was the only subtest on which the student performed at a below average level. However, one needs to take into consideration that those reasoning skills were measured with only seven test items (as compared with other reasoning skill subtests that were measured with at least twice as many items) and then ask, "How well did those seven items sample the complete domain of skills?" Obviously, correctly answering two out of seven items reflects some sort of deficiency on the part of the student. However, it should not be quickly assumed that that particular level of performance is worse than correctly answering 12 out of 23 items ("Figural Reasoning") or 7 out of 18 ("Verbal Reasoning"). These also reflect poor student performance, but they may be more accurate measures of the student's skills since they were based on a greater number of items. In other words, they

> "I guess I would say I look at individual scores first and then see if they match in the trend of the class. Because sometimes those individual students might not be in the trend and that provides some fairly unique challenges. Because then it simply means it has to be more individualized because if I'm changing my teaching to meet the natural trends in the class just generally, but this student isn't in that trend then I have to modify that."
>
> —Jeff Burkett,
> *Sixth-Grade Teacher*

sampled a greater proportion of the entire domain of items addressing those specific skills.

Therefore, it is important to examine not only the raw scores, percentile ranks, and the like, but also the total number of items possible on a given test prior to making any intervention decisions (Mertler, 2003). Consideration of this fact is likely more crucial when examining the test results of individual students for purposes of designing instructional intervention strategies. Once again, teachers should exhibit great care to avoid the over interpretation of individual student's test scores.

"It's not enough to look at the whole class. You have to look at each individual child, and making sure that [the individual] child gets what he or she needs."

—Martha Fether,
Elementary School Principal

The process for examining test results to help guide the development of intervention strategies for individual students is essentially the same as that shown in Figure 7.1. It is important to remember the primary difference—you are essentially revising instruction for one individual student and making make instructional

Figure 8.2   Steps in a Generic Process for Identifying Curricular Areas in Which Students Are Deficient (Focusing on Individual Intervention)

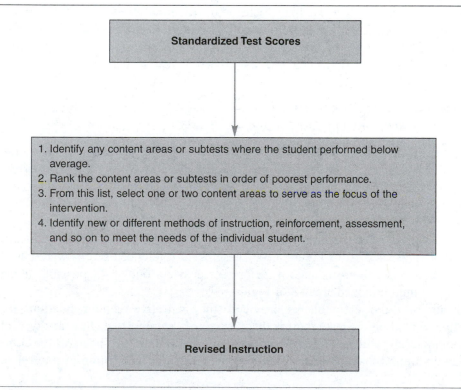

"I look at the individual reports and I basically look at are they low in the subject area. Are they middle or are they high compared to most students? That gives me a little bit of a baseline."

—Amy Kenyon,
First- and Second-Grade Teacher

decisions accordingly. A process for using standardized test data to guide intervention decisions is presented in Figure 8.2.

This process begins by identifying from provided test reports any content, skill, or subtest areas where a given student performed below average (or poorly, but not necessarily below average). If more than one area is identified, they should be ranked in order of the perceived severity of the deficiency or weakness. The one or two highest-ranked weaknesses should then be selected so as to serve as the focus of the intervention for a particular student. Finally, new or different methods of instruction, reinforcement, and/or assessment should be identified, developed, and implemented to meet the needs of the individual student.

Examples

Three examples of individual student test reports, their interpretations, and discussions of how teachers might design interventions as outlined in Figure 8.2 are presented next. These examples focus on instructional decisions at the individual student level. The three examples in this module use the Gates-MacGinitie Reading Tests (GMRT), the TerraNova Achievement Test, and the Dynamic Indicators of Basic Early Literacy Skills (DIBELS) test, respectively.

Example 1: Sixth-Grade Student's Reading Achievement Test Results

Each student in Mr. Fernandez' sixth-grade class was tested in the fall using the GMRT. Most of his students performed at or slightly above the average performance of the national norm group on both vocabulary and reading comprehension. However, one student, Thelma Brimer, demonstrated comprehension scores that were well below the average (see Figure 8.3). She scored in the 20th percentile, or the 3rd stanine, on the reading comprehension subtest of the GMRT (as shown in boxed areas #1 and #2 of Figure 8.3). These norm-referenced scores were based on her actual test performance of 22 correct answers out of 48 possible items (as highlighted in boxed area #3 of Figure 8.3).

In addition, the test publisher provided some narrative recommendations for Thelma. Stated on the test report is that her scores "suggest that she reads typical school materials with a below average level of understanding." The narrative comments continue by stating that "Thelma may need help in learning to interrelate

Figure 8.3 Sample Individual Student Test Score Report

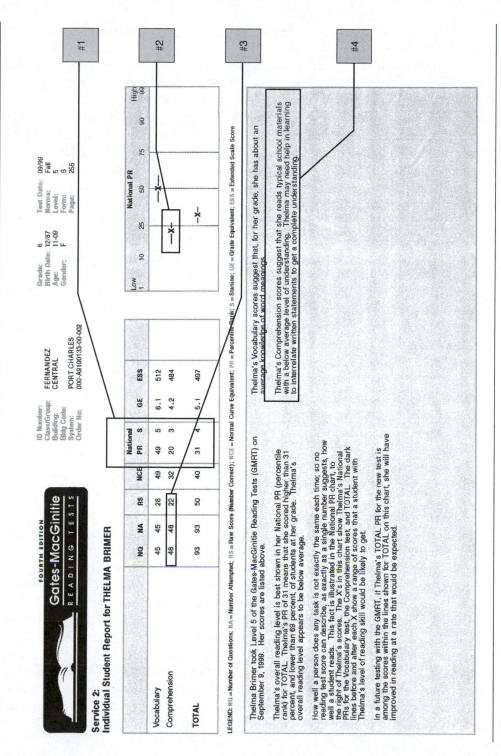

written statements to get a complete understanding" (as shown in boxed areas #4 of Figure 8.3).

Based on this information, Mr. Fernandez decided to conduct several additional assessments to determine Thelma's instructional reading level. He determined that she was clearly reading at a frustrated level for a typical student in the sixth grade. He then proceeded to identify from his classroom library several leveled books at her appropriate reading level. Once he had selected several chapter books for Thelma to read, he scheduled a brief amount of time each day for he and Thelma to engage in a period of oral shared reading of a randomly selected chapter from the books.

Each day they share read to each other for roughly 20 minutes. Following each oral reading session, Mr. Fernandez posed both oral and written comprehension questions to Thelma. They reviewed the correct answers to the questions. By engaging in this activity with Thelma, Mr. Fernandez taught her to identify important words in each question and then to locate those important words in the reading passage. For example, Mr. Fernandez might have provided her with a question such as "What color was the basket in which Susie placed her fruit?" He taught Thelma to identify the important words in the question (i.e., color, basket, and fruit in this example) and then to locate those important words in the reading passage as a means of finding—and, eventually, being able to recall—the correct answer to the question. Mr. Fernandez also encouraged Thelma to draw pictures of what she had read and also suggested the use of drama (i.e., having Thelma act out portions of what she had read) to reinforce her developing reading comprehension skills. His goal for Thelma's intervention strategy was to see her spring reading achievement scores improve, in particular with respect to the performance of the sixth-grade norm group.

Example 2: Fourth-Grade Student's Achievement Test Results

Ms. Shen had always thought of herself of a traditional teacher, especially in the areas of mathematics and science, and was also aware that some of her students experienced difficulty in learning from this teaching style. She tended to lecture from overhead transparencies as her main mode of instruction. When she received her students' test results from the spring administration of the TerraNova Achievement Test battery, some of her beliefs were supported. After examining the individual results for her students, she recognized that her students performed fairly well on the mathematics subtests, but that was not the case on the science subtests. One student in particular, Ken Jones (see Figure 8.4), performed well into the "Low Mastery" level on four (i.e., "Science Inquiry," "Physical Science," "Life Science," and "Science and Technology") of the six science subtests (as shown in boxed area #1 of Figure 8.4). Based on his results, she believed that she needed not only to alter her instruction, but also to inform the fifth-grade teachers of the apparent relationship between this more traditional teaching style and the students' lack of understanding as evidenced by their performance on standardized tests.

Ms. Shen first decided to consult with several other fourth-grade teachers in the district. She quickly discovered that they integrated much more hands-on, experiential learning into their instruction, particularly in science. She gathered material that they shared with her, as well as researching some additional ideas for hands-on activities in the areas of life science, physical science, and life science. She was excited to incorporate these new activities into her instruction and decided not to wait until next fall to implement them. The last science unit of the fourth-grade year was on the topic of the environment. For example, she scheduled trips to a recycling center and required students to bring in to school examples of materials that could be recycled, along with products that were then made from the recycled matter. Her students, and especially Ken Jones, really seemed to have a renewed interest in science. In addition, the students performed much better on their unit assessment. Ken received a grade of B— much better than his previous unit assessment average, which was in the low C range.

Based on these results, Ms. Shen concluded that her new approach to teaching science would substantially enhance Ken's learning experience going into the fifth grade. She also believed that this approach would really benefit her incoming fourth-grade students and was excited to try it out next fall.

Example 3: First-Grade Student's Literacy Skills Test Results

Mrs. Johnson's first-grade class, on the whole, had been doing quite well in all tested areas (i.e., "Phonemic Awareness," "Alphabetic Principle," "Vocabulary," and "Fluency and Comprehension") on both the benchmark assessments and progress monitoring assessments of the DIBELS. However, one student, John Smith, seemed to be struggling with some aspects of the DIBELS assessments (see Figure 8.5). He seemed to be strong in "Phonemic Awareness," having surpassed the target goal in the December benchmark assessment (as shown in boxed area #1 of Figure 8.5). Similarly, he met the target goal for "Alphabetic Principle" in April. However, he was experiencing some difficulty in the area of "Oral Reading Fluency." He scored slightly below the target goal in December and did not show any improvement in the April assessment, although the target goal had increased (as highlighted in boxed area #2 of Figure 8.5). Essentially, this indicated that John was actually regressing in terms of his oral fluency skills with respect to the DIBELS goals.

Mrs. Johnson knew that John was in need of some individualized interventions in order for him to demonstrate his progression toward the grade-appropriate goals. She decided to implement the 1-minute weekly DIBELS oral reading fluency interventions. The purpose of these intervention activities is to provide continuing reinforcement of fluent reading skills. In addition, she decided to check John's ability to recognize sight words to see if that was an area in which he might

Figure 8.4 Sample Individual Student Test Score Report for Objectives

160

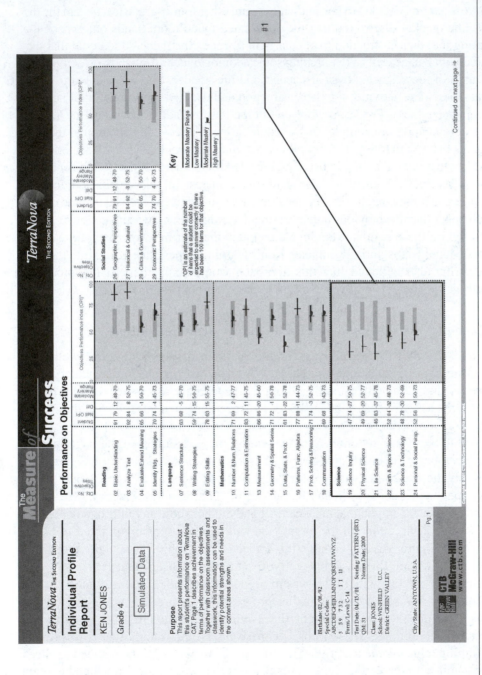

Figure 8.5   Sample Student Test Score Report

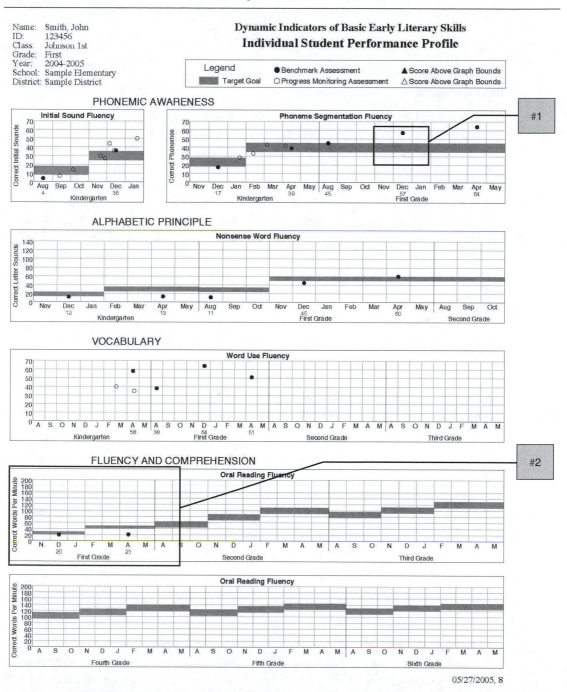

also need to remediation. If this was the case, Mrs. Johnson knew that helping him improve his sight word recognition would also increase his oral fluency.

Summary

In addition to being a useful source of information for guiding revisions to group instruction, standardized test data may also be used very effectively for guiding individualized instructional interventions. It is important to remember that individual student performance must be interpreted with caution, making sure that weaknesses are not identified from the over interpretation of test scores. This may result from placing increased value on poor performance on a subtest measured by only a handful of items. Consideration of this fact is likely even more critical when interpreting individual test results as opposed to group results.

The process for examining test results for purposes of developing individual intervention strategies is quite similar to that used for revising group instruction. Once content, skills, or subtest areas are identified from the test report as weaknesses, they should be ranked in order of importance or severity. The one or two highest ranked areas then serve as the focus of the particular intervention for that student. New methods of instruction, reinforcement, or assessment should be developed and implemented to meet the instructional needs of that student.

Activities for Application and Reflection

1. Obtain an actual test report for one student from any test you may use in your school or district. Closely examine the norm-referenced and/or criterion-referenced score information that is provided on the report. Briefly summarize the performance of this student. Follow the four-step process as outlined in Figure 8.1 and make a list of possible intervention strategies you could implement with this student.

2. Closely examine the sample test report for Martin Grant from the Iowa Tests of Basic Skills (ITBS) in Figure 8.6. Follow the process discussed in this module and demonstrated in the three examples to develop a plan for addressing any weaknesses exhibited by this student that you identify from your examination of these test results.

3. Carefully read the interview transcript with Jeff Burkett, sixth-grade teacher at Crim Elementary School, paying particular attention to his description of the process he developed to address individual student needs based on test scores, his district's curriculum, and his teaching. Discuss this process with your classmates or colleagues. Are there ways that you could adapt this process for your own classroom?

Figure 8.6 Sample Individual Student Test Score Report

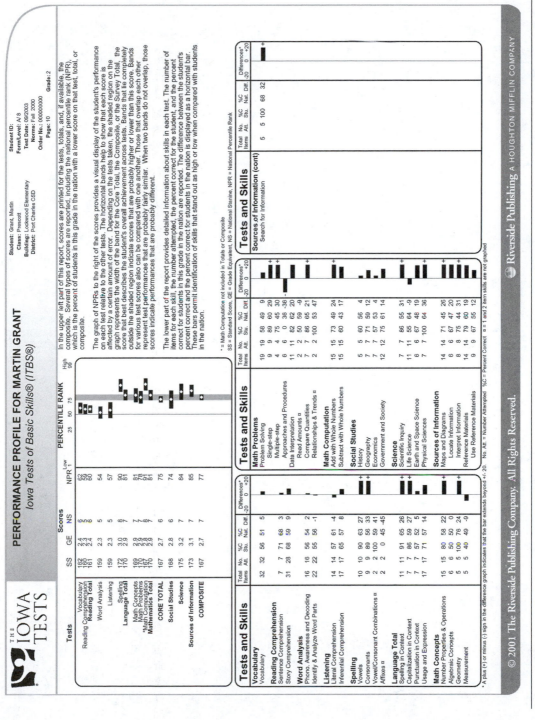

SOURCE: Copyright © 2001 by Riverside Publishing. Sample "Individual Performance Profile" from the Iowa Tests of Basic Skills (ITBS). Reproduced with permission of the publisher. All rights reserved.

Value-Added Analysis and Interpretation

In this module, the concept of *value-added analysis* and interpretation is introduced and discussed. There is a stark contrast between value-added assessment and more basic types of test data analysis. We will first consider what is meant by value-added; then we will examine a straightforward value-added process that can be used by teachers. Finally, we will consider one example of using value-added analysis.

WHAT IS "VALUE-ADDED" ANALYSIS?

By this point in this book, it should be very obvious that I advocate the idea that test scores need to be viewed as our friends and not as our enemies. However, using them as a single accountability tool is somewhat inadequate (Monson, 2002). For example, comparing the test performance of this year's fourth-grade students to last year's fourth-grade students—a common practice at various state and district levels—is known as *cross-sectional analysis*. Simply put, cross-sectional analysis, such as this example, is analogous to comparing apples to oranges. As all educators know, one group of students varies, sometimes drastically, from the next group. This notion of comparing one cohort of students to another has become the standard measure of school accountability, primarily by default since few alternatives exist (Monson, 2002). A teacher who has an extremely bright group of students one year will likely spend the entire next year cringing if next year's group proves to be more challenging or less proficient. Suddenly, it appears as if she is not doing her job very well because the test performance of the students in her class has decreased from last year to this year.

With increasing frequency, state departments of education as well as school districts and individual schools are beginning to examine students' test results in terms of gains over time. These types of analyses are typically referred to as *longitudinal analyses*. Instead of cross-cohort comparisons, individual student and cohort performances are being tracked along multiyear routes. In other words, school accountability and student performance are being scrutinized at the levels of individual student and collective (i.e., the same group of students) performance over multiple years (Monson, 2002). It is important to realize that these types of comparisons are much truer reflections of student learning—this is because they result in comparing apples to apples.

Often, educators find it difficult to agree on the amount of improvement or progress a given child should make in a particular school year. However, what we can agree on is that the role of educators is to take children and add value to them as a commodity, so to speak (Mahoney, 2004). We add that value to our students in a variety of ways—for example, we teach them subject matter, we model appropriate behavior for them, and we train them to be knowledgeable in a wide variety of life-based skills. All of these things add to their value as human beings and as future adults. Good teachers add value in numerous measurable and immeasurable ways. For example, we can measure the gain of a student in mathematics, but it is not possible to measure the impact of a teacher who motivated a student to want to learn mathematics (Mahoney, 2004).

As we all know, at any given grade level there are students who far exceed their state's standards for performance at that grade level. At the same time, there are those who fall far below the standards. Not only are the reasons for this discrepancy innumerable, they are also typically not factored into accountability measures. Over the course of a school year, how much improvement should we expect to see from those who already exceed the standards? How much should we expect to see from those already far below that criteria? Those are difficult questions to answer. In fact, I would guess that if you posed that question to several different educators, you would receive unique responses from each regarding expected levels of improvement for these students.

Here is another question whose answer might be easier to agree upon. Is it reasonable to expect that from year to year those students who enter a given grade level already far below the standards—for whatever reasons—will realize as much improvement as those who have already surpassed those standards? Most of us would likely respond in the negative. Perhaps, due to external factors (e.g., home environment), it would not be reasonable for us to hold such expectations. However—and realize that this point is crucial—if we do not factor into the equation those types of individualized factors, then we are in essence holding all students to the same standard. Many professional educators have argued and will continue to argue that this approach is simply not realistic. To get an accurate picture of each student's academic growth, the individual progress of each student must be measured from year to year. Realize that teachers have always tried to take a given child from point A to point B over the course of a school year, but the challenge has always been to measure their progress when every student's point A and point B is different (Mahoney, 2004). Therefore, each student's target may be different; but the important aspect of that fact is that each student has an appropriate target.

This is the essence of value-added analysis. Value-added analysis provides a new method of measuring teaching and learning. It uses the annual test scores that are now being collected for all students—as required by No Child Left Behind (NCLB)—and analyzes them to reveal the progress students are making each year, at both the individual and group levels. It has been formally defined as "any method of analyzing student test data to ascertain students' growth in learning by comparing students' current levels of learning to their own past learning" (Evergreen Freedom Foundation, 2003, p. 3). Instead of comparing students to each other or to a preestablished level of proficiency, value-added analysis compares students to themselves to determine if they are advancing academically; and if so, at what pace. With its focus on growth rather than on levels of absolute achievement, value-added analysis can vastly improve our understanding of the contribution that good instruction makes to student learning (Hershberg, Simon, & Lea-Kruger, 2004). As was previously discussed, this is the value that is added by individual teachers, specific instructional programs, and so on. While still a relatively new approach, value-added analysis is seeing greater implementation across several states. Value-added assessment has been in place in Tennessee (i.e., the Tennessee Value-Added Assessment System, or TVAAS) since the early 1990s when it was created by Dr. William Sanders. Variations have been since implemented in Ohio (Data Driven Decisions for Academic Achievement, or D3A2), Pennsylvania, Arkansas, Minnesota, Iowa, and New York. Individual school districts in Texas, Washington, Colorado, North Carolina, and Florida have also begun using a value-added approach.

By following individual students over time, value-added analysis factors in (rather than ignores, as is done in typical cross-sectional analyses) student background characteristics over which schools have no control (Hershberg, Simon, & Lea-Kruger, 2004). Not only can these factors not be controlled, but they also tend to bias test results. Essentially, students serve as their own point of comparison. For example, if a given student came from a home environment that did not foster academic growth, that would not count against him or her in a value-added system. The reason for this is because that student's performance is being compared only to his or her past performance—both of which came from the same home environment. The most unique contribution value-added analysis has made to the notion of school accountability is that it enables educators and the public to identify progress made by individual students, along with the extent to which individual teachers, schools, and school districts have contributed to that progress (Hershberg, Simon, & Lea-Kruger, 2004).

Value-added assessment also operates on the assumption that teachers clearly matter. A good teacher can create and facilitate learning regardless of what his or her students are like when they enter the classroom (Evergreen Freedom Foundation, 2003). Teacher quality is the most important element in determining how much students will learn over the course of a year. Excellent teachers are able to foster growth in students at all levels of achievement (Evergreen Freedom Foundation, 2003). This fact often is lost when simply examining aggregate test data or when comparing this year's students to last year's.

Simply put, value-added analysis follows the process as described below:

1. An individual student's past achievement is collected.

2. Using models created from previous similar students, an end-of-year level of achievement is predicted for that individual student.

3. A successful school year occurs if the predicted achievement level is met for the individual student; if the predicted level is exceeded, this fact denotes the value-added portion of instruction (J. Mahoney, personal communication, September 16, 2006).

A PROCESS FOR VALUE-ADDED DECISION MAKING

The most prominent, and perhaps most well-known, model of value-added assessment was developed by Dr. William Sanders. His model uses a mixed-model methodology involving a type of statistical analysis originally developed for use in agricultural research (Evergreen Freedom Foundation, 2002). This model incorporates extensive use of multivariate, longitudinal data arranged into complex statistical models. This is the nature of TVAAS, a state-level model of value-added analysis. One variation of the value-added approach projects test scores for individual students and then compares the test scores they actually receive at the end of the school year to those projections. Scores that exceed the projected values provide evidence that the instruction provided during that school year was highly effective; scores that are mostly below projected values suggest that the instruction was ineffective (Hershberg, Simon, & Lea-Kruger, 2004). This approach considers student-related factors such as the pattern of previous test scores, both of the individual student as well as those of other students in the same class. If a given student's performance is below projected scores while students with similar previous academic histories in the same classes have done well, this is evidence of a student effect—that is, variables such as the home environment that are beyond the control of teachers and schools—that can be considered outside the range of an individual teacher's influence (Hershberg, Simon, & Lea-Kruger, 2004).

Value-added analysis provides educators with two patterns of instruction that characterize their classrooms:

1. which students are the focus of their instruction (previously low, middle, or high achievers); and

2. how effective has their instruction been in providing those students with a year's worth of growth from wherever they began at the beginning of the school year. (Hershberg, Simon, & Lea-Kruger, 2004)

Teachers can meet regularly and, using these test data, can discuss how to change their instruction in whatever direction is warranted.

At its simplest level, value-added assessment is like a pre- and posttest given to students to determine what they have learned in a particular course (Evergreen Freedom Foundation, 2002). Unlike simple achievement tests, value-added analysis also provides results that can be compared across classrooms and years. Value-added assessment and analysis must utilize tests that have the following characteristics:

1. The tests must be highly correlated with curricular objectives.

2. The tests must have sufficient stretch to measure the progress of both very low and very high achieving students.

3. The tests must have appropriate reliabilities. (Sanders, 2003)

For the most part, well-established standardized achievement tests will meet these criteria, whether they are norm- or criterion-referenced (Evergreen Freedom Foundation, 2002). In states that have state-mandated tests at a variety of grade levels, the first criterion is easily met. Statewide tests are based on statewide curricula, which are also reflected in what is actually being taught in classroom across that state. In essence, this is the parallel alignment between curriculum, instruction, and assessment that we discussed in Module 3. Violations of the second of Sanders' criteria typically do not pose any sort of major problem either. The only cases he cites are a few criterion-referenced tests that were very narrowly focused on mid-level grade skills (Sanders, 2003). Similarly, the third issue of acceptable reliability is typically not a problem for tests with more than 40 items.

Again, because students' scores on these achievement tests are compared with their own prior test scores, external factors such as home environment or socioeconomic status (SES) essentially have no impact (Evergreen Freedom Foundation, 2002). In other words, the SES level of a particular student cannot have an effect on test performance since various test scores are all coming from the same student, who has the same SES characteristics. This would not be the case in situations where students in Mrs. Taylor's fifth-grade class at a given elementary school in the Midwest, for example, were being compared to a national norm group. Students in the norm group would possess a wide variety of differing characteristics, as would the students in Mrs. Taylor's class. Straightforward comparisons of test scores, especially over time, become somewhat muddled due to these uncontrollable factors such as student, teacher, or school characteristics.

Figure 9.1   Steps in a Generic Process for Value-Added Assessment (Focusing on an Individual Student)

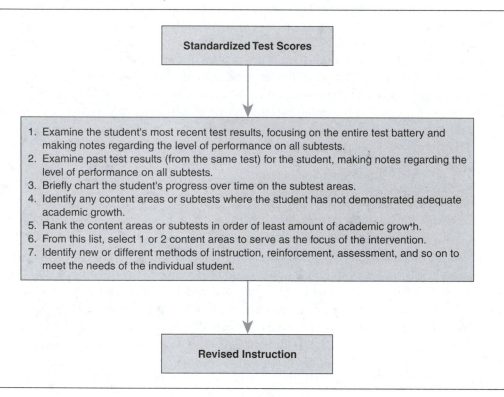

Standardized Test Scores

1. Examine the student's most recent test results, focusing on the entire test battery and making notes regarding the level of performance on all subtests.
2. Examine past test results (from the same test) for the student, making notes regarding the level of performance on all subtests.
3. Briefly chart the student's progress over time on the subtest areas.
4. Identify any content areas or subtests where the student has not demonstrated adequate academic growth.
5. Rank the content areas or subtests in order of least amount of academic growth.
6. From this list, select 1 or 2 content areas to serve as the focus of the intervention.
7. Identify new or different methods of instruction, reinforcement, assessment, and so on to meet the needs of the individual student.

Revised Instruction

For our purposes here, we will consider a relatively simple process (at least in terms of the various types of value-added models and processes) for using value-added assessment. This process, as shown in Figure 9.1, is relatively similar those previously examined in Modules 7 and 8. The primary difference between this process and the earlier ones we have examined is that we are now including the past test scores of the student in addition to the current test performance.

This value-added process begins by examining the most recent test results for a given student. It is important to make notes about the performance across all of the subtests or content areas since the focus in value-added analysis is not solely on areas of low academic performance. Past test results are then studied and similar notes made. It is crucial to be sure that all test scores that are examined for the student are results from the same test. For example, it would be appropriate to note the performance across several years on the Metropolitan Achievement Test, 8th edition (MAT8), Stanford Achievement Test (SAT10), or statewide achievement tests. The following would be an acceptable approach for a student currently in Grade 6:

Grade (Teacher)	Test Scores
3 (Jones)	Statewide 3rd Grade Reading Achievement Test—Fall Statewide 3rd Grade Reading Achievement Test—Spring
4 (Smith, B.)	Statewide 4th Grade Reading Achievement Test—Fall Statewide 4th Grade Reading Achievement Test—Spring
5 (Williamson)	Statewide 5th Grade Reading Achievement Test—Fall Statewide 5th Grade Reading Achievement Test—Spring
6 (Stone)	Statewide 6th Grade Reading Achievement Test—Fall Statewide 6th Grade Reading Achievement Test—Spring*

* These results are the current test results.

For this given student, this reflects another level of the apples-to-apples comparison we discussed earlier. The interpretation of academic growth would likely be much more accurate than monitoring progress across a variety of tests. Therefore, it would not be appropriate to interpret the progress made by the student as determined by several different measures. This amounts to a variation of the apples-to-oranges comparison for that particular student. For example, the following would likely result in a less accurate picture of growth or progress:

Grade (Teacher)	Test Scores
3 (Jones)	3rd Grade Metropolitan Achievement Test—Fall Statewide 3rd Grade Reading Achievement Test—Spring
4 (Smith, B.)	4th Grade Metropolitan Achievement Test—Fall Statewide 4th Grade Reading Achievement Test—Spring
5 (Williamson)	Statewide 5th Grade Reading Achievement Test—Fall 5th Grade Iowa Tests of Basic Skills—Spring
6 (Stone)	Statewide 6th Grade Reading Achievement Test—Fall 6th Grade TerraNova Achievement Test—Spring*

* These results are the current test results.

The third step in the process is to combine the notes made during the first two steps. I recommend that this be done in some sort of chart so that it is possible to see everything laid out before you on one piece of paper. For example, using the SAT10 subtest categories and fictitious data, an individual student's progress or growth would then be displayed as follows. Note that both norm-referenced scores (provided first in each column as a percentile rank) and criterion-referenced scores (the number of items answered correctly and the total number of items) are provided in the chart.

Subtest	Grade 3—Fall	Grade 4—Fall	Grade 5—Fall	Grade 6—Fall	Growth?
Word Study Skills	50* • 23/32**	59 • 25/30	60 • 26/30	62 • 25/30	–
Reading Vocabulary	50 • 24/30	46 • 22/30	52 • 25/30	55 • 34/30	–
Reading Comprehension	53 • 36/54	53 • 35/54	55 • 36/52	60 • 40/54	–
Mathematics Problem Solving	58 • 33/48	54 • 30/48	60 • 35/48	58 • 28/46	–
Mathematics Procedures	54 • 18/32	74 • 26/32	78 • 28/32	70 • 24/32	+
Language Mechanics	44 • 14/24	46 • 15/24	52 • 17/24	46 • 15/24	–
Language Expression	40 • 18/28	36 • 13/24	38 • 14/24	45 • 15/24	–
Spelling	48 • 19/40	73 • 30/40	72 • 29/40	73 • 30/40	+
Science	62 • 27/40	69 • 30/40	67 • 28/40	69 • 30/40	–
Social Science	35 • 19/40	40 • 22/40	42 • 23/40	75 • 35/45	+

* Value indicates a percentile rank.
** Values indicate the number of items answered correctly and total number of items.

The fourth step in the process is to identify any subtest areas where the student has and has not made adequate progress from year to year as well as over all years collectively. In the example above, notice that there was considerable academic growth during third grade (as indicated by the improvement in Grade 4 scores over those made in Grade 3) in the areas of mathematics procedures and spelling, as well as in social science during Grade 5. In most of the other areas, however, there has not been adequate progress made by the student—an indication that significant learning has not occurred. These are noted in the rightmost column where a minus sign (i.e., −) indicates that adequate growth has not occurred and a plus sign (+) indicates that the student has made demonstrated good academic progress.

The remaining three steps in the process basically mirror the latter steps of the processes we have examined previously. The content or subtest areas in which the student has demonstrated the least amount of growth are ranked, beginning with the most severe area. From this list, the teacher would then select one or two of those areas to serve as the focus of any intervention or other instructional strategies. Finally, new or different methods of instruction, reinforcement, or assessment are developed and implemented over the course of the school year to help the student experience appropriate academic growth.

Example

One example of test reports, their interpretations, and discussions of how teachers might design value-added interventions as outlined in Figure 9.1 for an individual student (in this case, our own son, Addison) are presented next. The test score information provided are excerpts from the reports we received at home regarding his performance in the second and third grades. In these reports, only the norm-referenced results were provided and are shared here.

Example 1: Individual Student's Second- and Third-Grade Achievement Test Results

Our son, Addison, took an achievement test battery early in both his second- and third-grade years. The norm-referenced results for his performance in second grade are shown in Figure 9.2(a), and in third grade are shown in Figure 9.2(b). In second grade, Addison scored relatively average or slightly below average across the subtests. His lowest performance was in Reading Vocabulary (27th percentile; 4th stanine), while his highest was in Science (75th percentile; 6th stanine). In all other areas, he scored in the 5th or 6th stanines.

In the third grade, his performance was much more varied. His best performances were in Mathematics Concepts and Problem Solving (91st percentile; 8th stanine), Language (84th percentile; 7th stanine), and Social Studies (82nd percentile; 7th stanine). These all represented dramatic increases over his performance in these same areas in the second grade. However, his performance in Spelling dropped considerably (from the 40th percentile in the second grade to the 11th percentile in the third grade) as did his performance in Reading Comprehension (from the 51st percentile to the 28th percentile).

The next step in the process is to combine all of this test data into one common table, allowing us to see any trends, patterns, or other areas of concern. Compiling the information from these two sets of test results into one chart would give us the following:

Subtest	Grade 2—Fall	Grade 3—Fall
Sounds and Print	42 • 5*	36 • 4
Reading Vocabulary	27 • 4	47 • 5
Reading Comprehension	51 • 5	28 • 4
Mathematics Concepts and Problem Solving	60 • 6	91 • 8
Mathematics Computation	48 • 5	57 • 5
Language	44 • 5	84 • 7
Spelling	40 • 5	11 • 3
Science	75 • 6	76 • 6
Social Studies	45 • 5	82 • 7

*Values indicate the percentile rank, followed by the stanine.

Upon examining this information, it appears that Addison should have received focused instruction in several areas during the remainder of third grade. In rank order of importance, those areas would be

1. spelling,

2. reading comprehension, and

3. sounds and print.

Although Addison's performance in Sounds and Print did not show a substantial decrease, it was still relatively low across the two years, which is why I added it to the list. Based on this list, spelling and reading comprehension should have been the focus of his third-grade teacher's attention as well as of his parents' at home (to which I can honestly attest was the case).

As an aside, it is interesting to note that Addison received a great deal of spelling instruction in first grade, hence his average performance at the beginning of second grade. However, he received very little spelling instruction in the second grade, which was evidenced by his very low score in spelling at the beginning of third grade. I point this out because—contrary to the popular belief of some—standardized test scores do quite often strongly support what actually occurs within the classroom.

Summary

Value-added assessment and analysis is defined as any method of analyzing student test data to determine students' growth in learning by comparing students' current levels of learning to their own past learning. It is seen as a valuable

Figure 9.2(a)   Norm-Referenced Achievement Test Battery Results for Second Grade

Addison C Mertler

Student Profile

Student Age: 7 Yrs 00 Mos
Student No.:   0000654321
School: Kenwood Elementary
District: Bowling Green City
Grade: 2
Test Date: 09/04

			National Grade Percentile Bands						
Tests and Totals	**Raw Score**	**National PR-S**	1	10	30	50	70	90	99
Total Reading	69	35–4							
Sounds & Print	29	42–5							
Reading Vocabulary	16	27–4							
Reading Comprehension	24	51–5							
Total Mathematics	47	55–5							
Concepts & Prob. Solving	24	60–6							
Computation	23	48–5							
Language	26	44–5							
Spelling	22	40–5							
Science	25	75–6							
Social Studies	21	45–5							
Basic Battery	164	44–5							
Complete Battery	210	48–5							

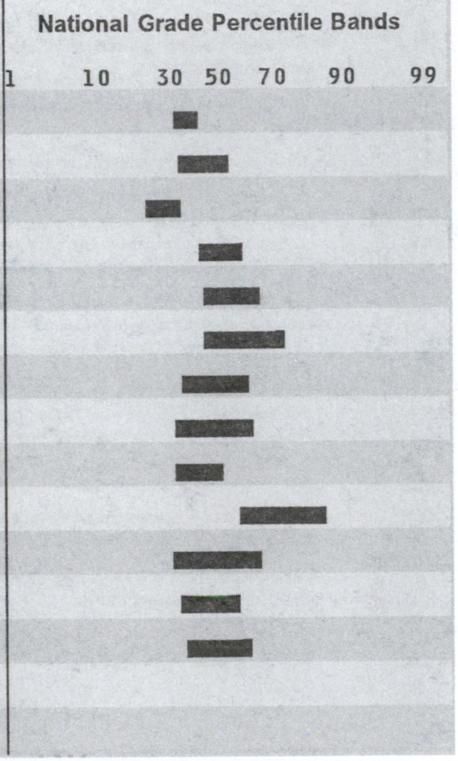

Figure 9.2(b) Norm-Referenced Achievement Test Battery Results for Third Grade

Addison C Mertler

Student Profile

Student Age:	8 Yrs 00 Mos
Student No.:	0000654321
School:	Kenwood Elementary
District:	Bowling Green City
Grade:	3
Test Date:	09/05

Tests and Totals	Raw Score	National PR-S	National Grade Percentile Bands
Total Reading	60	34-4	
Sounds & Print	17	36-4	
Reading Vocabulary	21	47-5	
Reading Comprehension	22	28-4	
Total Mathematics	55	76-6	
Concepts & Prob. Solving	33	91-8	
Computation	22	57-5	
Language	34	84-7	
Spelling	14	11-3	
Science	24	76-6	
Social Studies	25	82-7	
Basic Battery	163	51-5	
Complete Battery	212	58-5	

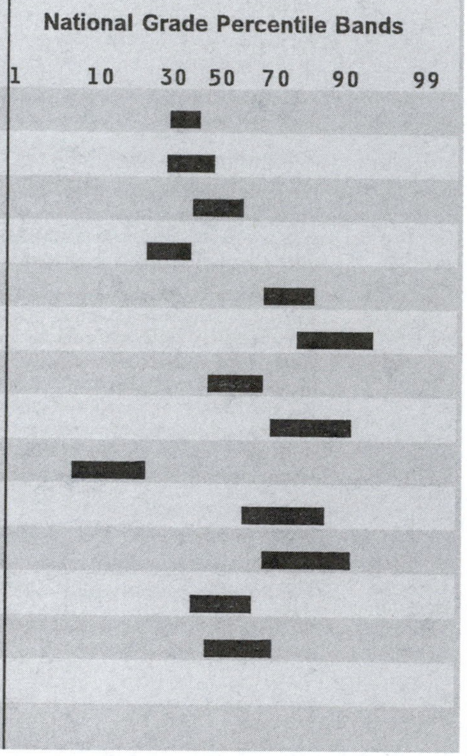

longitudinal analysis approach as opposed to a more typical cross-sectional one. This permits teachers and administrators to make more meaningful comparisons across years, by comparing apples to apples, so to speak. This ultimately results in truer reflections of student learning.

An important aspect of this approach is that we are adding value to a child's education by closely looking at the amount of individual gain experienced by the particular child. The wide variety of factors that can impact undesirable cross-sectional analyses (e.g., comparing this year's fourth-grade students to last year's fourth-grade students and seeing declining academic performance) are essentially factored out. Each student serves as his or her own control, or baseline, for comparison purposes. Additionally, it becomes easier to see the impact that individual teachers or instructional programs are having on particular students.

Value-added assessment can take on many forms, ranging from complex statistical models to fairly basic pretest (i.e., beginning of the school year) and posttest (i.e., at the end of the school year or early in the next school year) comparisons. At the teacher or school level, the latter form is more realistic and practical. The process begins by examining recent test scores against past test results—looking for patterns, trends, or clear areas of weaknesses. Combining this information into one table allows teachers to see these multiyear patterns. Any areas where the student is not making meaningful academic progress should then be targeted for reinstruction, differentiated instruction, or additional reinforcement.

Activities for Application and Reflection

1. What advantages and disadvantages do you see with value-added assessment, especially when compared to the approaches discussed in Modules 7 and 8?

2. Closely examine the sample test report for John Smith from the Dynamic Indicators of Basic Early Literacy Skills (DIBELS) in Figure 9.3. Follow the value-added process discussed in this module to develop a plan for addressing any areas where progress has been limited for this student.

3. Carefully read the interview transcript for Martha Fether, elementary school principal, paying particular attention to her pre- and posttesting comparisons. Discuss her description and school-wide practice from a value-added analysis perspective. What characteristics of her school's practice make it a value-added approach?

Figure 9.3   Sample Student Test Score Report

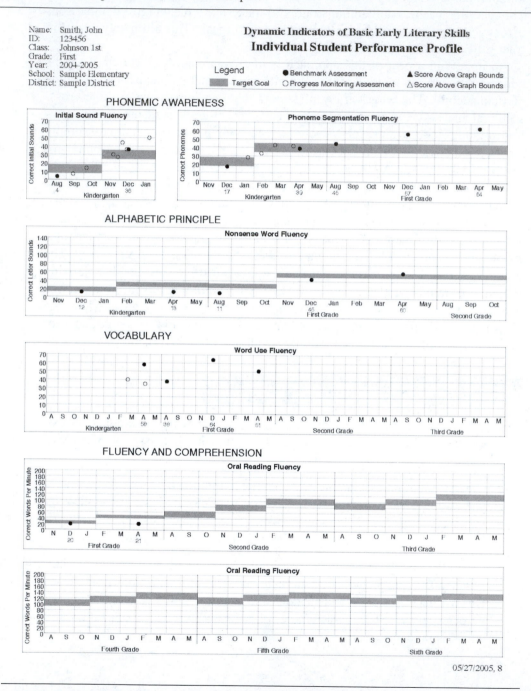

SECTION IV

Case Studies

*Interviews With Teachers
and Administrators*

District and School Profiles

Interview Transcripts: Teachers

Interview Transcripts: Administrators

DISTRICT AND SCHOOL PROFILES

Bowling Green (Ohio) City Schools

Bowling Green Schools have embraced the idea of data-driven decision making through a series of processes and procedures that have been central-office driven during the past five years. The district has made progress on the state report card rating system and has moved from being a Continuous Improvement district to one that is Effective, and as of the 2005–2006 school year, has attained a rating of Excellent.

Crim Elementary School

Crim Elementary has moved from being Effective on the state report card rating system to being Excellent. A principal who has wholeheartedly bought into the concept of data-driven decision making has led this effort. Crim is leading the way for other schools in the district by sharing its experiences.

Bowling Green High School

Bowling Green High School is actively engaged in data analysis and data-driven decision making because of the interests and efforts of the high school administration. The high school has met by department to review the Ohio Graduation Test (OGT) results and then has made plans for further instruction in those areas that students are having difficulties.

Interview Transcripts: Teachers

Jeff Burkett
Crim Elementary School

Sixth-Grade Teacher

Math, Science, and Reading

Twenty-Four Years of Teaching Experience

Craig Mertler: As you well know, some teachers just don't like standardized tests. Why do you think they don't like standardized tests?

Jeff Burkett: I think there's a lot of pressure. There's pressure to have students perform because it's a reflection on ourselves as well as the student in the classroom and the school, the school district, the state, etc. I have no problem being held accountable for what I teach. What's frustrating is that it's one test, one day, one little snapshot picture of a student for two and a half hours of their lives. But I have no problem being held accountable for what I teach. I wish there could be a more broad-based way for us to be accountable besides standardized tests. But that's the challenge and that's obviously why there hasn't been something else because it's difficult to think of something.

CM: Do you believe that it's important for teachers to know how, to have the *knowledge of how* to interpret their students' standardized test performance?

JB: Absolutely. I think if a teacher is truly a professional, wants to do the best they can for the students, we know that students perform differently; and if the teacher wants to know how a student performs, then they should look at all of the various ways that a student performs in different projects. And testing is one of those. So why wouldn't you look at the results. It just makes sense to me that you would include that.

CM: And so not only is it important for them to know how to do it, but I gather you also feel it's important that they actually do it. It's not just a matter of having that knowledge, but you actually have to do it.

JB: Absolutely. We assess students' writing. We assess other pen and paper tests that students take. We assess how well they work in a group. We have checklists, we have portfolios, we have other project-based things, and test scores are just one of the things that you should add to the magic list. So if you want to help meet students' needs and I do, then I can't ignore test scores. I don't think that

I should solely look at them, but certainly include it in the repertoire that a teacher reviews.

CM: You have a multitude of other sources of information that you use and you have access to this information, so why wouldn't you use it as one additional source of information?

JB: Sure.

CM: It is not the be all, end all, nor should it be.

JB: Right. And sometimes we're threatened by the 2 point font that the results come out in. But with the correct prescription of glasses one can read the results. [Laughter . . .]

CM: In light of the fact that you think that it's important to interpret those scores and use that information, can you explain why you think that it's important that teachers maybe should like standardized tests. And I use the term like kind of loosely there.

JB: Pleasant feelings about, is that what you mean by like? [Laughter . . .]

CM: Maybe more pleasant than what we typically do as a society in the whole because, again, you know that most people that I know don't really love standardized tests.

JB: Oh I think it's a fact of life. I don't particularly enjoy going 55 miles per hour. It's just another thing in my list of life. It's wasted energy for me to get all cranky about. So, if I look at standardized testing as a way to help students achieve better, then I'm happy as a teacher. That seems to me to be the essence of what a teacher should be. So yes, we don't have to particularly like them, but we have to face the music. I think it's important for a teacher to show and have their students feel an aura of invincibility with tests and to feel confident. And if a teacher has a strong negative attitude about standardized tests I think that's very difficult to hide with students. And even with sixth graders. I think they're very keen and can really determine a teacher's true feelings, however poor the attempts may be at masking what it is. If the teachers are bad mouthing the tests and [saying], "Oh we have this to do," then I think that's how students approach it. But if we coach and we say, "Yes, this is going to be a challenge for us but we're going to work hard"; and even though deep down I wish I could do something different, I can't let that show to the students. I think that's vital to have the teacher have this aura of confidence building to give to students.

CM: It's all part of test preparation.

JB: Right. So even though I may not like it, I accept it and learn to deal with it and see what the best ways are and then I can have the students best approach it.

CM: How long ago did you personally begin this idea of, or this process of critically examining your students' test scores?

JB: It was probably about four years ago.

CM: How did that process start for you? Was it something that you bought into right away? Were you a little bit hesitant about it at first or

JB: I think I can be brutally honest and say it was principal inspired. We had a retreat for teachers and we were attempting to find some building goals. And of course, finding an objective that's measurable and observable. Test scores obviously came up, so . . . We came to an agreement as a staff that that was what we wanted to approach . . . and it was our principal's impetus. As well as knowing then about AYP [Adequate Yearly Progress], and what that would mean from year to year. That was the impetus. And again, there were some people that didn't like that impetus but I embraced it and said let's figure out how we can make this work.

CM: I already know the answer to this question a little bit, but I'm curious to hear your explanation of it in terms of its importance. What kind of support do you get from your principal in this process in your building?

JB: Well I think it's gargantuan. Martha [the principal] provides teachers with inordinate amounts of data and I don't think she does it to overwhelm us. I think that the things she provides for us help us see what the trends are with students across certain tests and the certain substrands of the test. We have had inservices on how to interpret data. Those have been very helpful. We have had guest speakers come to school to help us learn how to interpret data. One of the other things I think has been vital is the opportunity for teachers to share their own ideas with each other of how they're using data in the classrooms. And, you know, we don't live in our own bubble and what one teacher dreamt of one nightmarish night, tossing and turning, another teacher can use down the hallway; that's been very good for us as a staff.

CM: How critical do you think that support is school wide, whether it comes from your principal or from other teachers?

JB: I believe it's ultra critical. It helps you see that there is light at the end of the tunnel. Why should education be a lone-ranger job? It never has been and why should it be with testing. So I think we should embrace it; I enjoy a principal who prods and nudges and challenges the staff to do things differently. Sometimes teachers get into this rut of doing the same thing over and over. We have ups and downs in our careers at certain times. For me, in my 24th year . . . well, over the past four years, I've enjoyed the difference in approaching how I teach. And I've had to make some changes and some of those have been difficult for me.

CM: But not a bad thing?

JB: No. No.

CM: Can you share a little bit with me about how you actually go through this process of looking at your students' test scores. What is it that you do and what kinds of information do you use in the process?

JB: For sixth graders I look at their third-grade reading scores [on the Ohio Achievement Tests, or OAT], their fourth-grade scores [on the OAT] and then their fifth-grade scores, on either the MAT8 [Metropolitan Achievement Test, 8th ed.] and/or the achievement tests. And so I'll make a list of students that did not pass the reading and math in particular because those are the subjects that I teach. Then I will make a list of the students that passed one or the other, sort of partial passing. I'll make another list of students that were within five points of passing—and this is the list that I'm most intrigued by. I will readily note who has or hasn't passed but also what the differential was. Then I'll strand it out. I call it stranding it out. I'll look at what areas, particularly in math, the student was weak in.

CM: And so when you do this are you looking mostly at individual test reports or are you looking across the grade level, or do you do both?

JB: Both. I look at the scores for the class, you know, math, geometry strand. How well did we do with that? But I guess I would say I look at individual scores first and then see if they match in the trend of the class. Because sometimes those individual students might not be in the trend and that provides some fairly unique challenges. Then it simply means instruction has to be more individualized because if I'm changing my teaching to meet the natural trends in the class just generally, but this student isn't in that trend, then I have to modify that. Do you want to know specifically how I do that then?

CM: Sure.

JB: Well, I decided one sleepless night, to find a way to have students be able to see everything it was that they were being tested on. Not as a way to overwhelm them, but as a way for them to have a checklist if you will of all the concepts. So I took all the learning outcomes from the achievement tests and I put them into what I call user-friendly terms and I listed them under each of the subjects. So I have a math achievement test checklist and I had the different strands listed. And I listed them as "I-Can" statements. [For example,] "I can define what a scalene triangle is. I can define what a rhombus is. I can define what parallel lines mean." There were quite a few, about 116 math statements. And then on the right-hand side I made four columns, a *self* column, a *here* column, a *family* column, and a *teacher* column. Now I did this for all the students because I didn't want to try to single out the students who need extra help. I provided this in a three-ring binder. Students study each concept. When they think that they know it, they initial it and put the date in the box under the first column for *self.* Sometimes during class we'll pair up and if you and I were doing that I could sit here and say, "Craig, what do parallel lines mean?" and if you told me the correct answer then I would put my initials in your box on your checklist under *here.* The *family,* I don't require a family box to be filled in for all students. Obviously your high achievers do because anything the teacher gives, [they will] complete. But my students that need the extra assistance, I will contact the home and try to have an older brother or sister, aunt and uncle, and/or parent help them with that. And, of course, after three levels there with my, I would call, my at-risk students, then I also would conference with them for the fourth column (*teacher*). I give them this binder as the post-Christmas gift, the first day back in January. We call them ATbs for lack of a better word. They're

"Achievement Test bibles," lower case bible, of course. But just to emphasize the importance. Inside, they also have a glossary. We printed off the glossary from some math textbooks. We take some notes during class and so they'll have their note section which is on a different color paper so we'll have "A-1" which is the "I can" statement, for example, just to use the scalene triangle. Then in the back they'll have a little section; it'll say "A-1" and it'll be blank. So the day that we cover geometry notes they'll take notes in that little box. Not little box, maybe a fifth of a page. Then if they need to study what "A-1" is, they go back in their reference notes and they can see that. So everything they need to prepare for successfully meeting the "I Can" statement is in this three-ring binder. Everything.

CM: That's fabulous.

JB: Well, it takes awhile. Because you start in January and obviously if the test's in May. That's the overall picture of how I do it. Then I would meet obviously before all this in small groups with the students that I have identified via their test scores that I have made from my lists. And I will highlight certain "I Can" statements. For example, I might say, "Craig, based on your third-, fourth-, fifth-grade scores, you want to really work hard at section B in reading," so I'll highlight that and the students know that those are areas in which they need to show a little more effort. And I haven't met a lot of students that don't want to do well. I really haven't. I have had mixed results with the home support obviously with average students because a lot of times we know that that's why students are at risk because they don't have a lot of home support.

CM: But don't you think that that level of buy-in, if you will, from the students is reflective of your attitude which is something that you talked about before.

JB: Yes.

CM: If you're not downplaying it and if you're not criticizing it, then the students tend to have a more positive outlook toward it as well.

JB: Absolutely. We have a lot of students that love sports analogies and I do see myself as a coach and they understand that. They know you have to work hard at practice. So I use that analogy a lot about the fact that you're going to perform during the game as well or not as well as you practiced. And so practicing for the achievement tests is vital. The ATb, their playbook. If you go into a game cold, then chances are you're not going to do as well. But we know our opponent. We know who we're playing. We know the strategies they have. We know what plays they're going to run. So we work on meeting it. So that's, that's a nutshell sort of how I approach it and I've had a lot of success with it.

CM: When you put some of that responsibility back on them, which is one good way to get them to buy in to the processes, it's not just something that you're doing for them?

JB: Sure. Right.

CM: They have to do it for themselves that way.

JB: Another fascinating tie in to all this has been, all the things on TV that have embraced knowing trivia. *Who Wants to Be a Millionaire. Jeopardy. Quiz Bowl.* I mean, there are a lot of students that enjoy that kind of competitive thing and so we'll do a lot of game show reviews during class, but, you know, the students that do best have studied their ATb, of course, and they've got a lot of boxes checked off.

CM: With everything else you have to do where do you find time to do all of that?

JB: That's a great question. I approach my time in class after January as sort of four-day mini-units to cover everything. During the fall, I do my basic content teaching. But starting in January it's really what I call spiraling mini-unit reviews. Because I want to cover every single item that's going to be on the test between January and the test. So we'll do four-day mini-units. I'm still teaching the content standards. I'm still doing what the state says I should do, and just mixing it up a little bit with how that's done. So I don't see it as extra time. I just see it as time spent differently.

CM: That's a nice way to look at it.

JB: Well I'm not working harder; I'm just working differently than what I had been. I work hard; yes, it takes some time to write the "I Can" statements, but guess what . . . ? Hopefully, standards last six or seven years and you don't have to redo them and you can use it year after year.

CM: Even if the standards were revised, they're not going to be completely overhauled because there's still that basic foundation of knowledge that students should have after sixth grade in the area of math.

JB: Right. Yes. The teachers at Crim were asked to share some of their strategies with other teachers in the school system. And so I shared the old "I Can" statements and it sort of took off with a lot of other intermediate teachers.

CM: That is very impressive. I say that very sincerely. Let me ask you one last question. Imagine that you are standing in front of a room full of teachers from another district and they are getting ready to embark on this journey of looking critically at standardized test scores. What kinds of advice would you give to these teachers who are brand new to this process from what you've learned over the past four or five years?

JB: Well I think my first piece of advice would be that you have to come to terms with it in your own heart. And whatever you need to do in order to accomplish that, you need to do it. The students will be able to see that energy. They will be able to feel it. They will be able to know how you feel about it. So if you can come to terms with it, do a retreat, acupuncture, whatever it might be. [Laughter . . .] Seriously, though, I think the best way is by teachers talking. By teachers talking and looking at and asking themselves this question: How can we best prepare students for this component of their education? It is important. They may not particularly like the format, but that's not for us to decide.

So since we can't decide, we just accept it. I don't believe there's a single teacher out there in America that doesn't love when the lightbulb goes off above a student's head, and there are different ways to make that happen. So if teachers can take some time and have the support of their colleagues, their administrator and the school system, and we have had that, and it makes a big difference.

Interview Transcripts: Teachers

Sue Garcia
Crim Elementary School

Primary (K–3) Intervention Specialist

Eight Years of Teaching Experience

Twelve Years as a School Psychologist

Craig Mertler:	As you are well aware, there are teachers out there who really don't like standardized tests. Why do you think they don't like standardized tests?
Sue Garcia:	I think a lot of it has to do with the pressure that they feel for student achievement on those tests, and they sometimes need to abandon what they feel as good teaching strategies or effective instruction to make sure that kids are ready for those standardized tests. I think the standardized assessments have frustrated a lot of good teachers because they [are tempted to say], "Okay I know what I need to teach and I'll need to adjust this and do this but now I have this big time bomb that's ticking that changes the way they typically do things." And the emphasis on the standardized tests and that trickle down effect, you know, in order to be able go to third grade you have to do this in second grade and first grade instead of trusting curriculum and trusting teachers and intervention that it's all going to fall together. I know I get real crazy because of having kids with differing needs, trying to make sure that they understand the format because all of my students participate in all areas of those standardized assessments with accommodations. And sometimes you don't know exactly what accommodation a child is going to need until you've gone through it a few times.
CM:	That's what I hear a lot, which makes pretty good sense. It's the notion of the pressure and then the associated frustrations that goes along with that. Do you believe that it's important for teachers to know how to interpret standardized test data?
SG:	Yes. I do. At least enough to figure out what they can do in their own classroom to change that. To look at class data from DIBELS [Dynamic Indicators of Basic Literacy Skills] or to look at information from the [Ohio] achievement test and to be able to figure out that here's an area that kids didn't do well on. If I give an end of the level test and five of the six kids miss something, then that's not their problem. I didn't teach it right. So I need to come up with a different way

to say, "Okay we have to do this before we can move on." But I think I understand how to interpret test results and then how to turn that interpretation into what we do in the classroom—I think that's the part that's missing sometimes. I think teachers can look at that and say, "Oh, this group of kids didn't do well on context clues." For example, it's sometimes about the format of questions and I think that that's something that some really good teachers do is teach kids the format of the test, not only the content of the test.

CM: Test-taking strategies . . .

SG: Absolutely. I have eight third graders all with varying degrees of disability. When we worked on the third-grade reading achievement test, three of those students passed it on the first time in October. I was so excited. We started practicing and working on the format; for me it's more of a format issue. My kids don't know what to do with the question. They can get through some of the bits and pieces. But we had something—"What's a stupid answer." And we never used stupid in my room, but we were allowed to use stupid for this practice test and they actually learned how to cross out the bad answer, the stupid answer, or the tricky answer.

CM: That's my next question because it kind of builds on that. Do you think it's important for teachers to actually practice the interpretation? I mean, it's one thing to know how to do it; it's another thing to actually do it on a regular basis or once a year or however often you may do that. Do you think it's important for them to do that in light of this kind of information gathering we're talking about?

SG: I think they have to. I mean there's so much emphasis put on those achievement tests and to figure out how well we're teaching. But if they're not given the time and the opportunity to look through [the test results], I think the kids are not going to benefit. And they're going to be stuck in the rut. Now I've worked in I can't tell you how many different school districts and how many different buildings as a psychologist and as a teacher and I don't see that happening a lot.

CM: I'm going to get to something about your building in a minute too, but I think you're right. I think you've got a situation here that is somewhat unique in that for the most part, you've got a building-wide effort.

SG: Well, Martha affords me the opportunity to use my skills as a psychologist in a lot of different ways. But I have heard teachers say this makes more sense. Some of the things I found myself actually doing for teachers that first year and into that second year I don't have to do anymore. Teachers are now saying this is what I think I have to do on my own. So I think that that has been really good.

CM: But that speaks to a level of support across the building too. And that maybe teachers shouldn't feel that they're kind of in this alone; even though they're looking at their students' scores and what that teacher is doing in his or her classroom, it doesn't necessarily have to be confined to those four walls. You can go outside and look for some assistance and some alternative interpretations.

SG: And I think that happens. I've had to be in a unique position because I'm teaching first, second, and third. So I kind of know where they have to be, and this year if I look at my second-grade group and think, "Oh my goodness, that third-grade achievement test!" I have six kids on kind of a nonreader boat. So I'm thinking, "Okay, what do I need to do now so that when we get to that point, you've got a fighting chance of showing the state of Ohio what you really do know how to do," without getting muddy through the format and some of those other pieces.

CM: You obviously value the practice of interpreting test scores. Can you explain why you think then that, generally speaking, teachers should like standardized tests.

SG: I mean, I hate them. I understand the value of them. But I absolutely hate them. And I do understand their purpose. It doesn't make me like them any better.

CM: I use the term like very loosely. You value the importance of doing this. You think it provides important information, but you hate the idea of the test in general. So how do you resolve that conflict in yourself?

SG: I hate the idea of the test because I watch what it does to my students. I watch them for a week saying, "I hate learning. I can't do this. I know we practice Mrs. Garcia, but I mean . . ." I hate what it does to their little bodies. [I try to tell them,] "I'm here with you. If you're not learning it, it's not always your fault that you haven't learned it. I'm not doing my piece." I think the problem is it's just one of those hoops that you have to jump through as a teacher. And I think that's the part that teachers don't like about it. I think a good teacher isn't going to mind one more piece of evaluative [information]. But I think it's what those results are used for and how it reflects on one week of a child's life or one day of a child's life.

CM: How long ago did you personally begin this process of looking critically at students' standardized test scores?

SG: Not until I was a psychologist. I mean, the first five years I taught, in the late 80s or 90s, this wasn't there. You took the Iowa [Tests of Basic Skills] and life went on. What I know now as a psychologist, I get to do again as a teacher. I always wanted to go back to teaching again because I kept saying now I know all this other stuff. I need to get back in the classroom and meld those two pieces together.

CM: And the other stuff being . . . ?

SG: School psychology stuff. I'm a school psychologist who hated testing. I mean I think it provides valuable information, but it's only one piece of what a child knows or can do. So when I was able to work in districts in which I could look at all kinds of information on kids, that's when I really started to figure out what does this tell me about this child. What does this tell me about this teacher.

CM: I think you've hit on something there that [standardized testing] is just one source of information and they're not going away. What kind of support do you get in this process from your building principal?

SG: I get lots of support. I think she relies on me heavily to do some of the things that I do, some of those stats. I think I can deliver it to teachers, and I think my rapport with teachers is really good. Sometimes the packaging is real important, and you have to get teachers to look at data or do something with it.

CM: Can you kind of give me an overview of how you individually go through this process of looking at scores and using that information to make whatever various decisions you might use that information for?

SG: I think DIBELS is the one that I use the most because it's kind of longitudinal. I have emergent readers. I mean I have kids who are walking through the first-grade door and don't know all the letters of the alphabet. I think DIBELS helps me monitor their progress; and if I'm providing good instruction, then it's going to show up in some of those DIBELS scores. And I have found out this last quarter that when we didn't practice it three days a week like we were doing, some of those scores dropped. That tells me those kids didn't have that skill as well as I thought they did, so now we need to go back and review a little bit. But that's okay.

CM: But that's excellent because it's a decision that you're making from those test scores. So it's some information that you're using along with the other things that you see on a daily basis.

SG: I have to keep track of what the general education classroom is doing, so that if I have a student identified who I feel has made enough gains that can go back into one of those general groups, that can happen. And I think that progress monitoring through DIBELS has done that for me. We've had seven kids in first grade alone cycle through my class and back into a typical reading group.

CM: With all the responsibilities you have as a teacher, where do you find time to do this kind of stuff?

SG: At home. I do a fair amount of it at home, before school, you know if teachers come in after the DIBELS results come out, and everyone's flocking to my room, they say, "Okay, what am I doing here?" I used to do a lot of it, printing out of those reports and things for the teachers. And now they're saying, "Okay, remind me how to do that." So they're taking a lot of ownership for those pieces. Finding the time just happens.

CM: Let me ask you one last question. Imagine that you are sitting in a room full of teachers in a different district who are just going to begin this process. What kinds of advice would you have for them?

SG: Don't lose your own teacher instinct when you're looking at all this data because there's always a way to look at that data to help you quantify what your teacher instinct tells you. I mean teachers have really good instincts. I think that with all this data teachers are losing some of that ownership.

CM: That's very good. Excellent.

Interview Transcripts: Teachers

Amy Kenyon
Crim Elementary School

Teacher

First and Second Grade

Seven Years of Teaching Experience

Craig Mertler:	Admittedly, some teachers don't like standardized tests. Why do you think they don't like them?
Amy Kenyon:	I'll have a child who can't read but excels in math. If the student was identified, it would be documented that they have that discrepancy and you'd be able to help that child. But what about the one who doesn't have low enough scores that say he or she is LD [learning disabled]. They're right in the middle and their reading isn't as strong, and yet they have to read the math [items]. They have to read the science [items]. They have to read the social studies [items]. It's all a reading test. It's very hard to be able to sit down and say they can do social studies or they can't when everything's based on their reading.
CM:	Do you think that just serves as a source of frustration for teachers who have students that kind of fall into those categories of reading difficulty but not necessarily content difficulties?
AK:	Yes, exactly. I know that doesn't extend across all the grade levels. For instance, in first grade I can read the test to them. But second, third, fourth, etc., I cannot. The test booklet is huge; it's overwhelming to the students. And also I've heard among the fourth and sixth-grade teachers in the past if you're assessing math and you want to know if they can multiply, don't ask them to multiply and then graph, etc. . . . three different areas in one question. If you want to know if they can multiply, ask them multiplication.
CM:	Do you believe that it's important for teachers to know how to interpret standardized test scores?
AK:	Yes, because they do have some validity to them. They need to be able to build upon their weaknesses for each of the children. For example, when we look at test scores in the past and how we can help the kids and meet the building goals,

we have found that writing about their passages or writing about the math problems is an area of weakness; and so as a district goal, we want them to do more written work and interpretation.

CM: So let's build on that for a second. I ask you if you thought it was important for teachers to know how to interpret. Do you think it's important for them to actually practice, on a regular basis, the interpretation of test scores?

AK: I do because when you only do it once a year, it's easy to forget the details and the interpretations of the scores. Should I just look at the mean, do I look at the raw score, do I look at stanine score . . . ?

CM: You obviously value the practice of interpreting test scores. Can you talk a little bit more about why? Based on this notion of interpreting standardized test scores, can you explain to me why you think the teachers should like standardized tests.

AK: No, because I don't like them. Some of the test items are written above the grade level. And so that soured me from getting more into the test, not that I was very pleased with them anyway. But still, to find out that they were able to use words that are more difficult when they be able to decode them, it really just turned me sour.

CM: Well then it becomes, like you say, even more of a reading test in that situation. Now there seems to be a little bit of a conflict here because you tell me you don't like standardized tests, yet you do treat them with some level of importance . . . you value the information that you get from them. How do you resolve that conflict?

AK: Well, I understand the value of some testing. If they could keep it as a reading test that would test their reading and then science and social studies maybe could be more hands-on, it would not be such a level of frustration for the children. However, I understand you do need some testing. I just don't particularly like the way they set this one up. I know it's a work in progress. So that is how I resolve it. I understand that there is some validity to it, although I do not like how they base everything solely on that test.

CM: Speaking from a personal perspective, how long ago did you begin critically examining test scores?

AK: Well, looking at data . . . maybe seven years ago, but even more so with Martha coming in as a new principal. She is data driven 100% all the way. I think she has been here five years now.

CM: How did you begin that process? When it was first presented to you, how did you feel about it and how did you get started into it?

AK: I was very standoffish because again, that was a conflict with me and I just pushed it away and ignored it. However, with the staff meetings we were expected to bring the data. Martha really pushed it. She's my principal. I need to open my eyes and accept it. Not necessarily open my eyes, but I had to be more accepting of it and that's okay. I need to push aside my bias.

CM: What kind of support do you get from your principal?

AK: Tons. She loves data. She'll help us out if we're running out of ideas or we're frustrated. I can always go into her office and say, "Look, I don't know how to do this. How am I going to get this concept to my children?" She's there. She's there to support us.

CM: Do you think that type of support is critical to the process in this building?

AK: Yes. If you don't have that support, you almost want to give up because parents will see the support or lack thereof from the principal and they treat you accordingly. So if the principal doesn't value you, the parent doesn't value you, and then obviously that trickles down to the child.

CM: Good. Can you share with me how you individually go through this process of looking at your students' scores, taking that information and then being able to use it? What's the process that you individually go through?

AK: Okay, well you can go back to your question about the importance of reviewing regularly. I go through it once a year and so I don't use [achievement tests] per se to guide a lot of my instruction. At the beginning of the year, we have a staff meeting. We talk about the importance of building goals. We want 75% at proficiency or better. We're also looking for more written work in response to reading, math, problem solving, and the like. So those are goals specifically that I'm working on in the classroom that I have shared with the students as we review different tests that we do academically outside of the [achievement tests]. I also looked at the data that I have on [in-class] math [tests]. And that is what I really look at, interpret that data, looking at how well they understand the concepts. Do I need to go back and reteach? So I use test data but not the [achievement tests] 100% of the time.

CM: I think you've hit on a really key point and that is that standardized test data is just one source of information. You use it in conjunction with all the other sources of information that have about your children's academic performance. I think that's key because I don't think anybody's advocating to scrap everything that you're doing in the classroom and focus all on standardized test scores. Not at all. But it's one other piece of information and it sounds like that's how you treat that. When you look at reports that you get back on student performance, do you tend to focus more on the individual student reports, or do you look at your group reports, across your class?

AK: I look at the individual reports, and I basically look at are they low in the subject area. Are they like middle or are they high compared to most students? That gives me a little bit of a baseline. We looked at the data that we received from the [achievement tests] or that MAT8 and the OLSAT [The Otis-Lennon School Ability Test]. When we get those scores back we . . . compare for each test where each child is and then we group them accordingly. That gives us our baseline in order to build for each of the students. Every six weeks we give another reading test. In second grade it's every five. And we just build upon that data. And then in math, it's every three-four weeks they'll get a test depending on the speed and rate at which we are able to go through the lessons. So the [achievement tests are] really just a foundation.

CM: When you look at the reports, what types of scores do you focus on?

AK: I know the stanine is important. When we go through the identification process, we use the stanine that is reported.

CM: Okay. With all the responsibilities that you have as a classroom teacher, how do you find time to fit this in with everything else that you're doing?

AK: It's very difficult, and that's probably one of the reasons that I look at it at the beginning of the year. We meet with the building [staff] and say, okay these are goals, and then I honestly put the [achievement tests] aside.

CM: But you're using that as a basis at the beginning of the year for helping make a lot of decisions that you enter into the school year with as far as grouping students and curricular focus. Is that correct?

AK: Exactly. And then they're pushed aside as other testing that now is more recent, and I feel it really gives more of a true test of the students. In math, we have [math tests] that we can use daily and then we have the test to say okay does this make sense for this child.

CM: Do you think this type of professional activity helps you do your job better?

AK: Well, possibly. I use so much data that's outside of the standardized testing, but it's not the sole source of what makes me become a better teacher. I think it's a matter of being able to look at the everyday assessments, formal and informal assessments of the children, and further education is what makes me a better teacher.

CM: What kinds of advice would you give to teachers who are just beginning to start this kind of process of looking more closely at standardized test data? What would you tell them if you were sitting in a room with teachers in a building who were just beginning this process? What kinds of advice or experiences would you share with them?

AK: Standardized testing is a great tool [for some teachers] and they utilize it. They understand it. They utilize it monthly, weekly, whatever. So I would tell them to search it out for themselves and discover what works for them because it might be of importance to them especially at the beginning of the year in gathering data and finding out information individually about the children. They also need to do that with an understanding that it is accurate and reliable but there is still room for error . . . what is that term?

CM: The standard error of measurement?

AK: Thank you. Yes. There's still room for that. And so they need to understand that it's just not 100% for each child.

CM: That's very good advice.

Interview Transcripts: Teachers

Ellen Sharp
Crim Elementary School

Teacher

First and Second Grade

Twenty-Nine Years of Teaching Experience

Craig Mertler: In talking about standardized tests, as you well know, there are teachers who just absolutely despise standardized tests. Why do you think those teachers have a real dislike for standardized tests?

Ellen Sharp: I'm not a 100% sure, but I can't say that I love them with first and second graders. So, you know, within the first three weeks of school handing them a number #2 pencil and saying, "Welcome to first grade. For the next five mornings we're going to do this" is, I think, asking a lot of first graders. But I don't know if it's an accountability thing, perhaps indicating to them that they haven't done their job. For those kids who have difficult time taking tests, it's strenuous to try to run the day and get everybody on the same page and follow the directions. I always have questions about going too far with redirecting or trying to keep kids on task, and that kind of thing. So, but I do see its importance. I mean, so I can live through a week of it.

CM: Let's talk about that importance for a second. Two separate questions. The first one is, do you believe that it's important for teachers to have the knowledge about interpreting test scores?

ES: I think it's important. At the primary level, I found that it was more important to me with the students coming in as first graders who I knew nothing about, as opposed to the students who I lived with and come in as second graders because I know them. For me, what's interesting is that it was good to have that information. The information the kindergarten teacher sends along can be used to do some comparisons to see if we have a child who's overachieving or who's underachieving according to the standardized test. As a looping teacher with the second grade, it's nice to see if how you think you know the student in terms of those test results matches or if there are some gaps or some things that don't make sense to you to be able to take a look at what's going on.

CM: Since you value the practice of interpreting test scores and using that information, do you think that you could explain why you think that maybe more teachers should like standardized tests?

ES: Well, first of all, I think one of the reasons that I value it so easily is because I've worked 18 years in special education where the instruction for children revolved around tests, whether they were informal, standardized, or whatever. So I didn't know any other way to teach when I went from special ed. to general ed. other than to be assessing to find out what they know, what they don't know, and to individualize their instruction. The importance I think is that the data we get from assessment drives our instruction. I think that's what's difficult for a lot of general ed. teachers. Because especially those who have kind of been teaching for awhile, it seems as though they kind of have a set way of teaching, kind of teaching to the middle and not really individualizing their instruction. When you start forcing the issue that a child didn't do well on the test and rather than giving the reason that they don't have a lot to work with, it's their parents' fault, it means that maybe the way they're being instructed is not working for them and so you have to try something a little bit different for that child. Of course, that means more work, which means doing things differently than the way you've done them for the last maybe 5 or 10 years.

CM: That's a good point. That's a very good point.

ES: I think that here at Crim we've certainly done a lot of inservices about how that instruction can work differently and what that means.

CM: You hit on something with the inservices and the kinds of training that you've had to support this as somewhat of a school-wide effort. What kind of support do you get from your principal in this whole process as a building?

ES: Well, I think that Martha has currently given a lot of support in the area of DIBELS. I'm not sure that we could handle the DIBELS testing without her support and without Sue's. I think Sue is a real key player too. I think we have a great advantage of having on staff a special ed. teacher that has a psychology background. She's willing to do some extra things. I feel like without her support I don't think we could be where we are with it. It's just been part of our philosophy and the way that we have determined how to instruct in the first- and second-grade classrooms. I think we've always had a lot of information. More so than we might have had 10 years ago because that's kind of been our philosophy and the way we've approached it. I know that's not district wide. I mean, I know that's a philosophical kind of thing. We happen to all be on the same page philosophically.

CM: How do you think you all came to be philosophically aligned? Do you think it started that way? Four or five years ago? Or is that more of a growth process?

ES: When we went to the multi-age program, there were four of us, two of whom are not here now. Probably of the four of us, there were two of us who were on the bandwagon. And it was all based again on the fact that we weren't meeting kids' needs very well. We needed to do something different. Test scores didn't look good. And the students were not performing on that fourth-grade test the way that, of course, everybody wanted them to. At least we had two people who were willing to give it a go. And I think that sometimes maybe one or two of us did a little bit more of the leg work or more of the work to get the other two on board; but after a year or two, we were so thrilled with what we were doing and the good things that were happening made sense. And since we've replaced two teachers, you can kind of get a feel for whether or not you think those [new] teachers are where they need to be.

CM: Can you tell me a little bit about the process that you go through in terms of interpreting your students' test scores? How you actually do that, and then what you ultimately do with the information that you take off of those reports?

ES: And you're referring to the standardized tests, right? Because I don't do a whole lot with the standardized test at the first and second grade. What I interpret and really play around with are some of the other assessments that we do at the beginning of the year to determine groupings of students. When those scores come in, I take a look to see if their scores kind of match with where we've grouped them based on the informal assessments that we've done to kind of put them where they need to be. Now I will tell you that there was one child this year whose standardized test scores came back much, much higher than I would have ever expected because he has lots of behavior issues. He's not an identified student within special handicapping conditions, but his behavior was so bizarre that I really, truly did not know what was in there, you know, cognitively. Very bright. So immediately after seeing that test score and seeing that he had that kind of ability, I regrouped him. I put him into a different group because, I'm thinking, I'm not challenging this child enough; so does that mean the behavior occurs because I'm not challenging him; or if I challenge him, what differences will I see?

CM: Do you think that this type of professional activity, by that I mean being able to actually look at test scores, regardless of what kind of test they're coming from, helps you to do your job better?

ES: Yeah. I think it depends on whether or not I make the choice to change my instruction based on what the test gives me. If I still continue to teach to the whole class when I have a child that is falling behind or needs enhancement based on these scores, what good does it do? But if I make the choice to consciously and with a lot of effort try to change what I'm doing or gear it more towards the needs of the students, then I think it's very important. I don't think you have to spend hours and hours to do that. But I do think that in a general ed. classroom there are some things you can do that aren't real painful.

CM: Can you give an example?

ES: Well, one of the things that I do, that I think is real important, is to look at kids and group them according to their strengths. And they change constantly. I don't think that when we group kids, it's a grouping that stays all year long; and I think it's a different way of looking at your classroom; it's a different way of coming at it. But I think it really meets the needs of kids better than deciding that all these kids go here and all these kids go here, and that's the way it's going to be the whole year. The kids come and go from one group to another based on what their strengths, and that requires benchmarking, assessing, and knowing that it's time to move.

CM: I think everybody has said something about the fact that one of the things that all this process has either forced you to do or encouraged you to do is to look a little further outside your own classroom walls for ideas, for assistance, for collaboration. Not that you weren't doing that before, but that there's a maybe a little bit greater push to do that now from having more information upon which to base decisions about what do we need to do differently, how can we do it differently. We know we need to do something . . .

ES: Right.

CM: . . . but how do we do it, and how do we get there and so forth. Let me ask you one final question. Imagine that you were sitting in a room full of teachers from another district who are just getting ready to start this process of really looking closely at test scores for the same purposes that your staff has engaged in doing here. What kinds of advice would you give those teachers for whom this was going to be something brand new?

ES: Don't try to do it all in one year. Pick either a subject area or a test. Start with baby stuff. I mean you can't do it all. But if you can see the advantage of doing it with a subject area or with a particular test and really work to maximize that information and use it and really, really stay consistent to it for a year, then I think you can build on that, from year to year. And maybe you know, if you don't start with your whole class, maybe start with at least a group of students to track and to really use the test information. And I think the support, inservice, administration, etc., would need to come with that in terms of that group that's starting it. It's nice to have a really informed administrator and someone who can assist along the way and be well informed of what they're talking about. I think sometimes there are administrators who don't really know about the test or really how to have it benefit. So I think inservice for teachers is important. I think it's also probably important for principals or administrators to also get that inservice.

CM: But you didn't start it four or five years ago and then all of a sudden, after year one, everything's in place. And I think the perfect piece of evidence to support that is that you went from being a school that was rated as Continuous Improvement to a school that was rated as Effective to a school that is now rated as Excellent. That fact provides evidence that it's a building process that you are going through.

ES: Right. And I think it is important to a staff that's beginning something like this is that time needs to provided during the school day to reflect and to collaborate and [work with other teachers]. I think one of the most exciting things I had happen last year was that in the spring, we were able to gather the first-, second-, and third-grade teachers; break kids into classes for the following year; and to place them into classrooms based on how we could meet their needs as was being described on their DIBELS testing. We need the time to be able to do that, and so I think that those are the pieces that kind of make it, that fine tune the process, and I think that those are the things that sometimes just get shoved out of the way because there's not time to do it; so making the time available to be able to do that, I think is real important.

Interview Transcripts: Teachers

Cori Boos
Bowling Green High School

Mathematics Teacher

Algebra and Integrated Math

Five Years of Teaching Experience

Craig Mertler: As you well know, there are a lot of teachers out there that just despise everything to do with standardized tests. Why do you think they feel that way about standardized tests?

Cori Boos: I think that group of teachers that we're referring to are just kind of the older generation. I think they feel a lot of stress from it because they're going to have to not necessarily completely change, but they're going to have to adapt some of their instruction so that it matches the standards. And I think that pressures them and they feel like less of a professional because someone didn't believe that they were already doing it. I think they almost kind of get defensive about it, and the approach that they take is that it's just not worth it.

CM: Taking that into consideration, do you think it's important for teachers to have that knowledge of how to interpret standardized test scores?

CB: Oh, absolutely. First of all, the tests are not going to go away. A lot of people in that "I hate standardized testing" group think if they just ride it out, it'll all pass. And I truly don't think that that's going to be the case. It's just going to get more severe, and the testing's just going to grow. If they don't adapt, then they're going to miss the pieces that we need to also take into consideration. We should be teaching test taking as well as the material that they need to be taking the test on. And those two grouped together need to be part of the daily classroom.

CM: Is it also vitally important that they on a regular basis actually practice this interpretation of test scores?

CB: Yeah, I think that they should take into consideration in all of their assessments that they give the kids, that it kind of mimics the practice test; and I also think that if they look at data that we have available to us maybe based on some weak areas and concentrate more strongly on those, then hopefully the growth will come.

CM: Since you value the practice of interpreting standardized test scores and using that information, why would you argue that teachers should like standardized tests?

CB: Well it's only going to benefit the kids. I mean the more they stand behind what they're doing, the more benefit the kids are going to get. They'll reap the benefits. But if you stand up there and say, "Well, this is what I'm doing because this is what I'm supposed to be because you're going to have a test," you know, where's their trust? And it all trickles back to the fact that if they don't believe in what the state is doing, so why should the kids believe in passing the test?

CM: How long ago did you personally begin this process of looking at test data?

CB: Well, as far as the actual data that you got back from the test, probably three years ago. That was strong at the charter [school I used to teach at] because we didn't meet AYP there, and so there were some severe concerns of where we were headed and what we were going to do. I've spent time with Diane [the assistant principal] and they laid it out a lot nicer for you and a lot of the prep work is done and you're just handed the information, which is almost too easy. But even so, teachers kind of resist using it. As far as just adapting my lifestyle to the standardized testing era, since I only have five years in it was almost immediate. I got one year of teaching done, and then out came that blue book in math that said here's what you're going to teach. So I've actually redesigned two or three curriculums just in math in my short five years to align to the state standards.

CM: What kind of support do you feel that you get from your administrators in this building?

CB: That's what's going to be expected of us [here]. Now as far as the data, it's wonderful what Diane and Jeff [the principal] do as far as administrators. It's all done for us. They lay it out. And even with the practice test that ninth graders take, I helped her run all of the data analysis for it. We ran it through scantron, and we just handed it to the departments. And so again, it's not something that they have to go digging for, it's just naturally provided. "Here's the data. Please do something with it."

CM: How critical do you think that support is to the process of teachers being able to look critically at test scores and then use that information?

CB: Well I think it all goes back to what I said before, that it depends on the approach of the administrators. If the administrators also support the standardized tests and approach the staff with "this is why we're doing it, not because the state tells us, but because it's really going to benefit our school . . . It's going to benefit our kids and not because they're going to all pass the OGT, but because they're going to be smarter and they're going to be more successful in the real world." It's all about approach.

CM: Can you tell me briefly how you go through that process of looking at scores and then what you do with them? So in other words, you get score reports from your students in your math classes. Then what do you do with that information?

CB: Well, I use it to drive my instruction. For example, in our ninth-grade practice OGT that we took, if 38% missed this question, then it's not as important as the question that 62% missed. So maybe that topic is something I need to hit a little bit heavier. Since I'm new here and I teach both algebra and integrated math, my kids got shoved altogether as far as the data analysis. And next year I want to be sure to split those apart because I teach the classes differently. So it really didn't gauge for me exactly the numbers that I wanted to see. It didn't show as a whole; it put it altogether, but it didn't show in algebra what I didn't cover, and it didn't show in integrated what I didn't cover. It just showed weaknesses and strengths of both combined. And because they're covered at different times, next year I want to give a lot more attention to how that's run.

CM: With all the responsibilities that you have as a classroom teacher, where do you find time to do this extra stuff?

CB: I guess I don't really see it as extra stuff. I see it as part of my professional planning.

CM: Where do you think you would put this kind of activity on your professional list of priorities?

CB: Well, I think it has to come pretty high. I mean if you're not instructing what's going to be on the standardized tests in your lessons, then you're not preparing your kids. And that's my job professionally is to prepare my kids not only for the test but for the future, and they're directly related. I mean I can't do one without doing the other. If I don't use the data to drive my lessons to prepare my kids for the next step in their ventures, then I'm not doing my job.

CM: I think you've already answered this question, but I'll ask it again. Do you think that this type of activity helps you to do your job better?

CB: I do. I do. I think it gives me direction. I am not a book teacher at all. Currently, I'm working with a lot of book teachers. And they will say to me, "What do you mean? That's what the next page is. That's what's next." And I am not teaching that next because I can cut and paste in my mind and pull things from here and there and put it together and create units without a book. I can do that. Plus I spent two years at a charter school where we didn't have books. And I had to just pull resources from everywhere. And I taught the standards without a book. Amazingly enough people, some people, don't know that that could happen.

CM: That's the mind-set . . . that you're talking about, that's difficult for some people to change and look at it a little bit differently. I have one last question for you. Imagine that you are standing in a room full of teachers from another district, all of whom are new to this. The district has decided that they are going to start down this road of looking at test scores and trying to use that information to help them make decisions. And obviously some of those teachers are probably going to be apprehensive and some of them are going to be negative. What advice would you give to those teachers as you're standing in front of them?

CB: I would sell them first on the fact that it's not going to be very different from what they're already doing. It's just going to be maybe like something extra to drive their lesson plans. It's not something new. It's something to enhance what you already do, and that's kind of the thing where a lot of districts fall short in redesigning their curriculum, and it all kind of blew up in their faces because they thought that it was so brand new and so different and they didn't take the time to see that the standards were their curriculum. It just needed to be cut and pasted so that it fit into what they were already doing. And you have to take small steps with it. I don't think you can shove something down their throats right away and expect it to be successful.

Interview Transcripts: Teachers

Sara Caserta
Bowling Green High School
English Teacher
English 10 and College English
Seventeen Years of Teaching Experience

Megan Newlove
Bowling Green High School
English Teacher
English 9
Three Years of Teaching Experience

Craig Mertler: When you think about standardized testing, as you well know, there are lots of teachers out there who really dislike standardized tests. Why do you think that's true? Why do think teachers really have this just incredible dislike for everything to do with standardized tests?

Sara Caserta: I think the pressure it puts on the students and the fact that they're already under stress. I think it adds to that stress. [Standardized testing] may reveal things that we already knew. We already knew they were a low reader, then you put them through a crisis that just validated [the fact that] they're a low reader. We knew that going in.

Megan Newlove: Yeah. I think it puts a lot of pressure on the teachers and students. And sometimes I guess I feel this more than people who have been teaching for a longer period of time, but it just feels like there's so much I need to get in in a school year, along with all the testing. I feel like there's never enough time in the school year to get through everything that the state says we need to get through. But also you know as a teacher, you're a human being. You have things that you feel that are important; and maybe some of the things that you feel are really important that you'd like to be able to spend more time on, you can't do that because of the standards and because of the testing. There's just so much pressure placed on the district.

SC: So it might be like a creative project, where you don't have time to get it in that way. Whereas it might have been more fun, more complete for the student, now you just want to get through the information. We try to cover so much as opposed to the Japanese that decide to cover three things really well as opposed to twelve things like we do. We try to, as Megan said, cram in so much in such a short amount of time.

MN: I think that teachers who teach ninth grade and tenth grade at the high school really feel that pressure the most. It really is a lot of stress.

CM: You are the ones who, like it or not, have the primary responsibility of getting everybody ready for the Ohio Graduation Test (OGT).

MN: Right. And we take that seriously. We know what the Ohio state test is and what the consequences are for a student who doesn't pass. You care about the students and you want them to pass, and you want them to do well and to take it seriously, but you don't want to scare them to death; and so it's kind of hard to find a balance.

CM: Factoring in what you just told me about the downsides of standardized testing, do you think, and then why or why not, that it's important for teachers to know how to interpret standardized test scores, that they have the knowledge of how to do it?

SC: Oh yeah, I think it's invaluable. I think that because when you go through the data from the OGT, sometimes it will reveal maybe one aspect of one area that we're not hitting enough of. "Okay, we really need to focus on this particular area . . ."

MN: I guess the way I kind of look at it is, if we're going to [examine test scores], the situation is what it is. This is what we need to do and you can fight it or accept it and obviously we accept it. But I think when you analyze the data, it can be overwhelming at first too. Personally, I'm not a math person; but when you can learn how to analyze it and then going that next step further and learning how to apply that to your classroom, some of the things that when we [found with] our data analysis were very eye opening.

SC: And we were really happy with what we were doing; our data showed us that we were doing something right.

MN: So I think when you're sitting down and reevaluating where you need to go next, the data analysis does help because it shows where we were strong and then the areas that we really need to work on. And I think it helps with time management. I think it makes you more effective as a teacher because I know that my students do very well on vocabulary. If there's going to be a situation when I need more time, I know I can probably take some time away from vocabulary and spend more time over here on something that we did not do as well on. So that is very valuable.

CM: Do you think that there would be any other mechanism for having these "eye-opening experiences" that you've had when you've seen things revealed to you in your test scores, if you had not had the test scores to look at?

SC: I do diagnostics at the beginning of the year; most teachers do. You do a writing diagnostic. It's not perfect. I do a reading diagnostic. It's another window. Like I said earlier, a lot of times the OGT [scores] will come back and I'll say, "Okay I knew that about this student. It didn't tell me anything I didn't already know." Or sometimes I'll be surprised saying, "How did they pass that?"

CM: I think you hit on something that I argue in favor of all the time which is that test scores are not the answer to everything, but they are one additional piece of information that you take into consideration with everything else that you do whether it be an external type of assessment or diagnostics that you do, or if it's a unit test or if it's an informal writing assessment, or something like that. That's what helps paint the pictures that you get of your kids.

SC: Well, because a kid can have an off day.

CM: Sure. Since the two of you obviously have found some value in looking at students' test performance, why do you think then that teachers should like standardized tests? I use the term like very loosely here.

SC: It's another piece of data, although I'm not sure that it outweighs the stress associated with it.

MN: I think you can look at the standardized test as something that can be positive if you know how to analyze the data and you [practice] that. You sit down and you look at it, and you really put that into practice that you can, as a teacher, see some value in this. But for a teacher who wouldn't practice that, I think . . .

SC: Right, that it would be a [useless] exercise for them, I suppose.

MN: Right. The kids have to do it so let's try to make this as worthwhile as possible. How can we turn this thing that can be very frustrating into a tool that we can, you know, kind of use to make us better and to be more effective? If you look at it that way, I think it's [about] your attitude, how you view it, and what you decide as a teacher, you know, what you decide to do with the test scores.

SC: I think the student has to see value in it. You have to see value in it so the student sees value in it. What does this tell us about you? How can this help you? Otherwise, it was another purposeless test for them too. [In order to be effective] the student has to see a purpose in the data, the teacher has to see a purpose in the data, and the data has to be used.

MN: If found that fact really important in my class this year because we gave the ninth graders their practice test during OGT week. And you know I found as a teacher I really had to sell them on the idea that they were going to have to take these tests. And I really knew that if I didn't get them to try to take it seriously, that that data really wasn't going to be useful to us because if the kid blows the test off and leaves all the constructed responses blank because he doesn't feel like writing it out, what does that tell us? Nothing. So what I told my students was that this is important because it will give you an idea about how you might perform in the future on the test. It doesn't guarantee anything but at least it gives you an idea and of course it's important to us as your teachers, and administrators, and things like that. But it's important. If you're asking a student to sit down and to put that much time into a test, I think that student deserves the respect of, you know, here's why we're going to do it.

CM: Well, I'd like to compliment you on that because that's one of the biggest things that you read in testing literature, that there's got to be this positive motivational directive, if you will, that's coming from teacher to student because if the teacher doesn't buy into the test, there's no way you can expect your kids to buy into the test. And then what you end up with is an exercise in futility because the kids end up with scores that really don't mean anything. And you can't use them for anything. So in that sense, you have just wasted a week if not more if you factor in your prep time.

SC: And you're setting them up to be retested again. I always joke with my kids, "How many times are we taking this [test] guys?" "Once!" And it's all of that positive feedback. You can do it.

MN: We've had more dialogue going on between the ninth-grade teachers and the tenth-grade teachers. And I think that's very important, especially for [Grade] 9 teachers. And so we'll say, "Okay, I do that in [Grade] 10 or I'll make sure I spend more time on it." What can we do down in [Grade] 9 to maybe focus more on certain things so that when you get them they'll be better, stronger at this. And that helps.

CM: Prior to this process of looking at test scores and item analyses, would you have had this degree of collaboration?

SC: We used to do ninth-grade writing assessment, so there was a dialogue. It was only in the realm of writing, but we did have an excellent collaboration: talking about the data, utilizing the data for placement. Well where should these juniors go? Should they be taking college English? Should they be taking senior composition? Where should they go? And so it helped with placement and other things. But it opened up that dialogue for us. In a way, I guess the Ohio Graduation Test data has us working through this course of study that we're teaching now and has opened up the dialogue between us.

CM: What kind of support do you get for this process from your building level administrators?

SC: Our vice principal, Diane Tache, is . . . well, we call her Data Queen. [Laughter . . .] Every copy [of test reports] are provided. Every piece that you would need. I can't think of anything that [she doesn't provide]. There isn't anything left undone. She has come to our department [meetings]. We've gone through [the results] and we've selected out item numbers to analyze. "Okay, why didn't you do well on this or why would the kids maybe have missed such a good question," going back and looking at the question, analyzing how the question was set up. And it's been good. She's been very good at supporting that.

MN: I think she's done a great job letting us know what we need to do and then helping us, guiding us through the process. I really do think we have a tremendous amount of support from the administration here. As a new teacher, this could just be so overwhelming and scary, but I feel like we really are supported by the administration.

CM: Do you think that support is critical?

SC: Sometimes you need a tutorial just to go through what the numbers mean. Because everything's written in code by letter, by number, by plus sign, by minus sign, and so in a way you need to be led through the code. If you didn't lead teachers, I think, through the coded language of the data, I have a feeling that if you handed them the data, and I'm only guessing on this, that it would go in some drawer. I'm not necessarily so sure that they would be able to interpret the data to all that it might reveal without some kind of guided lead.

CM: I think if you don't have that knowledge of what all the symbols mean and how to make sense of them, it's overwhelming and it's just easier to say, "I'm going to worry about this another time. I don't have time to deal with this right now." And it goes in the [cumulative] folder and it goes in a filing cabinet and it never surfaces again.

MN: The other thing that was so important about what Diane did was she brought the English department together because we found with all these different sets of eyes looking at the data that you really see a lot more within the numbers. And people were saying, "Oh my gosh, look at this! Oh, look here."

SC: They would notice something in a question I hadn't noticed. Or, "No wonder why the kids said it was letter A because see they were looking at this." I wasn't maybe seeing it the way someone else was, and so I think not just interpreting the data, but then talking with one another, you know . . . more eyes, two eyes are not enough. You need multiple eyes to look at something.

MN: Right. I think that's a key part of that. That when the teachers do that stuff, they do it together. It really made a huge difference.

SC: And that requires time, resources, and money—and I realize that requires an enormous amount [of each]. For some districts that could be the end, right there—this is never going to happen. But if you want to make use of the data, you're going to have take the time and resources and the money to make it effective. Otherwise it's going to end up in a filing cabinet.

CM: So you see it as an investment.

SC: It is an investment. The problem with the investment though is that the test scores are going to come back in May. That's a bit of a problem because what's going to happen then is those teachers are going to say, well you're almost finished with these kids anyway. So I think there is only one missing piece—where that data needs to be moved to maybe the next teacher like whatever your failures are. What were they missing, and that would go to the next teacher. And that might be a kind of a nightmare. I don't know how you would do that, but let's say they failed the math test. Well those OGT math scores then from May I think should go to the teacher that they have next. They can analyze what it is that they need. I'm not sure that piece is happening yet. Now we give the ninth-grade [practice] test as she said, and many schools don't do that I'm finding out. And so we do it specifically because we want to know [and be able to report to the next teacher if they] had a really rough time.

MN: Giving a practice test takes a tremendous amount of time and effort on behalf of the department, especially I guess the English department because we had to grade all of the constructed response answers, so that takes time and effort.

CM: There's probably a huge issue of professionalism and you two value it enough to know that it's going to take us a lot of work and a lot of time to do this, but it's going to help us in the long run.

SC: And it helps our communication. That's one way it helps us to connect.

CM: Can you just kind of briefly walk me through the process that you use. So you get these test scores back . . . ?

MN: Diane actually prepared a folder for all of us. We had a data analysis meeting and the English Department sat in a circle. We sat down and Diane led us through the data. We looked at different charts and different graphs of the data and then we broke down the results with the test next to us so we saw, "Oh, on item 17 we see that the students, wow, they really struggled with that one." They struggled with this, so we need to spend more time on it.

SC: And I thought it was interesting that I got to see her explaining how they calculate AYP.

MN: That was interesting.

SC: That's kind of an administrative concern. It's really all of our concern, and I think I didn't see it as all of our concern until she explained how it is actually calculated. I had no idea on how that was really done.

CM: Do you think that this kind of professional activity helps you do your jobs better?

MN: I think anytime that you can sit down with other teachers and talk and really collaborate about anything, it makes you a better teacher. As a new teacher, I really take so much from the other colleagues who have more experience, and that's so valuable. We really value working together and talking. And a lot of times during the day you just don't get a chance. You know, you feel like you're kind of in your little cave of a classroom and then you're working, working, working, working, and then it's time to go home.

SC: There's always a new way of approaching something, and that's what I learn from the new teachers; and then I learn from even our student teachers in the building. I learn from them in watching them and getting ideas; otherwise, you're locked into how you've always done it. You have to continually be working and changing. And that's what the data can help you to do to some extent. It's kind of a reality check; it sounds cliché, but it is. I might need to find another method for doing something. I need to find something else.

CM: Last question for you. Imagine that you are standing in a room full of high school teachers from another district. They are getting ready to embark on this same kind of journey. They've never really looked at their OGT scores before, critically, to help guide anything that they do. They're going to start doing this. What kinds of advice would you give to those teachers if you were standing there in front of them, based on the experiences that you've had?

SC: I think I'd tell them to be open to trying, to learn from it. That it might be overwhelming, but that if you don't try, you're not gaining anything. The test is already here. It's not going to go away. As we know, more tests are on the way. It's not just the tenth-grade test. So since it is the reality that we live in right now, try to be part of shaping the reality and using it. Otherwise it's going to be a pointless activity, not only you, but also for your students. And it's a disservice to them, I think, not to try to analyze this data and make use of the data.

MN: I think it's about attitude. Teachers have a lot of resentment towards these tests because of the pressure that they've placed on the teachers. And when you resent something and you feel frustrated about something, it's easy for a teacher to say I don't want to do that. But it's about how you approach it. And you can accept it or not. We all need to accept it and deal with it. And if you really look at it as something that can be a really valuable tool and make you a better teacher, it's not a bad thing. That's a good thing. I guess the other thing I would add to what she said is I really do feel like when these teachers do this, it's something they should collaborate on. It shouldn't be something where a teacher is sitting at the edge of her desk, looking at the data and trying to make sense of it. It needs to be something that they do together.

Interview Transcripts: Teachers

Joe Hudok
Bowling Green High School
Social Studies Teacher

World and American History

Eight Years of Teaching Experience

Craig Mertler: When you think about standardized testing, as you well know, there are lots of teachers out there who just really don't like standardized testing. Why do you think that's the case for a lot of teachers?

Joe Hudok: The biggest reason I think, and this is just based on my own personal experiences with the people that I work, is we have a very professional but also a very, how can I put it, mature faculty. They've been here a long time. People hate change. And the thing I hear the most is, "I'm going to have to change the way I teach, and I don't want to have to change the way I teach. I'm not going to teach to the test or this is going to mess up what we've been doing for 20 years, 15 years." I think that's a huge reason. People just don't like to change what they've been doing. Another reason is I think that some people fear that they'll be tracked with numbers that come out of these tests and they'll somehow be a reflection on their performance as a teacher. I hear arguments all the time about well, you can't compare my class to so and so's class because they have an honors class and I have inclusion classes. Those are the two biggest reasons for me. I don't think it has much to do with not wanting to do extra work. I think it's just they feel that they are going to have to change, to things that they aren't comfortable doing.

CM: Taking that into consideration, the fact that a lot of teachers feel that way, do you think that it's important nonetheless for teachers to know how to interpret standardized test data?

JH: Absolutely. The biggest reason is we are being measured as a district and as a school. We always talk in departmental meetings about how we're not measuring you against this guy or this guy. But I do. I like to use the numbers to see how my kids did on this and that. I use the data we generated from the OGT test last year to see what areas did I not hit—what areas should I have stressed more—because it was real specific. And [you know], this isn't going away. And you better learn how to interpret [these scores] for yourself and use it to your benefit rather than just leaving it up other people's interpretations.

CM: Very good. So you value that process of interpreting standardized test scores. In light of that, why would you argue that teachers should like standardized tests? And I use the term like very loosely here.

JH: I'm kind of a stats junky. I like raw numbers that tell me how my kids did. I like to know that 95% of my kids passed this question or 85% of the kids in my classes passed their OGT. I think that's the biggest reason. It's not maybe the best measurement, and it certainly shouldn't be the only measurement. But it's a measurement of your effectiveness, based on the stuff they want the kids to know.

CM: How long ago did you begin really looking at test scores?

JH: I kind of got into it with the proficiencies with the ninth graders. The kids had taken tests as eighth graders and then the first couple of classes of freshman I had, the only kids I had taking the standardized test were kids that hadn't passed [in eighth grade]. And I got interested in it just to see what this kid could do any better based on this year's class. And then with the OGT, it became even more important because I needed to know if I was covering the things I'm supposed to cover. Are my kids getting it or do I need to change something about the way I'm doing it?

CM: What kind of support do you get in this process from your building level administration?

JH: Diane Tache is unbelievable. She's the OGT queen. She's got the coordination of the task and just her helping us get ready, whether it's workshops with people talking about writing to the task or for getting together as a department to talk about sequencing. And then with this distribution of the data that she gave us last year, she's been unbelievable in terms of supporting our efforts in trying to get these kids through these tests. I don't know how she could do a much better job than the one she's already doing.

CM: Do you think that's critical to you as teachers being able to do this?

JH: If Diane didn't drive the bus on this, I would think that the majority of my department wouldn't tow the line. I don't think they would get involved. I teach with some guys that are very professional and do a wonderful job, but they're not interested in this at all.

CM: Can you share with me how either you individually or your department actually goes through this process? So in other words, Diane gives you reports back from OGT or she gives you item analyses, things like that. What do you or what does your department do with that information from that point?

JH: We sat together as a department last year and at the beginning of this year. We went item by item through each of the test questions. What we really looked at mostly were the percentages of kids that passed each question. If there's an abnormal percentage of kids that didn't pass it, then we asked questions. Why?

Did we not get to this? Did we cover it differently? Was there an aspect of it that we left out? Do we even offer this at the high school? Do we offer it at the freshman and sophomore levels before they take this test? After the practice OGT, we ended up changing the entire sequence of our whole department. We had to switch some things around . . . we got rid of a course. We moved world history from the sophomore year to the freshman year and American history from the junior year to the sophomore year. So for us it changed completely what we do, or actually just maybe more than anything the sequence in what we do. Because the test is given in March, there were some things that we didn't get to until April-May; and we had to move these back to the front. I know for world history, specifically, we used to start at prehistory and then cover medieval times, and now we start at the Renaissance in week one and two and get going from there just to get everything in we need to get in. So it changed a lot of what we do.

CM: With all the responsibilities you have as a classroom teacher, how do you find time to do this on top of everything else?

JH: Diane and the administration has been really good as far as making time for this. We spent at least part of one day and then some other times during the school year where she'd get us a substitute, and we'd meet as a department. Otherwise, it'd be difficult. The way she presented the data was pretty easy to interpret for me anyway. We had a list of all of our kids, and we had a list of how they did on each of the different sections of the social studies component of the OGT; and it doesn't take too long to run through that and just to see, "I didn't cover that" or "Gee, I need to look at this." So I don't think it's a tremendous amount of time, but you definitely need to take some time and look at it.

CM: Where do you think this falls on your list of professional priorities?

JH: It's important. For me, [it affects] my day-to-day planning, and it also [affects] the individual needs of all my. The fact is these kids can't graduate from high school unless they pass this test. And that's pretty important to me and it's very important to them, so it's in my top ten. I don't know where it ranks specifically, but it's up there.

CM: Do you think that this type of activity has helped you to be able to do your job better?

JH: Absolutely. I didn't have to overhaul my whole style of teaching, but it made me more mindful of the things that are on this test. And I don't teach to the test. But I do tell students specifically, after I've taught a lesson I've taught for the last eight years, "In your notebooks, you can you highlight this. It's something that we know is going to be on the OGT." So I mean it's changed a little bit about what I do, but it doesn't drive it.

CM: Imagine that you are sitting in a room full of teachers from another district and this district is just getting ready to embark on this kind of venture. Teachers have never done it before. The administrators have never done it before. They think it's going to be worthwhile but the teachers are hesitant, some of the administration is hesitant. They're looking to you for some advice from somebody who's done it. What kind of advice would you give those teachers about this process?

JH: Standardized testing is never going to go away whether it's an OGT or [something else]. You've got to learn to interpret your results because your school is being judged by that. Just because we don't hold individual teachers accountable or measure them against the data, doesn't mean another district isn't going to. What I tell people is since we have to give the test and since your kids have to pass the test, why not use anything at your disposal that's going to help you help those kids. And this is a good tool. It's not the only tool, but it's a good tool because if you get good data and it's specific enough, you can tell how every single kid that you had performed on the geography component, the history component, etc. If you get an item-by-item analysis of each of the questions, you can tell that 50% of your kids failed this one or 25% of your kids failed that one. So I tell people to use it to their benefit and be happy. Embrace it because it's not something that's going to go away. Just find something that works for you. Find data that is useful for you and use it.

Interview Transcripts: Administrators

Martha Fether
Crim Elementary School
Principal
Twenty-Two Years of Experience in
Education (Six Years in Administration)

Craig Mertler: As you well know, some teachers—as well as some administrators—don't really like standardized tests. Why do you think they don't like standardized tests?

Martha Fether: I think because a lot of teachers today are, I would say, more in their 40s and 50s. Accountability really wasn't stressed [when they began teaching]. I was fortunate that I had a special ed. background, so of course we were always looking at IEPs [Individualized Education Plan] and looking at seeing where the kids were and looking at numbers. I don't think classroom teachers really have had the opportunity nor the training to really understand what standardized testing can do and can help them to become better teachers. The other part of it is that some people are nervous about accountability. You know, their complaint is that they are teaching to the test. Well, you're always teaching to a test, so I can't say that that's a good excuse. I think it's more about change—that it makes them more accountable.

CM: Do believe that it's important for teachers and administrators to know how to interpret standardized test scores?

MF: Yes, yes I do. I can remember when I first started out as an administrator having a teacher look at her achievement test scores in math and it was maybe 50% [passing] and a typical response was, "Oh, okay, I didn't do very well. Maybe next year I'll have a better class." I think it's important that they understand and look at each of the individual item analyses that really gets to the heart of what they are doing, why they are doing it, and if they are doing it correctly so as to make changes. I think we take it one step further here at Crim because we're not just looking at standardized testing, but we also look at Progress Monitoring [which is a portion of the DIBELS testing]. I feel this is equally if not more important because the standardized testing for us typically take place in the fall. Therefore, in the spring, we can do a pre- and posttest kind of analysis. The MAT8s are done in the fall [only] so it's not really a comparison [within the same] year. We're looking at what went on in third grade, how that looks in fourth grade, and so on and so forth. So I think that it's important that we look at the Progress Monitoring so that when we go to take those standardized testing we are ready to cover those areas that need to be covered.

CM: Do you also believe that it is important for both teachers and administrators to actually practice that interpretation of standardized test scores and why?

MF: Yes, I think that we look at the indicators which are supposed to go with bad achievement testing [scores], then I guess we are looking at that standardized testing on a daily basis. Looking at the numbers of the individual students though, that's where I feel the Progress Monitoring comes into place and that's still a way of looking at standardized testing. So I feel that the practice comes into play when we're taking those indicators, looking at where children are with those indicators, based on their previous testing so that we know that if Johnny did really poorly in the reading process, and then look at the item analysis to say that on this question we only got 20% right and it's on the reading process, maybe it's not just Johnny with the problem. We need to really address these issues and look at our indicators with that. So in a way, we actually practice it every day.

CM: Okay. That's exactly what I meant. Since you obviously value the idea of interpreting standardized test scores, can you explain why you believe that teachers should like standardized tests?

MF: Well, that's a good question, and here's the reason I say it's a good question. Having a special ed. background, I did things really different as a special ed. teacher. I was always looking at leveled books. I was always looking at the number of sight words they could get. I was looking at their math problems. So I was always a numbers person to begin with, which was a little bit different than most special ed. teachers that I've been with. I started that process and I felt it was important. Now this was before it really became vogue to really address where kids are at. My kids had to go back and look at their numbers. Every nine weeks we looked back and reflected on their writing, and we had portfolios that would we would check and say, "Wow, this is what I did. Look what I'm able to do now." I didn't look at it as a measure of somebody looking down on me if things didn't quite go right. I looked at it as a measure of this is what I need to do to improve. I think teachers are starting to gain the understanding; but again, it's that background. It's the education that they came up with that really they didn't address individual students. They [were taught to address] the whole class. I don't think we've done a good job as far as training, and I don't really see us still doing a very good job as I see the student teachers coming in and having conversations with them. We're still looking at the book and not really at the individual student. It's not something that somebody is judging you on, as if you're not doing a very good job. Let's do it smarter. Everybody's working hard, there's no question about that. But can we work smarter? Can we look at what the research says? Can we look at how we could do this differently? And so I think the teachers are getting there.

CM: That's all part of that mind-set.

MF: It is. It is a mind-set. Absolutely.

CM: What kind of support do you think that teachers need in this process?

MF: Time. Time, time, time . . . The problem that I see is that we have a week after the students are all gone in the summer and a week before the students come back in the fall. We have time to really look at data to make some important decisions. To have that time available where we're not interrupted; where they don't have to go make lesson plans up for somebody else to come and see their classroom; that they can sit down and really have good conversations. I've tried to build in collaboration time before school starts, so we could get our building goals together; we could look through the data; we could start to look at our needs for the kids so that the first day of school we're up and ready to go. We can't do that now because we don't have that time. Ideally, I would love to be able to have meetings twice a month where we can sit and not have students in the building and just have time to talk with teachers. So the biggest thing is time.

CM: Well, speaking of time, with all the responsibilities that you have as an administrator, where do you find the time to do this?

MF: As far as the looking over the data?

CM: Well, that aspect, but also finding the time to help organize your teachers. How do you make that work?

MF: Well, it's my top priority. During the summertime when I'm supposed to be on vacation [laughter . . .], I do a lot with the data. I put together a huge spreadsheet with all the MAT scores, all the DRAs [Developmental Reading Assessment], the DIBELS, for each of the grade levels, so it's kind of a longitudinal look at the children. And I get that organized in the summer, and then I send that out to the teachers, usually by July once we get all of the achievement test scores back. So I make it a top priority because I don't think you can go anyplace else unless you have that. I can't have a conversation with a teacher if I don't have that data with me. So I guess it's just a matter of prioritization.

CM: What do you do with reluctant teachers as far getting them to buy into this process as being a valuable educational one?

MF: Well, again when you have the data in front of you and it's pretty black and white, it's nothing that's going to be skewed from one view or the other. By making the time, it allows me to have more time, if that makes sense. So when I have students who have not shown progress, I can sit down with the teacher and say, "Look at where we're at. What are we going to do differently?" This building is a good building with good teachers. There are still teachers who are not doing what they should be doing and I think you're going to always find that. So what I try to do is involve a lot of teachers. And they have seen success with what the teachers are doing as far as the individualized attention that they're getting. I think that it's just kind of snowballing. When we started out at the Continuous Improvement level, I found that once a child was nonproficient he or she stayed right there. It never changed. So if we had a good class, we did well. We had a bad class, we did poorly. And so, the tough part was trying to get them to realize that we don't need [to do it this way]. So once we got that, our scores started to go up and as you can see I have charts all around the building because they need to see and the kids need to see that's how we're doing. That's when they bought into it heavily. And then when we went from Continuous Improvement to Effective, and then last year we went to Excellent. They bought into it . . . boy did they buy into it. But it's taken five years. And we're not there yet, but we're close.

CM: But I think that's important for people to see too, that this is not something that is going to necessarily give you the kinds of results that you're looking for overnight, but rather from one school year to the next school. It's a process.

MF: Right.

CM: Imagine that you're sitting in front of a large group of teachers from another district just getting ready to embark on this journey of looking at test scores and that kind of thing. What advice would you give those teachers?

MF: Well, I think you have to first and foremost tell them that it's a philosophy. Anything in education is a philosophy. The thing I would want them to know that this is a changed way of thinking. The data speaks for itself. We're going to have achievement testing, so that's not an issue; the crucial aspect is that progress monitoring piece. [Teachers need] to embrace data, and realize not that it's going to make you look bad, but it's going to make you say, "Okay, what can I do differently that I wasn't doing before with this child." So that's where the philosophy comes into play that data truly is my friend, as I tell them. . . . Now, we're actually family—it's not just friends, it's family here. And getting them to understand how important that is. The bottom line is with No Child Left Behind, we don't have a choice. You have to change. Your choice is how you want to change. It's not enough to look at the whole class. You have to look at each individual child and make sure that that child gets what they need. And I'll give a good example. We had a third grader last year. She improved on her reading achievement test by 70 points. She didn't pass it. That's a [negative reflection] on us, but what a gain! We celebrated that gain just as much as we did for those children who passed. It's not just about getting children to be proficient. It's also looking at those huge gains and congratulating people and making them feel good. And the students feel good. It's amazing.

CM: It's a change of mind-set. It's about getting teachers to see the value and maybe change their philosophy a little bit.

MF: Well, it's really no different than with children. With children, you need to build upon their success so you start at the low end. You're going to have teachers who are starting at that low end and you need to just compliment them as they're making changes. So it's taking those small steps and understanding that everybody embraces change differently. You know, it's a perception. But the biggest thing that I think that scares teachers is that they feel that the numbers are showing that they're not a good teacher. That's the mind-set . . . not to take it personally that someone's going to come down and say you're a bad teacher. I define bad teachers as being teachers who will not look at their data and will not make changes based on that data and to try something that is different that's going to make that child successful. And there's a big difference between those two perceptions of bad teachers.

Interview Transcripts: Administrators

Diane Tache
Bowling Green High School
Assistant Principal
Twenty-Seven Years of Experience in
Education (Thirteen Years
in Administration)

Craig Mertler: As you well know, there are a lot of teachers that do not like standardized testing. Why do you think that is? Why do you think that there are teachers that just are negative about standardized testing?

Diane Tache: Many years ago, a lot of teachers went into education for the freedom to be able to do whatever they wanted and be creative with whatever they wanted to do. So a lot of times you will have teachers, especially in the elementary level, they have very special interests. And they bring those interests into the classroom. With accountability and standardized testing, that world has to be realigned a little bit. And it doesn't have to mean that the creativity goes away, it just has to be realigned. But, for example, for teachers who have been used to teaching [units on] dinosaurs for five years in a row and you tell [them] that dinosaurs is not covered at their level and needs to go somewhere else, it sometimes creates a real tough task for teachers to be able to either hand off what they love to teach and also have to make new plans to change on a yearly basis. The other thing I think with teachers is that we've never had to be totally accountable at a certain grade level, at a certain moment in time. You know, the final product is that the student receives a diploma at the end of the year. They graduate from twelfth grade and that pretty much signifies everything they've done K through 12. Now, with the different levels of standardized testing, it's taking a new look because every year with accountability and testing, teachers are having to really do more self-reflection of what they've done, how they've changed instruction to meet student needs, and then what the outcome, through data, actually shows.

CM: Why do you think it's important for teachers and administrators alike to know how to interpret test scores and also actually practice that interpretation of scores?

DT: I think it's important because oftentimes when we were looking at curriculum and things like that, again, teachers teach what they learned about, what they were good at. And it could have been all over the board in terms of what students were coming out of their classrooms with, but by having the data and being accountable for a certain amount and coverage of content at your grade level, it provided some standardization, which we desperately needed in education. It also allowed teachers to be able to see the assessment piece on a larger scale. One of the weakest areas when we evaluate teachers is their daily assessment of whether or not students learned what you had set out for them to do and what they're still weak in that you need to revisit the next day or the next week. A final standardized assessment also helps teachers to think twice about it. If you think about curriculums from years gone by, you'll see that dinosaur theme over and over again. And if you ask students even what kinds of things have you learned every single year in math or in reading, they'll tell you. It's year after year after year, so when you have a curriculum that has some accountability and actually has some benchmarks and standards, then everybody begins on one page. Over and over in math classes both elementary and middle school you'll see that data analysis and probability, for example, are always the last chapters in the book. You can ask every student that has gone through that, have you ever gotten to these chapters? The answer will be no. Now with accountability, you've got teachers thinking it through, thinking smarter, saying, "Okay, I need to get through this material so I need to do curriculum map to make sure I do." And so they end up working smarter but not harder.

CM: Since you obviously value this practice of looking critically at test performance, why would you argue then that teachers should like standardized tests?

DT: As an educator, you want students to be able to walk out with a diploma that means something. All students need to have certain skills when they leave— math skills, reading skills, writing skills, communication skills, etc. However, in years gone by, the level of those skills could be everything from very very minimal to accelerated and beyond. I think it's time for a target, and I think teachers should want a target because teachers want to do good things. And if they can see that they are really making a difference, then I think as professionals they will continue to seek out other strategies to continue to improve in those areas. So that's why I think all teachers need to look at data and embrace it, and say, "How can I do a better job for students? How can I make sure that the students coming out of our school are competent in those areas?"

CM: How long ago did you personally begin the process of looking at standardized tests scores and how did you begin that process?

DT: It was the craziest thing. I was principal in [another district] in one of the schools and I was asked to go over to the elementary building to be the principal in a school that had not had good scores on their proficiency tests for a couple of years. They were really in dire straits. In addition, the district was not where the district superintendent thought we ought to be. We had a meeting, a summer retreat, and one of the things that came up was the goal, and I quote, "Proficiency, proficiency, proficiency." So when I got to the elementary building, the scores from the previous administration had just rolled in. Oh my . . . I'm a science teacher by background, so I'm into data, numbers, and things and like that. So I started to play around with it one summer, just to see. In addition, the [previous versions of] tests go online. Okay, well it makes sense to me that if you're going to fix a problem we've got to know what the problem is first. I took the tests, starting with math, to see what we were doing. Sure enough, there is a probability, data analysis, measurement section. [The students] were doing horrible things in that area. I started to share that with a few teachers, and some of them were very intrigued by it. And so I said, "Well, I think one of the things in professional development that we should consider is hiring some subs, taking the teachers out of their classroom," because we tried it after school and that was a disaster. It was boring. But, my fourth-grade teachers, my third-grade teachers, my fifth-grade teachers were very, very interested because they saw where this whole thing was going back to. So we pulled them out, got subs for them, got them some food, and I did a little rendition to convince people to look at this. It was amazing. I started them off. They took the bull by the horns, and they were intrigued. They wanted to see those test questions. They wanted to see how kids answered them. They got to the point of being able to identify strategies. So that's how that got started, and I did it for Bowling Green City Schools as a guest speaker for the administrators. But they weren't really buying into it yet. But after a five-year stint in my previous district doing it, we went from meeting maybe one indicator to meeting all five year after year after year because we came right back with the data.

CM: What kind of support do you believe that teachers need in this process, and how critical is that support?

DT: It is vital because you can show them data, but if they really don't want to buy into it, and sometimes having that district report card, even though some people really are offended by the fact that we have to be graded, plays on teachers' minds because teachers want to do good and they want their students to do well. So it's very visible for them and they want to do well. But then you've got to be able to teach them how to do it. Believe me, sitting with eight math teachers who have had 25 plus years of experience, they're not real thrilled about having to take a half a day away from their algebra II class and have a sub to come in and sit with me; but as people started to really look at that data, what has happened is that they've started to see some things that need to be fixed. And also what we have to do is say, "Okay, do you have some ideas on how to fix it? Okay, what's it going to cost in terms of support materials?" And that was one of the first things that we did was after we saw some issues and did some realignment in social studies, for example, we had to get some new materials for them. Professional development kinds of things that were out there . . . we encouraged people to go. We want teachers to learn—that's a key component. But what are you going to do when they do learn? Because if you're not willing to back it up with what they as teachers and the diagnostic people say we need to have, then it's going to go nowhere. It's kind of like going to a doctor and the doctor says you need surgery. But, "Oh by the way, we don't have the instruments to do that surgery, so just go on back and just deal with it," and the same with teachers. You've got to be able to support them with what they want to try and do and then continue that over and over so that it becomes second nature. Now after three years of doing data, I don't even have to convince them about coming down and taking a half day to do this. I just sign it up and they just come. So it's part of our culture now.

CM: With all the responsibilities that you have as an administrator, where do you find time to do this?

DT: It's got to be top priority. Testing and accountability are here. They're not going to go away, so we need to embrace it and go. Now that I've got the teachers on board, it's a real easy one. I get things prepared. On July 1, those tests are online. First thing I do is I have those ready to go so that the teachers could actually start using them in the classroom. As soon as the final data comes, I will go ahead and get that stuff ready to go and get them in here to do it. You've got to have a belief that it works and I've seen it work.

CM: How do you deal with reluctant teachers if they don't really buy into this process you have? What do you do in that situation?

DT: We still a few of those yet. We have some experienced teachers who have always done it this way. "I only have a couple more years to retirement, so I'm going to continue to do what I've always done." One of the things that came up last year for the first time was individual teacher results. And you know our principal and I looked at that and I even told them, "We're not judging you, because we don't have time to do that. We're looking at the big picture, not the individual." But I gave every teacher their copy, only for them to see. For some of them, you could see that that self-reflection was starting to kick in when they're seeing the district had 75% pass that item and the rate in their class was at 55. If you believe that your teachers are professional, they'll do it on their own. A few of them would come in and chat privately about ideas. And we told them up front, we weren't looking at that in terms of the evaluative process or that it we're going to get on your case about it. It's for you to do some self-reflection. And if you go in there with a nonthreatening approach that that's what you want them to do, good teachers will take it upon themselves to do what they have to do.

CM: One last question. You've had this happen so you kind of can speak from direct experience. But imagine that a couple of years down the road, you're standing in a room full of teachers and/or administrators from another district, brand new to this process. They've decided they're going to embark on this journey. There's a lot of apprehension. There's a lot of reluctance. There's some excitement. What advice do you give to those educators sitting in front of you?

DT: What I would say to them is let me come over and do a session with some of your teachers and let me show you how they can get as excited. How to work smarter . . . . How to develop instructional strategies collaboratively. One of the things that we did at the elementary level from the beginning is, "Okay, if I'm doing measurement, I want that art teacher and that phys. ed. teacher and even that music teacher to work with fractions, to do some of the same things when I'm doing it." You get that interdisciplinary approach, and then it works so well in the elementary building. But when you see teachers buying into that, they're going to go with it and they're going to be excited about it because somebody has the answer. You can show teachers what's wrong, and you can rant and rave; but if you don't offer and provide them a pathway for a solution, it's not going to change. When I came to Bowling Green, they weren't ready to because they weren't at crisis state. Now everyone's at crisis state. So they're all looking for a diagnosis and a solution. I think people are getting smarter about it. So administrators have to be curriculum focused because if they're managers, they're not going to get the job done as well as those that are into instructional leadership for change. If they're managers, it's not going to happen because it's not in part of their culture of importance. So that's what you have to do. You've got to get them in a crisis state where we've got to do something. And, honestly, AYP is pushing that envelope.

CM: AYP has put everybody in some sort of crisis state . . . this year, next year, the year after . . .

DT: Right, it's coming to a school near you!

Interview Transcripts: Administrators

Kathy Zachel
Bowling Green City Schools
District Assistant Superintendent
Thirty-Seven Years of Experience in
Education (Twenty-Nine Years in
Administration)

Craig Mertler: As you're well aware, there are a lot of teachers out there as well as administrators who just despise everything there is to do with standardized testing. Why do you think that's the case for those individuals?

Kathy Zachel: I think it's because they don't understand what the purpose of testing is. I think it's because they feel that testing has been put upon them and they have not been taught how to see testing as a tool. Granted, just like anything else, it's not a perfect tool. Nothing's a perfect tool in our profession. But it's a tool. And it can give you a lot of information if you know how to dig the information out of the results.

CM: Why do you believe that it's important for teachers as well as administrators to have the knowledge about interpreting standardized test scores, not necessarily to do it yet, but just why do you think it's important for them to have an understanding of how to do that?

KZ: I have a strong belief that assessment drives instruction. That's a deep philosophical belief of mine because I believe unless we really know what the strengths and weaknesses of our students are, that it's impossible to deliver the instruction that is necessary to help our students to be able to achieve at the next level. So I think if we don't give enough attention to the test—if we just sort of get the test, give the test, don't use the data, and throw the test scores in a drawer—that it serves no purpose. It's an exercise in futility.

CM: Some people would interpret your comment about assessment driving instruction, probably not the way that you intend it to be interpreted. Can you explain what you mean when you say "assessment drives instruction"?

KZ: When I say assessment drives instruction, what I believe is that if we really want to have students learn what it is that we're trying to teach them, we've got to know what they already know about a subject or what they don't know about a subject.

We've got to know how they learn and what their strengths are in terms of the learning process because if we don't know that basic information . . . Let me put it like this, if I'm not an auditory learner and someone's standing up there telling me everything about the civil war, I may never get it. Whereas if I'm a real visual person and I read it, maybe I'll get a lot out of it, but still might not get the whole piece, as much as if I would use several modalities. So I guess I just believe that if we really want kids to learn what it is we're trying to teach them, we've got to really know how they learn and what they already know before we start—otherwise, we're spinning our wheels.

CM: Why do you think it's important for teachers as well as administrators to actually practice this notion of critically looking at standardized test data?

KZ: I guess it's because we believe that all kids can learn. We have said that. I mean when I started Teacher's College in the mid-60s, that was the mantra and at that time, individualized instruction was the name of the game. Everyone had to have an individualized plan. So I guess that was the influence. During my first couple of years of teaching in inner city schools, I had to try to adjust teaching strategies to meet a wide variety of needs; I couldn't do it as a group. I guess it just made me really focus in on what they already knew because we had to build on what they already knew; otherwise, they'd get bored.

CM: Based on your belief in terms of the potential value of standardized test scores, can you explain why you believe that teachers should like standardized tests?

KZ: I think they should like it from the standpoint that it's a way at getting additional pieces of information about a student. I think any time that we can have another little piece of the puzzle, if you will, it's helpful. And again I think you have to be careful because if you're only counting on one instrument, that's not going to cut it because you can make some false judgments. But if you have several pieces of information and you're looking at different facets of the child's learning styles and learning abilities, you could start putting together a little picture, especially if you look at it over time.

CM: How long ago did you personally begin the process of critically looking at students' standardized test scores?

KZ: Probably about 10 years ago, in the mid-90s. I started looking at it a little bit differently and really got to concentrate where I really would start digging, digging, digging, and making all the graphs and charts and things. It was just sort of one of those things that evolved. The literature was also helping me think about that because I read a lot in professional journals, and I was reading about [examining test scores]. So I started asking questions and started hearing people talk about it at meetings, not a lot mind you. I would honestly say that it's become the hot topic now. In the last three years I've heard more about it than I ever heard in the last 10.

CM: What kind of support do you think that teachers and building-level administrators need in this process?

KZ: I think first of all, they need to know that they can do it. I think they need to feel confident. I think a lot of times people feel like, "Oh, I don't know anything about statistics. I don't know anything about this stuff. Oh, no, don't ask me to do that." I think they need to be shown that it's not as hard and it's not nearly as complex an activity as they would believe it is. I think they need to break down some of those barriers. Second, I think they just simply need to be shown—and they need to see some modeling of it—how it's done and how it can be done efficiently. And then third, taking it a step further, is showing them how it really fits into actual practice. How do you use this? So you've got all these numbers and you've made these graphs, so what does it mean and how are you going to gear your instruction now? What does that mean for instruction? Of course, each of those steps has a lot of smaller components.

CM: Do you think that this kind of support is critical to teachers being successful in doing this?

KZ: I think so. I think if they're missing the support, they're going to shy away from it and they're going to put it off. You can mandate all you want, but it's not going to happen. I mean it's just that you've got to get down there with them and show them how this works and what it all looks like. I think if they see it and you show them and give them some examples, it really helps them immensely. If they can see it and understand how to use it, they'll use it. For example, with DIBELS, that's one of the things that's so powerful because you see *exactly* where the weaknesses are in that sound-letter relationship. You say, "Oh, wow, I need to work more on getting the kids to understand that letters and sounds are connected." How they do that then is up to their own creative venue.

CM: How do you provide that kind of support from the district level to the teachers in the individual buildings?

KZ: One way is to bring in someone from the outside. Other times it would be just simply working with the building principal first, and then maybe getting the building principal and a couple teachers from the building on board, then having them go back and teach their colleagues, and then being available for consulting. Sending people to conferences is another way. I mean, sometimes with a lot of these ideas you're an expert 50 miles away from home, but not in your own backyard, so sometimes it's necessary to have people go out. Other things I've tried along the way is having people go see other people who are doing it. Sometimes that goes over better than saying, "Well, professor so-and-so says this and that . . ." "Well that might be fine, but do they really know the constraints of my job?" You've got to find what works. Each group of teachers, each group of administrators, each school district, has its own little profile. Here we found that it worked having someone come in, talk to a whole group of teachers and administrators, and then from there we did some work with individual building principals and then from there it went to the teaching staffs. We went back and worked with building principals and teaching staffs together and it's taking hold. Now, I'm the first to say that in some buildings it's caught on more than in others, but that's the way it is. But everyone in this district understands. Whether or not they buy into it and actually do the examination of the scores, they know that data is important.

CM: You talked a lot about working with groups of administrators, administrators working with groups of teachers, groups of teachers coming back and working with the entire staff. Do you think that collaboration is an important part of this process?

KZ: Oh yeah, I think it's real important because I think if you say, "Okay, we have these 400 kids in our schools that we've tested and we have to start looking at their data." Well, looking at 400 test scores can be a pretty daunting task if you will, especially if you're looking at a lot of different factors. So if people within a building can work on things together, if first-grade teachers only work on the first-grade tests, and second-grade teachers work on the second-grade tests, etc., it just makes it a smaller chunk. I think whenever you can chunk things out and you're also talking to your colleagues, someone may see things a little bit differently and have a different take on it, then some conversation starts. You gain a better understanding and deeper insight when you do it together. If you're doing it by yourself, it becomes a pretty tedious task.

CM: With all the responsibilities that you have as an administrator, where do you find the time to do this kind of thing, especially in light of the example that you just gave? In other words, where on your list of professional priorities do you think that this kind of activity falls?

KZ: Well, I really value this activity. Unfortunately, I find myself always putting it off to summer. Even though we give some achievement tests in the fall and even though we give our state achievement tests in the spring, I can't really do anything until summer. It's even becoming difficult to do it then. But I still have been able to manage to keep up with it in the summer. Now how that transpires down the road, I don't know as we get more and more tests. If push comes to shove I mean I could probably even do it at the end of the day or come in early. I'd just make it a point.

CM: How do you deal with teachers or administrators who are reluctant and have a hard time buying into the process?

KZ: Keep talking to them. I talk their ears off. Give them articles to read—because I read so much—and I keep on trying to convince them. I try to show them examples. I can honestly say there have been a couple of people in the process of doing this that haven't budged one inch, and I'm not going to change them. There are a lot of other variables that play into that. But for the most part, I've been pretty successful. At least they'll hear me out; and even if they don't want to get involved, they'll let me have access to a couple of staff members and I can work that way. But the other part of it is that the teachers who aren't on board are feeling a little bit embarrassed by the fact that they don't know about this stuff and so they're sort of saying, "Where'd you learn about that?"

CM: They're in the minority now . . .

KZ: Yes. Oh, they're a definite minority. They're saying to other teachers, "How did you do that?" I've seen those conversations take place. I noticed that when we've had grade level meetings, they actually talk about this stuff, so I know it's coming along. Sometimes it's so hard to see the forest through the trees because it's been such a slow process. Just because you bring someone in or you have a presentation, this doesn't happen overnight. It's been a slow process. This is six years of working here in this district to get [where we are now], and now I think in the last year and a half I've seen the buy-in. It's coming around.

CM: I think you bring up another very good point that this is not an overnight or one-year kind of process where you get everybody up to speed and you're off and running. It really does take several years to kind of get it to a point where it becomes a district-wide kind of effort.

KZ: Well, we started off with a motto during my first year of getting this district to move in this direction. That phrase was, "Data is our friend." And I had pink neon slips posted in every principal's office, gave them to every team leader, every grade level chair, every department chair . . . "Data is our friend." Then I started talking about it and tried to show them examples. Then we had some interest [and we did some inservice sessions]. Then I hit them with another phrase the next year . . . "Assessment drives instruction." Then we worked on that piece in conjunction with the data. We brought in some curricular changes and new instructional materials that were meeting the content standards and doing all of the work that needed to be done to get in line with the state standards. Our next year after that was, "Focus on the goal." And we kept stressing that to keep them focused. Remember, don't let all of this stuff get in the way. Keep in mind what your goal is. Your goal is student learning. What do you have to do to get to student learning? Then, this past year, our motto has been, "Refine, refocus, reflect." And, honestly, I'm going to use that again because we're still not there. I think there are some things that we still need to do from a curricular standpoint to refine our instructional delivery. I think we need to refocus our efforts on some of these students who are still having somes difficulty, and then we need to reflect. We need to really bring in that reflection piece where we think about what has really worked for us, what hasn't worked for us. If something has worked, why has it worked? If something hasn't worked, why hasn't it worked?

CM: Last couple of questions. I want you to imagine that you're standing in a room in front of a bunch of teachers from another district who have never done this before but they're getting ready to really begin to look hard and critically at their students' standardized test scores. What kinds of advice would you give to those teachers?

KZ: First of all, I'd say start slowly. Don't try to do too much too fast. Number two, I think I'd say try to understand that the reason you're doing this is to enhance your students' learning. Understand that it's related to student achievement and student learning. That's the whole reason you're doing this. And number three is also to understand that you may find some things that you're going to have to change along the way and that may be a little unpleasant because you think you've been doing things the right way, but the reality is that when you really look at what the numbers and what the data say, you may have had a false perception about what was going on in your classroom. You really need to think about what those numbers are saying to you. I would also encourage people find others who are doing this and visit them and talk with them. If you haven't done this, there are a lot of people who have become very good at it and they're practitioners just like you are. So go talk to them.

CM:　Now you leave that room. You go to another room down the hall and in that room are building and district-level administrators. What advice do you give to that group of people?

KZ:　I think that, first of all, they have to commit to the process. In other words, they have to understand what the process is. It's fine to have building principals leading the charge; but if the people in central office have no clue about what this is all about, it's not going to fly in the long run because it has to be a district effort, especially in smaller districts. It may be in the urban districts where you have a 100 schools, you could have little pockets and people can do this on their own. But in the smaller school districts, central office definitely has got to understand the process. And if they're not going to buy into it, then they've got to stay out of the way but at least support the effort. I think the other thing is, if they're really interested, they need to be careful not to dominate the discussions. They need to let the teachers and the principals come to their own realizations. What I mean is you could have an administrator who might, for example, be a test coordinator that is a wiz at understanding all of this stuff. But he or she cannot become the dominating force because it's got to come from the buildings. If the building [staff] don't buy into it, if it's coming from up above, it's just not going to fly as well as when you have it coming from the grass roots. Also, I think they have to understand that it's going to take time. You can't say, "Okay, I'm coming into this district as the new superintendent. This has never been done and, by June, I want everyone to be buying into this process." Doesn't work like that.

Interview Transcripts: Administrators

Hugh Caumartin
Bowling Green City Schools
District Superintendent
Thirty Years of Experience in Education
(Eighteen Years in Administration)

Craig Mertler:	As you well know, there are a lot of teachers and a lot of administrators who just absolutely despise everything there is to do with standardized testing. Why do think those individuals feel that way about standardized testing?
Hugh Caumartin:	We're making a great transition right now in the area of teaching. I remember talking to a gentleman who was the director of a library when libraries were going through this tremendous change—librarians being the gatekeepers of all knowledge to the computerized, Internet world. Instead of being the gatekeepers, they were now expected to teach people how to be their own gatekeepers and how to access information that only they could give out in the past. The battle within the library industry was very difficult because the librarians just had a very difficult time making that transition. I think there's a similar phenomenon going on in education right now because teachers are going from what was considered the art of teaching to much more of a science of teaching. And that's not to say that there still isn't significant amount of art. A good teacher is an artful teacher. But right now, given all that we're faced with—No Child Left Behind, state requirements, the tremendous diversity that we are now realizing in the general ed. classroom—you need an awful lot of information to be able to effectively educate each and every child that walks in a classroom. We're in that transition stage of going from an art to a science. There's a lot of resistance because I think a lot of the teachers who have spent considerable number of years on the art end of it are saying, "You know, I've been able to do this my own way and I've done it very successfully." Well, maybe not as successfully as they thought, number one; and number two, the scope of what they're doing has changed dramatically, particularly because of having incredible diversity of students that they're seeing in

their classrooms. But as with all professions, there is a tremendous amount of resistance to any change. The ones who embrace it, really understand where they're at and how effective it makes them as a teacher. But they've got to get to that point. And a lot of people, some people are more accepting of change than others and some are extremely resistant. So I think I see two things. One is to go from the art to the science you need to use data-based decisions for students in developing their educational programs, and that requires an incredible amount of leadership on the part of the principal. If you don't have that leadership, that change is extremely difficult to effect. You will get the principals who want to protect their staff and other supporters. When you see a building principal who is a leader, who knows what it is that they're trying to accomplish, knows how to do it and then is committed to making sure that happens, the transition definitely occurs and it occurs relatively quickly. The teachers realize how effective they've become, and they see the results of their change—it's now their new professional approach to the business of education.

CM: And so you see that support as being a really critical component in that process?

HC: Yeah. I think if support isn't there, it isn't going to happen. As in any field of work, you will have some people by their very nature embrace change or for whatever unique reason they latch onto something and they see the light and off they go. But for the vast majority of people, it's going to result from leadership on the part of the building principal and then, at some point, you get to that critical mass level where there are enough teachers in the building who have bought into the program who are doing what it is that you want them to do. That brings on the rest of them. You're always going to have your 10% that probably will never get there. But that's becoming more and more difficult for teachers because, now for example, in Ohio, your name is connected to the scores of your students. So, if you're not producing, it becomes very difficult to hide. It's not good . . . it's not bad . . . it just is.

CM: Why do you think it's important for both teachers and administrators to critically look at test scores?

HC: I think that's the most effective and efficient way to find out are kids learning. It's that simple. But more importantly, if you know how to interpret it and use it, it not only tells you whether or not kids are learning, but it can show you how you can change what you're doing—well what they're doing—so that they do start to learn. So as far as diagnosing what the problems are and then coming up with remedies for those problems, it becomes a very effective tool. You used to do it as an art—flying by the seat of our pants. I'm sure sometimes that did work. I think there were probably some very, very gifted teachers who somehow, someway just were able to do it. Geniuses in the field. Fact of the matter is not everybody in the classroom is a genius this way we can provide any teacher with the skills necessary to be effective. Maybe not great, but effective.

CM: I'm guessing that when you started your career as a superintendent, this was not something that you did as a district. Am I right about that?

HC: No. I mean, you had tests but they were individual tests developed within the district, usually within the classroom, and kids passed or failed. Some tests were harder than others and some were easier than others. That was back in the old days when principals were basically building managers. They didn't get into much of the educational side of the equation. They were running the building. And now there's a huge demand being placed on principals to become, it's so overused I hate to say it even, but instructional leaders. I think I look at them more as instructional supporters where they have to know the key things—or at least where to find the key things—and then provide the leadership to the staff to make sure that that's the direction you're going, and then support them in that process. But that wasn't the case way back when.

CM: So with all the responsibilities and time commitments that you have as a superintendent, where do you find time in your day or your month or in your school year to take on, as a district, all of this new stuff?

HC: Well, I'm fortunate that we have an effective assistant superintendent who's in charge of curriculum and instruction, and one of the reasons I wanted to bring her on board was because she knew this material. Her learning curve was ahead of most everybody else's, and I thought that was critical. Then, as a superintendent, the only thing you can do is set the stage and hopefully provide the resources and some vision and direction. The work gets done at the building level with support from the staff, and in this case it happens to be our assistant superintendent. It is not a job that a superintendent, any superintendent, can do on their own. It is a matter of delegating that responsibility and hopefully having the people in place that accept that responsibility to get it done.

CM: As the leader of a district, where would you put this critical examination of standardized test scores on your list of professional priorities?

HC: Well, if you're going to get it done right now and especially at the stage we're at, it's a daily number one. That's not to say other alligators don't crawl in your swamp and distract you for a time. But I think when it comes down to educating kids, if you believe that developing useful student data, interpreting it, and using it as a decision-making vehicle is the way to go, then it's something that has to be done every day with full commitment towards doing it. That's what we do—we educate kids, and interpreting standardized test scores is going to help us get where we need to be. But you'd better be committed to doing it—it's a very consuming effort, very consuming.

CM: How do you deal with reluctant teachers or administrators, people who don't really buy into the process, and they don't see the value in it? As a superintendent, how do you deal with that?

HC: I think with principals, it's probably easier because you have a little more control [over them and their expectations]. If it doesn't happen, then we've got some issues that we have to talk about, and those could be career decisions. It's not as easy with teachers. I think you want to make sure that you have people in the building that have some sense of leadership in terms of how to get this done. Then you will find those people working with the teachers within the building who are willing to get on board and give it a try. As they become convinced, more will get on board and it's an eventual process that, as I said, at some point reached a critical mass and away it goes. It really takes hold. There will always be a few that just don't get it, but you can't let that dissuade you. You've got to continue to work with them. If it's severe enough where the job just isn't getting done, then nobody likes to think of going in and using termination as a solution. Sometimes it is—it would be a severe, severe case, but sometimes it is.

CM: How do you think that this type of professional activity has helped you to be become more effective at the job of educating children as a school district?

HC: The ballgame's change so much. Back before students with a lot of critical needs were included in a general education classroom—back when I first started getting in education—they were just shipped out to a special education class or to a special school somewhere and what was left were the kids who were able to take the educational program and be successful with it, for the most part. Those days are long, long gone. So we've got to change how we do it. And again, when you look at the average classroom in Bowling Green, it will have kids with IQs from 70 to 120, with one that child might that be autistic, maybe one or two that have severe behavioral issues . . . the list goes on and on. It just a tremendous number of issues that you're dealing with. They're all in one classroom, and they aren't going anywhere. I think one of the difficult habits that we are still trying to break in education is this magic wand approach that if we get this kid tested, either something magical will happen or he'll disappear from my classroom and it's not our problem anymore. That isn't how it works anymore. All you do when you identify a student is identify a student. You might get some more support from a special needs teacher, but the kid isn't disappearing. The same issues are going to be in your classroom from day to day, so you better figure out how to deal with it and handle it. I think if you really want your classroom to be as effective as it possibly can be—and your teaching as effective as it can be—you have to accept the fact that we need to look at it from more of a scientific angle, analyze the data, and make decisions based on that data.

CM: I want you to imagine that you're in a room full of teachers from another district who have never done anything like this before. What advice would you give to those teachers, as the leader of a district that's been engaged in this process for several years now?

HC: It's easy to say, but probably the best advice is just give it a try. It's a different way of approaching your profession or your daily job. But if you give it a try, you will see the results. That is an absolute guarantee. If you don't give it a try, your road is going to be very rough because the demands that are being placed on the educational effort are such that your name is going to be connected with how successful you are as a teacher. Your school and your district are going to be connected with how successful you are as a school and district. There's no where to hide.

CM: You now go down the hallway and there are, in a different room, the building administrators and the district-level administrators from that same district. What kinds of advice do you give them?

HC: They have an obligation to find out how to make it work. How does this whole thing come together? Or at least, where do I get the resources to enable my teachers to be able to do what it is we're expecting? I think in the whole equation where we have failed the greatest is with building administrators when we've told them, "Okay, you are no longer building managers. You are also building managers/ instructional leaders. God speed. Hope you do well. Catch you later." We have to make sure that we provide them with the necessary skills so that they can lead. You don't have to necessarily be an expert in something to lead, but you have to know enough about it to know what you don't know and how to get the resources in place. We have one elementary school that has really made incredible strides as far as improving their instructional delivery system. It's a very diverse school. It's got a good portion of its kids are on free and reduced lunches. It is a school where a lot of kids come from single-parent families. All the kinds of things that you typically think of a school that maybe would have some real challenges. They've hit the benchmark of Excellent. And I would attribute that to the principal embracing the concept [of data-driven decision making], finding out what the concept is about, and how to make it work in her school, and then accepting no less from the teachers. Then, once the teachers started getting a sense of what they could accomplish, it just took on life of its own. Those teachers are now being used in our district to tell other teachers of their success story, which is, unfortunately, resented in some circles. "Who do they think they are?" Well, I'll tell you who they are. They're the ones that are doing it. And they're the ones that are very successful. They've come from this point to that point. Might be a good idea to listen to them.

GLOSSARY

Ability test	A type of standardized test used to determine an individual's cognitive ability, such as potential or capacity to learn; often referred to as an *aptitude test*
Achievement test	A type of standardized test used to measure how much students have learned in specific, clearly defined content areas including, but not limited to, reading, mathematics, science, and social studies
Age-equivalent score	A norm-referenced test score that indicates the age in the norm group for which a certain raw score was the median performance
Aptitude test	A type of standardized test used to determine an individual's cognitive ability such as potential or capacity to learn; sometimes referred to as an *ability test*
Confidence interval	A range of scores within which we are reasonably confident; includes the student's true ability or achievement score
Constructed-response test items	Test item where students must recall from their own memories, or otherwise create, their responses
Criterion-referenced test scores	Test scores that compare a student's performance to some preestablished criteria or objectives
Cross-sectional analysis	The practice of comparing one cohort of students (i.e., this year's class of students, or perhaps an entire grade level) to another cohort (i.e., last year's class or grade level); this usually happens across different school years

Cut scores	Test score values that serve as the cutoff points between adjacent categories along some performance continuum
Data-driven instructional decision making	A process by which educators examine the results of standardized tests to identify student strengths and deficiencies
Derived scores	New score scales that result from transforming raw scores to know how a particular student's raw score compares to the specific norm group; also known as *transformed scores*
Deviation IQ score	A type of normalized standard score that provides the location of a raw score in a normal distribution having a mean of 100 and a standard deviation equal to 15 or 16 (depending on the specific test)
Diagnostic test	A specialized version of an achievement test used to identify the specific areas of weaknesses the student may be encountering
Difficulty index	A value equal to the proportion of students who answer a particular test item correctly
Grade-equivalent score	A norm-referenced test score that indicates the grade in the norm group for which a certain raw score was the median performance and is intended to estimate a student's developmental level
Group bias	A type of test bias that occurs when a test contains information or words that favor one racial, ethnic, or gender group over another
High-stakes tests	Standardized tests whose results can have substantial consequences for students, teachers, and schools
Item discrimination	A measure of how well students who scored high on the entire test perform on an individual item as compared to the performance on that item by students who scored low on the entire test
Linear standard score	A type of norm-referenced score that tells how far a raw score is located from the mean of the norm group, with the distance being expressed in standard deviation units
Longitudinal analysis	The practice of tracking individual student and cohort performances along multiyear routes, focusing on academic gains made over time for the same students
National percentile band	Confidence intervals that are presented around a student's obtained percentile rank scores

Norm group	The national sample of students that serves as the basis for the comparison for the scores attained by a given local group of students on a norm-referenced standardized test
Normal curve equivalent score	A type of normalized standard score that has a mean of 50 and a standard deviation of 21.06
Normal distribution	A distribution of test scores that serves as the basis for transformed scores; also known as a *normal curve* or a *bell-shaped curve*
Normalized standard scores	A type of norm-referenced score where the raw score has been transformed in order to obtain the same area beneath a "curve" representing the distribution of scores as is found in a normal distribution
Norm-referenced test scores	Test scores that compare individual student scores to the performance of other similar students
Percentile rank	A norm-referenced test score that indicates the percentage of the norm group that scored below a given raw score
Precision of performance score	A criterion-referenced test score that involves measuring the degree of accuracy with which a student completes a task
Quality of performance score	A criterion-referenced test score that consists of ratings that indicate the level at which a student performs
Raw score	A criterion-referenced test score, typically presented as the number or percentage of items answered correctly
Reliability	The degree to which the scores on a given test are consistent
Sample bias	A type of test bias that occurs when certain cultural groups do not have adequate representation in the norm group (the group to which student test performance will ultimately be compared)
SAT/GRE scores	A type of normalized standard score that is reported on a scale that has a mean of 500 and a standard deviation of 100
Selected-response items	Test items that have only one correct answer and that correct answer actually appears as part of the question; the student's task is to simply identify, or select, the correct option

Speed of performance score	A criterion-referenced test score reported as the amount of time it takes for a student to complete a task or the number of tasks a student can complete in a fixed amount of time
Standard error of measurement (SEM)	The average amount of measurement error across students in the norm group; also known simply as *standard error*
Standard setting	The process used to establish various cut scores
Standardized scores	A category of norm-referenced test scores that are obtained when raw scores are transformed to fit a distribution whose characteristics are known and fixed, usually a normal distribution
Standardized test	Any test that is administered, scored, and interpreted in a standard, consistent manner
Stanine	A type of normalized standard score that provides the location of a raw score in a specific segment of the normal distribution; they range in value from 1 to 9, where the mean is equal to 5 and the standard deviation is equal to 2
State-mandated tests	Standardized tests that are typically developed and implemented to meet some sort of legislative mandate within a particular state and have been implemented for accountability purposes
Test bias	A situation that occurs if and when a standardized test is in some fashion unfair to one or more minority groups
Test norms	Specific descriptions of how a representative national sample of students (i.e., a norm group) performed on an actual final test
Testwiseness skills	Student abilities in the use of test taking strategies during a particular standardized test
Transformed scores	New score scales that result from transforming raw scores in order to know how a particular student's raw score compares to the specific norm group; also known as *derived scores*
***T*-score**	A type of linear standard score that provides the location of a raw score in a distribution that has a mean of 50 and a standard deviation of 10
Validity	The extent to which a test—and more specifically, the resulting information it provides about a given student—is sufficient

and appropriate to make various educational decisions for which the information is intended

Value-added analysis   A newer method of measuring teaching and learning that analyzes annual test scores to reveal the progress students are making each year at both the individual and group levels

Z-score   A type of linear standard score that exists on a continuum that has a mean of zero and a standard deviation of 1

REFERENCES

Airasian, P. W. (2005). *Classroom assessment: Concepts and applications* (5th ed.). Boston: McGraw-Hill.

Borich, G. D., & Tombari, M. L. (2004). *Educational assessment for the elementary and middle school classroom* (2nd ed.). Upper Saddle River, NJ: Merrill/Prentice Hall.

Chase, C. I. (1999). *Contemporary assessment for educators.* Boston: Allyn & Bacon.

Cizek, G. J. (1996). Setting passing scores: An NCME instructional module. *Educational Measurement: Issues and Practice, 15*(2), 20–31.

Crocker, L., & Algina, A. (1986). *Introduction to classical and modern test theory.* Fort Worth, TX: Harcourt Brace Jovanovich.

CTB/McGraw-Hill. (2001). *TerraNova: Technical Quality* (2nd ed.). Retrieved March 10, 2006, http://www.ctb.com/media/mktg/terranova/other_media/tech_quality/technical_quality_all.pdf

Essex, N. L. (2006). *What every teacher should know about No Child Left Behind: Allyn & Bacon Start Smart Series.* Boston: Allyn & Bacon.

Evergreen Freedom Foundation. (2002). *School directors' handbook—Student assessments.* Olympia, WA: Author. Retrieved on July 25, 2006, from http://www.effwa.org/pdfs/education_directors_handbook6.pdf

Evergreen Freedom Foundation. (2003). *School directors' handbook—Value-added assessments.* Olympia, WA: Author. Retrieved on July 25, 2006, from http://www.effwa.org/pdfs/Value-Added.pdf

Gredler, M. E. (1999). *Classroom assessment and learning.* Boston: Allyn & Bacon.

Gronlund, N. E. (2006). *Assessment of student achievement* (8th ed.). Boston: Allyn & Bacon.

Hamilton, L. S., & Koretz, D. M. (2002). Tests and their use in test-based accountability systems. In L. S. Hamilton, B. M. Stecher, & S. P. Klein (Eds.), *Making sense of test-based accountability in education* (pp. 13–49). Santa Monica, CA: RAND.

Harcourt Assessment. (2002). *Metropolitan8—Technical Manual.* San Antonio, TX: Author.

Hershberg, T., Simon, V. A., & Lea-Kruger, B. (2004). The revelations of value-added. *School Administrator, 61*(11), 10–12.

Hogan, T. P. (2007). *Educational assessment: A practical approach.* Hoboken, NJ: John Wiley & Sons.

Kober, N. (2002). *Teaching to the test: The good, the bad, and who's responsible* (TestTalk for Leaders. No. 1). Washington, DC: Center on Education Policy.

Kubiszyn, T., & Borich, G. (2007). *Educational testing and measurement: Classroom application and practice* (8th ed.). Hoboken, NJ: John Wiley & Sons.

LaFee, S. (2002). Data-driven districts. *School Administrator, 59*(11), 6–7, 9–10, 12, 14–15.

Linn, R. L., & Miller, M. D. (2005). *Measurement and assessment in teaching* (9th ed.). Upper Saddle River, NJ: Merrill/Prentice Hall.

Mahoney, J. W. (2004). Why add value in assessment? *School Administrator, 61*(11), 16–18.

McMillan, J. H. (2001). Essential assessment concepts for teachers and administrators. In T. R. Guskey & R. J. Marzano (Series Eds.), *Experts in Assessment.* Thousand Oaks, CA: Corwin Press.

McMillan, J. H. (2004). *Classroom assessment: Principles and practice for effective instruction* (3rd ed.). Boston: Allyn & Bacon.

Mertler, C. A. (2002). *Using standardized test data to guide instruction and intervention.* College Park, MD: ERIC Clearinghouse on Assessment and Evaluation Digest Series, EDO-TM-07.

Mertler, C. A. (2003). *Classroom assessment: A practical guide for educators.* Los Angeles: Pyrczak.

Mertler, C. A. (2006, October). *Teachers' perceptions of the influences of No Child Left Behind on instructional and assessment practices.* Paper presented at the annual meeting of the Mid-Western Educational Research Association, Columbus, OH.

Mertler, C. A., & Zachel, K. (2006). Data-driven instructional decision making: An idea (and practice) whose time has come. *Principal Navigator, 1*(3), 6–9.

Miyasaka, J. R. (2000, April). *A framework for evaluating the validity of test preparation practices.* Paper presented at the annual meeting of the American Educational Research Association, New Orleans, LA.

Monson, R. J. (2002). Using data to think differently. *School Administrator, 59*(11), 24–25, 27–28.

National Center for Educational Statistics (NCES). (2006). *The Nation's Report Card.* Retrieved March 8, 2006, from http://nces.ed.gov/nationsreportcard/faq.asp

Nitko, A. J. (2004). *Educational assessment of students* (4th ed.). Upper Saddle River, NJ: Merrill/Prentice Hall.

Ohio Department of Education. (2004). *2004–05 Ohio school district rating definitions.* Retrieved July 15, 2005, from http://www.ode.state.oh.us/reportcard/definitions/rating.asp

Ohio Department of Education. (2006). Statistical summary of the Ohio Graduation Tests: March 2005 administration. Columbus, OH: Author.

Oosterhof, A. (2001). *Classroom applications of educational measurement* (3rd ed.). Upper Saddle River, NJ: Merrill/Prentice Hall.

Payne, D. A. (2003). *Applied educational measurement* (2nd ed.). Belmont, CA: Wadsworth.

Popham, W. J. (2002). *Classroom assessment: What teachers need to know* (3rd ed.). Boston: Allyn & Bacon.

Sanders, W. L. (2003, April). *Beyond No Child Left Behind.* Paper presented at the annual meeting of the American Educational Research Association, Chicago.

Spinelli, C. G. (2006). *Classroom assessment for students in special and general education* (2nd ed.). Upper Saddle River, NJ: Merrill/Prentice Hall.

Tanner, D. E. (2001). *Assessing academic achievement.* Boston: Allyn & Bacon.

Thorndike, R. M. (2005). *Measurement and evaluation in psychology and education* (7th ed.). Upper Saddle River, NJ: Merrill/Prentice Hall.

INDEX

About the Author

Dr. Craig A. Mertler is currently a Professor of assessment and research methodologies in the College of Education and Human Development at Bowling Green State University, Ohio. Dr. Mertler teaches graduate courses in quantitative research methods, introductory statistical analyses, multivariate statistical analyses, classroom assessment, and standardized test interpretation. He also teaches undergraduate courses in educational assessment methods. He is currently the author of five books (including *Action Research: Teachers as Researchers in the Classroom,* 2006), two invited book chapters, 14 refereed journal articles, two instructors' manuals, and numerous nonrefereed articles and manuscripts. He has also presented numerous research papers at professional meetings around the country as well as internationally. Dr. Mertler conducts workshops for both preservice and inservice teachers on the broad topic of classroom assessment—and specifically on interpreting standardized test scores—as well as on classroom-based action research. His primary research interests include classroom teachers' assessment literacy, assessment practices of classroom teachers, and Web-based survey methodology. Prior to teaching and researching at the university level, Dr. Mertler taught high school biology and Earth science, coached track and volleyball, and also advised various student groups.